D1196896

CORNELL STUDIES IN CIVIL LIBERTY

FREEDOM IN THE BALANCE:

Opinions of Judge Henry W. Edgerton
Relating to Civil Liberties

JUDGE HENRY W. EDGERTON

Freedom in the Balance:

OPINIONS OF

JUDGE HENRY W. EDGERTON

RELATING TO CIVIL LIBERTIES

Edited by Eleanor Bontecou

Cornell University Press

ITHACA, NEW YORK

PRINTED IN THE UNITED STATES OF AMERICA
BY THE VAIL-BALLOU PRESS, INC.

To

ROBERT E. CUSHMAN

Pioneer Scholar
in the Field of Civil Liberties

Preface

The opinions in this volume do not represent the whole range of Judge Edgerton's work on the bench, which is as wide as that of the court upon which he sits. They have not been chosen because of the philosophy which they reflect or their literary quality, although both of these aspects will interest and please the reader. Judge Edgerton's opinions in the field of civil liberties are important because they reflect one phase of the growth of freedom in this country. They are themselves a part of that growth. For that reason it is hoped that they will interest not only members of the legal profession but all those who are concerned with civil liberties today. They have been edited with that wider audience in mind.

Except in the cases of *Hurd* v. *Hodge* and *McDonald* v. *United States* the text used is that of the advance sheets. No changes have been made in the substance of the text, but passages have been omitted when they relate to issues other than those of civil liberties, consist of a catalogue of precedents or a list of quotations that might be confusing to the lay reader, or, as in the case of *Carr* v. *Corning*, are concerned with the analysis of facts that have a purely local and limited importance. For the most part footnotes have been omitted. In conformity with the present practice of the court, references that were originally in footnotes have been incorporated in the text. Because the opinions cannot be fully understood or evaluated without knowledge of the background of public opinion and legal theory against which they have been written, the headnotes and introductory statements are longer than would otherwise be necessary.

I must express my thanks to Robert E. Cushman, who conceived of this book, for the advice and moral support he has given throughout its preparation, to Judge Edgerton for his courtesy in answering my many questions and in refraining from comment or suggestion while doing everything in his power to smooth my path, to Virginia Rouse for her co-operation and invaluable technical assistance, and to the Fund for the Republic for financial help. Finally, I must thank Beulah E. Shields for the help she gave so freely in the final typing of the manuscript.

ELEANOR BONTECOU

Alstead Center, New Hampshire
August 1959

Henry White Edgerton:

A Biographical Note

Judge Henry W. Edgerton had not long been on the bench when it became obvious that his opinions were providing an important and brilliant addition to the law and literature of civil liberty. This they continue to be. As Miss Bontecou has made clear in her introduction, they rest upon sound legal principles, and for style and clarity they are legal literature at its best. The record of support of these opinions at the hands of the Supreme Court is most impressive evidence of Edgerton's stature as a judge.

As time went on, it was increasingly clear that it would be a serious loss if the Edgerton opinions were not collected, annotated, and published so that they might be readily available to the general reader. I take great pride, therefore, that with Judge Edgerton's consent this book appears in the Cornell Studies in Civil Liberty, which had its start under my editorship in 1943. A heavy debt of gratitude is owing to Eleanor Bontecou, also a distinguished contributor to the Cornell series, for undertaking the work of editing and annotating the opinions—a substantial task and one which she has carried through without reward save the sense of having honored a valued friend and at the same time rendered a public service.

It is indeed a privilege to have been invited to contribute a brief biographical sketch of Henry Edgerton and to add some comment about him as a former colleague on the faculty of Cornell University and as a long-time personal friend.

Henry White Edgerton was born in Rush Center, Kansas, October 20, 1888. Both his father and his mother were descendants of Governor Bradford of Plymouth Colony. His paternal grandfather was a country storekeeper, or, as he called it, a country merchant; and his maternal grandfather edited a country weekly and ran a printing press. His father, Charles E. Edgerton, and his mother, Annie White Edgerton, grew up in central New York, where the families of both had lived for several genera-ations. Charles Edgerton graduated from Hamilton College in 1882, spent some years in banking and in business, and then did graduate work in economics at Cornell and at Columbia. For the rest of his active life he was an economist with various government agencies in Washington, beginning in 1900 with the United States Industrial Commission and ending in 1918 with the Federal Trade Commission.

Henry Edgerton was the second of three sons. Each of his two brothers came to be a distinguished scholar: William, the younger, as an Egyptologist at the University of Chicago, and Franklin, the older, as an Indologist at Yale. Henry Edgerton married Alice Durand on June 28, 1913. Their son John, now an attorney in the Department of Defense, was born in 1919; their daughter Ann was born in 1921 and died in 1950.

As his family moved about, Henry attended the public schools in Binghamton and Ithaca, New York, and in Washington. He finished his sophomore year at the University of Wisconsin in 1907, then dropped out to serve for some months with a survey crew in Montana and some more months as a temporary special agent of the United States Bureau of Corporations. His last two years of college were spent at Cornell, where he was elected to Phi Beta Kappa in his junior year, was a member of the university debating team, and was class orator. A friend and fellow debater was destined to be a future judicial colleague, the late Chief Judge Harold M. Stephens. The year after his graduation from Cornell in 1910 Edgerton spent in Europe, much of it in France and several months of it attending lectures in the Law School of the University of Paris. Here he acquired a fluency in French which he has never lost.

Henry Edgerton entered the Harvard Law School in 1911 and received his LL.B. degree in 1914. His first law practice was with the firm of Davis, Kellogg & Severance in St. Paul, Minnesota, which he left after a few months to join the staff of the new Legislative Reference Division in the Library of Congress. He shortly returned to the practice of the law, this time with the firm of Warner, Warner, and Stackpole in Boston, and was admitted to the Massachusetts bar in 1916. In the fall of 1916 he went to Cornell as acting assistant professor of law. He returned to Boston in the fall of 1918 and entered the firm of Ropes, Gray, Boyden & Perkins (now Ropes, Gray, Best, Coolidge & Rugg). In 1921 he accepted a professorship of law at George Washington University and remained a member of that faculty until 1929. He was on leave of absence, however, during 1928–1929 and served as visiting professor of law at the University of Chicago. In 1929 he became a professor in the Cornell Law School and remained there until he went on the bench. While on sabbatical leave for the year 1934–1935 he was Special Assistant to the Attorney General in the Antitrust Division of the Department of Justice.

In the fall of 1937 Edgerton was nominated and confirmed as an Associate Justice (now Circuit Judge) of the United States Court of Appeals for the District of Columbia (now for the District of Columbia Circuit). He completed teaching the first semester at Cornell and was sworn in as a judge on February 1,

1938. He became Chief Judge in May, 1955, by statutory succession, as the senior member of the court after the death of Chief Judge Harold M. Stephens. He resigned his post as Chief Judge on his seventieth birthday, October 20, 1958, although the statute passed by Congress requiring chief judges to relinquish their functions as such at the age of seventy did not take effect until August, 1959. He remains, of course, a member of the court.

In 1956 Yale conferred upon Judge Edgerton the LL.D. degree. The citation read: "Lawyer and teacher, your career has had many distinctions, but none greater than the character of your service as a United States judge. You have brought to this difficult task of the judgment of men, not only the skill of a lawyer and the profound learning of a professor, but the inspired promptings of your own conscience. You are one of the truest voices of our constitutional tradition. Yale is honored to confer upon you the degree of Doctor of Laws."

Edgerton's stay at Cornell as professor of law lasted more than eight years. He taught, as most law teachers do, a variety of courses, but he developed a special interest in the law of torts, and his two-installment article on "Legal Cause" (*University of Pennsylvania Law Review*, 72: 211 and 343, 1924) remains a legal classic in that field. In *The Paradoxes of Legal Science*, Judge Cardozo, then Chief Judge of the New York Court of Appeals, comments on "the discernment and understanding with which he penetrates to the heart and essence of the problem." Two years later Edgerton published in the *Harvard Law Review* (39: 849) an article on "Negligence, Inadvertence, and Indifference: The Relation of Mental States to Negligence." Attracting wider attention than these because of its subject was his "Incidence of Judicial Control over Congress," which appeared in the *Cornell Law Quarterly* in 1937 (22: 299). This was reprinted in *Selected Essays on Constitutional Law* published in 1938 under the auspices of the Association of American Law Schools.

Teaching may not be one of the more spectacular professions, but a gifted and dedicated teacher achieves a kind of immortality denied to men in many other walks of life. There are a number of generations of Cornell law graduates who will insist that Professor Edergton was the finest teacher they ever had and that he left a lasting imprint upon them, not only as a splendid legal mind but as a man. He never met a class without the most painstaking preparation, and the students in those classes profited from his acute legal analysis and enjoyed the courtesy which he invariably extended to these younger friends. When he left to assume his seat on the bench, his students arranged a farewell dinner in his honor which was attended by practically every student in the Cornell Law School.

Twenty years later another dinner was held in Henry Edgerton's honor in Washington. It was attended by Supreme Court Justices, by judges from his own court, by distinguished lawyers, and by others in public life. But it had been planned and managed by Judge Edgerton's law clerks, as a tribute to his twenty years on the bench and as an expression of their admiration and affection. The relationship between a judge and his law clerk will, of course, be what the two persons involved, and especially the judge, make it. It can be rather impersonal and formal. But it can be much more than that. It can be an intimate and friendly association between an able and eager beginner in the law and a judicial scholar. The law clerk learns by doing, but he also learns by watching the judge as he reflects, questions, argues, decides, and writes. It is very highly personalized graduate work in law carried on under circumstances out of which lifelong friendships are formed. Among the things which Judge Edgerton must value most deeply is the loyalty felt for him by the young men and women who have served as his law clerks over the years he has been on the bench. As they come to take independent and responsible positions in the practice of the law, they look back on their clerkships with him as the happiest and most rewarding interval in their professional careers.

It is with diffidence that one comments in print upon the personal qualities of a friend with whom one may be having lunch next week. I have been acquainted with Henry Edgerton intimately for thirty years. Leaving out of account his eminence as a judge, I believe that all who know him see him as a man of unfailing courtesy, of great courage, of complete integrity, and inspired with a passionate loyalty to the principles of justice and human freedom to which he has devoted most of the years of his life. This book is, in a very real sense, a tribute to this last quality as well as compelling evidence of it. It is also a tribute to those who share Henry Edgerton's dedication to the cause of individual liberty under law.

ROBERT E. CUSHMAN

Contents

FREEDOM IN THE BALANCE:

Opinions of Judge Henry W. Edgerton
Relating to Civil Liberties

Introduction

Occasionally one can find in the records of the courts the visible evidence of the growth of a particular social institution. The cases reflect the developing social conscience and the attitudes of the public. The background of social controversy against which they are decided is made evident in part by the very facts of the cases, but perhaps even more by the varying opinions of the judges who decide them. In the process of growth, sometimes the law is molded by the force of current opinion, sometimes it leads and itself molds not only opinion but the institution that becomes an inseparable part of the fabric of our society. In the last three decades this has been true of the law of constitutional rights. The cases in this volume demonstrate the part played by one man in its development.

Henry W. Edgerton has served as an appellate judge in the District of Columbia during a turbulent period of world history in which issues of civil liberty and individual freedom have assumed a fresh importance both in the public consciousness and in the courts. When he first came to the United States Court of Appeals for the District of Columbia Circuit, economic depression had led to a revolutionary recasting of the social and economic structure of the country. The resulting extension of the power of the Federal Government over the lives of its citizens brought on a flood of lawsuits contesting the new laws and their administration. We were in the midst of preparations for war, and global war soon broke out. Ideologies alien to the democratic ideal as we understood it were among the weapons of the enemy. The suspicion of danger to our institutions bred intolerance of views that threatened traditional values. At the same time the challenge of an alien ideology and the example of countries in which individual rights were disregarded led to a renewed understanding of their importance to a free society. The result has been what Judge Prettyman has called "swirling currents of public emotion in both directions," amidst which the law of constitutional rights has developed rapidly but not always in one direction.

While we were engaged in open warfare, the principal threat to civil liberties came not from the Federal Government but from the activities of local officials and from the terrorism practiced by private persons against unpopular groups, especially the pacifist sect called Jehovah's Witnesses. Out of these activities there grew an important development of the law as to freedom of religion.

A few years later we were in the period that Justice Clark has called "a time of cold war and hot emotions" when the Government and the public became aware that international communism threatens the free world not only by force of arms and by economic competition but by internal subversion. Congress and the Executive took drastic steps to curb the Communist movement within this country and to make sure that all who served the Government or had access to its secrets should be of unquestionable loyalty. What the First Amendment forbids Congress to do directly to suppress that movement it sought to do indirectly by exposure of organizations and individuals whom it suspected of

Communist activities or sympathies. In the process freedom of speech was inevitably impaired, and accepted standards of fair play—due process in legal phraseology—were often ignored by both branches of the Government. The resulting struggle for the vindication of constitutional rights, in which the courts played an important part, became in many ways reminiscent of Lord Coke's fight against Star Chamber procedures and for the rights of Englishmen.

The drama of this phase of constitutional development has tended to obscure the fact that in the two decades of turmoil during which Judge Edgerton has sat upon the bench there has been substantial growth of the law implicit in the broad phrases of the Bill of Rights. In the early forties the Supreme Court took the position, since modified, that the constitutional guarantees of freedom of religion, speech, press, and assembly are so basic to a free society that they hold a preferred position in the law and that the presumptions are against any measures that tend to diminish those rights. Acting on this principle it ruled that speakers may not be barred from public streets and parks at the mere discretion of local officials and that the distribution of religious literature on the streets or in homes may not be prohibited or taxed. It reversed earlier decisions that children may be required to participate in the flag-salute ceremony in public schools in violation of their religious principles and that conscientious objectors may be barred from United States citizenship. It brought peaceful picketing within the protection of freedom of speech. Recently, for the first time, the Court declared specifically that freedom of association for the advancement of ideas is included in the right of assembly.

Since 1943, when the Supreme Court said that it is the duty of the federal courts to impose "civilized standards of procedure" in the administration of federal criminal justice, the rights of persons accused of crime have been given increasing protection and the standards of police activity have steadily improved.

In the last decades the Negro has been freed by a series of court decisions from his position of social and political inferiority. Discrimination on grounds of race has been banned at every stage of the process of jury service and voting. Contracts that forbid the sale or lease of real property to Negroes have been held unenforceable in the courts. The "separate but equal" doctrine that permitted separation of the races in trains, schools, and all public places has been interpreted more and more strictly and finally specifically overruled so far as public education is concerned. In spite of the intransigence with which this decision has been met in many communities, a general breakdown of segregation in other areas is occurring, partly as a result of decisions of the federal courts, partly by community action.

On the other hand, in the postwar years when the courts were confronted with the problems arising from the Government's anti-Communist program they faltered in their support of freedom of speech and conscience. Judges disagreed, but the majority saw the issue as the conflict between private right and national security in a time of national danger. Faced with this choice, they supported the Government although they recognized that the measures before them would in fact limit the freedoms of the First Amendment in areas far beyond the reach of the particular laws or regulations that were being challenged. They have continued to postpone any answer to the question of how far congressional committees or the Executive are limited by the requirements of due process.

There can be no doubt that the Government's anti-Communist measures, supported by the courts and probably by the weight of public opinion, have checked if they have not reversed the trend of the development of the law of constitutional rights, at least so far as freedom of speech is concerned. It is not yet clear how far the courts are prepared to travel along their present course in this area. The dissenting judges have not faltered in their opposition. As they have become more familiar with the realities behind the cases that are before them, the majority have scrutinized the Government's activities more closely, have refused to interpret executive power broadly, and have held officials to exact compliance with the letter of the law from which they derive their power and with the regulations that they themselves have issued. The courts have even added a new item to the catalogue of rights protected by the Constitution against arbitrary invasion by the Government, namely, the right to travel abroad. It is doubtful that one can long have progress in one area of civil rights and retrogression in another.

The Supreme Court is, of course, the final arbiter of all legal issues. Once it has spoken, a judge of a lower court is bound by what he understands to be its decision. The greatest number of individual lives, however, have been directly affected so far as civil liberties are concerned by the decisions of the United States Court of Appeals for the District of Columbia Circuit. Almost unnoticed by either the public or the legal profession, this tribunal has become one of the most important in the federal judicial system. Today, although its jurisdiction is limited to the tiny District of Columbia, many of its cases are of national importance. The volume of its work is equaled only by that of the appellate courts of two other circuits, the Second and the Fifth. It has played a dominant role in the decision of cases challenging the Government's personnel loyalty and security programs and the validity of the Attorney General's list, hearing all of those that have reached an appellate court. All but two of the appeals from the denial of passports have come before it. The great majority of the cases involving convictions for contempt in refusing to answer the questions of congressional investigators have been heard in the District of Columbia Circuit. The part played by it in connection with the industrial security program and the screening of military personnel is less important, but it has decided three of the five cases in those fields that have ultimately reached the Supreme Court. Because most of the high-ranking federal officials exercise their powers in the District of Columbia, the Court of Appeals has the major responsibility for defining the limits of executive power. More than one-half of all appellate cases brought in recent years to review or enjoin the acts of federal agencies—five times as many as in any other circuit—have come before it. The number of its cases in all fields that have been sufficiently important to be heard by the Supreme Court has been greater than in any other circuit.[1]

The responsibility of the Court of Appeals in the District of Columbia for establishing "civilized standards of procedure" in the administration of federal criminal law is unique, for it alone in the federal judicial system has the same wide jurisdiction as a state court over the whole range of common crimes. It alone is called upon to review the day-by-day practices of the police, who to the less fortunate are "the Law." The Court of Appeals also has the same power as a state court to make the rules of evidence for the lower courts in the District, and upon those rules may depend the jury's verdict of guilt or innocence. Its wide powers have enabled it to change the hundred-year-old rule as to the criminal responsibility of an insane person, which was formulated in England and known as the rule in *McNaghten's Case*. Under that rule, which has been only slightly modified in the American courts, an insane defendant is held liable for his criminal acts unless he did not know the difference between right and wrong or understand the nature of his acts. Today, in the District of Columbia, as a result of the decision of the Court of Appeals in the *Durham* case, no insane person will be adjudged guilty if his criminal act was the result of his mental illness. He will be committed to a hospital, not to a prison. The new rule has caused much controversy and has been difficult to apply but is clearly more in accord with modern medical knowledge and the demands of substantive justice than was the old.

[1] *Annual Report of the Director of the Administrative Office of the United States Courts, 1956*, Tables B 1, 3, and 5; *1957*, Table B 1.

Although the Court of Appeals is an intermediate court, for most of the individuals who come before it its decisions are final. Its judges as well as those in the lower courts in the District are bound by its decisions, whether or not they agree, until such time as they are overruled by the Supreme Court or by a majority of its own judges, sitting in banc. Four out of five of its decisions are not reviewed by the Supreme Court. For nearly ten years, for example, the decision in the *Barsky* case, which found no vagueness in the resolution of Congress establishing the Un-American Activities Committee, governed in all cases involving the work of that Committee that came before the Court of Appeals. Finally, after a number of persons had been convicted of contempt of Congress, the earlier decision was modified by the Supreme Court in the *Watkins* case. When, as in the *Bailey* case, the Supreme Court divides four to four in deciding an appeal, the judgment of the Court of Appeals becomes to all intents and purposes the law in all federal jurisdictions.

When Judge Edgerton came to the court in 1937, it had not yet attained the status of a circuit court in the federal judicial system. The volume and national importance of its work was steadily increasing, but it still was often thought of as a local appellate court in the District. At that time it was composed of five judges who sat in banc to hear all cases. In 1939 it was given one more judge, and in September, 1948, it was made the United States Court of Appeals for the District of Columbia Circuit. In 1949 the number of its judges was increased to nine. Today, in order to keep up with the work before it, these judges sit in divisions of three. Only when some question of exceptional public importance is before it or when the majority disagree with the judgment of a division does the court sit in banc. When this system was first introduced, cases were assigned and the members of a division selected by the Chief Judge. Judge Edgerton was one of those who brought about a change to the present practice by which the judges are chosen by lot under the direction of the Clerk of the Court without intervention by the Chief Judge. Opinions are circulated among all the judges, who are thus given an opportunity to modify them before they are made public. The system has not only distributed the work load evenly and made it impossible to pack a division with members of one outlook, but has also given each judge the fullest opportunity to make his influence felt. Each member of the court is now at least one among three rather than one among nine.

The men who compose the Court of Appeals hold widely differing social and legal views. With equally legitimate and skillful use of the tools of the law any two members may and do reach opposite results in cases that lie on the frontier of the law and require the weighing of values. Inevitably the determining factor in such cases is a judge's own philosophy, for, as Justice Frankfurter has said, where he comes out depends on where he came in. Yet the public knows little or nothing about the men who are appointed to the Court of Appeals in the District. The District Bar Association is, of course, interested in such appointments but is usually familiar only with the qualifications of its own members; no political penalty attaches to disregard of its recommendations. The District of Columbia has no representative in Congress to scan the achievements of prospective judges and report to the public. For good or for ill it is relatively easy for the President to make political appointments, to reward a "lame duck" in Congress, or to call a faithful but mediocre servant from a government department to be a judge on any of the District courts. It is equally possible, as was done in the case of Judge Edgerton, to disregard geographical limits and appoint a highly qualified legal scholar wherever he may be found.

Serving on the Court of Appeals in a formative period of the law, Judge Edgerton has had full opportunity to demonstrate his quality as a judge. He came to the bench from the Cornell Law School in 1937 and has served continuously on the Court of Appeals ever since, as Associate Justice, as Circuit Judge, as

Chief Judge, and again, after his seventieth birthday, as Circuit Judge. When he was appointed, his experience in the law had been primarily that of a teacher and a legal scholar, but he had already developed and set forth in an article in the *Cornell Law Quarterly* his theory of the qualities that make a liberal judge— the role he chose for himself when he came to the bench.[2]

The liberal judge, he wrote, will be tolerant of change and its advocates and will respect legislative acts that involve change. However, where legislative acts conflict with the right to advocate change, he will support the latter. He will not be the prisoner of abstract legal concepts or adhere to obsolete rules of law but will penetrate to the underlying realities of a case and modify the rules to suit the conditions of his time. He will not follow precedents blindly, a requirement upon which Judge Edgerton elaborated later, saying:

> The court holds that "the great weight of authority . . . compels us." This is a new rule and an important one. I think that it is erroneous. . . . Accordingly we should consider the weight of authority elsewhere for what it may be worth. . . . To let judges who lived and died in other times and other places make our decisions would be to abdicate as judges and serve as tellers. *Chaplin* v. *United States*, 157 F. 2d 697, 699.

Further, the liberal judge will always be aware of and will exercise, "within the limits of the judicial process," his right of free judicial choice and will be ready to be heterodox in his opinions. As to the substance of this heterodoxy, Judge Edgerton wrote that when he is called upon to engage in "interstitial legislation," and especially when he must weigh conflicting social interests, the liberal judge will give a little more weight than the orthodox to the interest of the "unprivileged minority." In that category he included married women, workingmen, foreigners, radicals,

---

[2] "A Liberal Judge—Cuthbert W. Pound," *Cornell Law Quarterly*, 21: 1–45, 1935.

criminals, and the unconventional. He added that "since appellate judges do their work with words their accomplishment depends in large degree upon the effectiveness with which they use words." When the Supreme Court first enunciated the doctrine that in weighing values the freedoms of the First Amendment should be given a preferred position, Judge Edgerton agreed; and when the Court retreated somewhat from that position, he stood his ground.

In his work on the bench Judge Edgerton has turned his precepts into practice. He has refused to accept the outworn fiction that a husband and wife cannot conspire together because they are one, *Johnson* v. *United States*, 157 F. 2d 209, or to base a decision on a landlord's liability for lighting the corridors of a building upon precedents created before the days of modern lighting. *Kay* v. *Cain*, 154 F. 2d 305. He rejected the rule that a plaintiff is concluded by his own testimony with the comment:

> The elusive distinction which these cases attempt rests upon the premise that "When a person testifies to facts in regard to which he has special knowledge, such as his own motives, purposes, or knowledge, or his reason for acting as he did the possibility that he may be honestly mistaken disappears. . . ." If he is human it does not disappear. Knowledge may be "special" without being correct. We little note nor long remember our "motives, purpose or knowledge." There are few, if any, subjects on which plaintiffs are infallible. *Leon Alamo et al.* v. *Del Rosario*, 98 F. 2d 328.

Judge Edgerton has consistently supported the liberal decisions of his court where police activities are in question, and in many of these cases he has written the majority opinion. In others his dissent has been vindicated upon appeal to the Supreme Court. In *Colpoys* v. *Foreman*, 163 F. 2d 908, 910, he epitomizes his position in the sentence, "Lawless invasion of homes is the more menacing to a democratic society when it is committed by public officers."

The record in cases involving the rights of defendants in criminal cases is similar to that in the police cases. Judge Edgerton was the first to write an opinion which found that the right of counsel had not been afforded when counsel assigned to an indigent defendant has proved to be incompetent. *Johnson* v. *United States*, 110 F. 2d 562. Exercising the power of his court to make rules of evidence for the courts in the District of Columbia, he has voted for those that give a defendant the fullest opportunity to prove his innocence. *Griffin* v. *United States*, infra, p. 225. He dissented from his court when it accepted the past record of a prostitute as, in itself, sufficient evidence of illegal intent on a particular occasion when she was on the street at night. *Beail* v. *United States*, 201 F. 2d 176. He has scrutinized closely confessions obtained by the police and, in a dissent to the admissibility of one, wrote, "From the point of view of one who is not sleepy and can go to bed when he likes, a person makes a bad bargain if he risks his neck for a little rest: but it is human to discount the future when one is suffering from an immediate physical need. We are told that Esau, being hungry, sold his birthright for a mess of pottage." *McAffee* v. *United States*, infra, p. 181. He spoke for the court in reversing a conviction for assault on a three-year-old girl, with the comment, "A repellent charge does not destroy the presumption of innocence or justify a conviction on evidence that is neither competent nor trustworthy." *Brown* v. *United States*, 152 F. 2d 138, 140. He disagreed with the other members of the court when they ruled that in deciding whether an indigent defendant may be allowed to appeal *in forma pauperis* the cost to the government should be taken into account. *Cash* v. *United States*, infra, p. 228. The Supreme Court agreed with him.

Judge Edgerton has been jealous of the rights of the insane. Insisting on strict compliance with the law as to the arrest of such persons, he wrote:

> In providing protection for persons whose relatives think or pretend to think that they require restraint because of mental

illness, Congress necessarily struck a balance between individual liberty and public safety. A policeman or a psychiatrist may think Congress should have drawn the line in a different place but may not make arrests on that theory. Some insane and some sane persons may well be thought dangerous, but even the most reasonable belief that they will do harm in the future does not justify doctor or layman in arresting them without statutory authorization and without a warrant. *Jillson* v. *Caprio,* 181 F. 2d 523, 524–525.

He refused to permit the confidential relationship between doctor and patient to be breached when the patient was a man charged with crime and committed to St. Elizabeths Hospital and the doctor was the government psychiatrist who attended him there. *Taylor* v. *United States,* 222 F. 2d 398.[3] He has consistently supported the rule in the *Durham* case.

In the difficult cases arising out of the Government's anti-Communist program Judge Edgerton has refused to accept the legal fictions that have been advanced to support it. To the contention that the Attorney General's list is not a public matter he replied:

> Appellees' ruling is said to be a mere matter of internal management. Even in such matters the Constitution governs. But there was nothing internal about the publication of the ruling. It was chiefly this publication that injured the appellant and its members and restricted the freedom of government employees. The right to hire and fire is not a right to broadcast statements that appellant, and so the members who compose it, are criminals or that they are subversive. *Joint Anti-Fascist Refugee Committee* v. *Clark,* infra, p. 121.

[3] Five months after this case was decided Congress amended the law of the District of Columbia as to the confidential relationship between doctor and patient so as to require a psychiatrist to testify as to mental competency in criminal trials where the defense of insanity is raised. P.L. 313, 84th Congress, 1st Session, August 9, 1955.

He rejected the argument that congressional inquiry into opinions does not restrict freedom of speech and conscience and wrote:

> There has been some suggestion that it restrains only timid people. I think it nearer the truth to say that, among the more articulate, it affects in one degree or another all but the very courageous, the very orthodox, and the very secure. But nothing turns on this question of fact. The views of timid people are not necessarily worthless to society. No one needs self-expression more. The Constitution protects them as it protects others. *Barsky* v. *United States*, infra, p. 48.

In these cases he has consistently taken the position that the erosion of constitutional rights is of itself a danger to the national security.

Insofar as the rights of Negroes are concerned, Judge Edgerton has been a pioneer. He was the first to write an opinion—a dissent —denying the validity of restrictive covenants banning the sale or lease of real property to Negroes. The first case in which this issue came before him, *Mays* v. *Burgess*, was not appealed, but in a second case, *Hurd* v. *Hodge*, infra, p. 250, he took the position that such covenants, even if valid between private individuals, were not enforceable in the courts. The Supreme Court agreed with him. He also wrote the first opinion, again a dissenting one, in a case that was not appealed, holding that segregation in the public schools of the District of Columbia is unconstitutional. This opinion he concluded with ringing words that have proved to be prophetic.

> It is sometimes suggested that due process of law cannot require what law cannot enforce. No such suggestion is relevant here. When United States courts order integration of District of Columbia schools they will be integrated. It has been too long forgotten that the District of Columbia is not a provincial community but the cosmopolitan capital of a nation that professes democracy. *Carr* v. *Corning*, infra, p. 273.

Judge Edgerton never forgets that as a liberal judge on an intermediate court he must convince both his orthodox colleagues and the members of the Supreme Court that his position is correct. At times his opinions read like briefs and seem rather bleak as he sets down the points of his arguments one by one and, in spite of his declaration of independence, piles up the precedents. At his best he shows himself to be a master of the legal craft. He is skilled in the use of the tools of the law, including the technicalities of pleading, to win his argument. It was his reliance on the last in the *Joint Anti-Fascist Refugee Committee* case that induced a member of the Supreme Court to join with four of his brethren to overrule the Court of Appeals. He can marshal facts with telling force. He has the gift of incisive and ironic phrase.

At times the critics have thought that the gate through which Judge Edgerton enters is too narrow, the path he follows too strait, and the philosophy that guides him too dogmatic, with the result that his decision in any given case is a foregone conclusion. There is also an impression that he is a confirmed dissenter. It is true that during the greater part of his service on the bench Judge Edgerton has found himself in what he considers to be the normal position for a liberal judge, that is, one of a minority among the orthodox. It may be that he believes that the dissent of today will be the law of tomorrow. However, a study of the cases in this volume will show that neither criticism is wholly justified. In seventeen cases he has spoken for the majority; in four others he has concurred in whole or in part with the judgment of the court. In only one case, *Pollak* v. *Public Utilities Commission*, infra, p. 27, in which he wrote the majority opinion, has he been specifically overruled by the Supreme Court. On several occasions a Justice of that Court has referred to one of Judge Edgerton's opinions with approval. He has dissented in twenty-one cases. In two of these the Supreme Court, on appeal, divided equally, four supporting the Court of Appeals and four agreeing with the dissent. In nine cases the Supreme Court over-ruled the Court of Appeals and supported Judge Edgerton's position. In several instances, when a case was not appealed, notably in the cases involving restrictive covenants and segregated education, Judge Edgerton has anticipated a later decision of the Supreme Court. It would seem that his philosophy of law has made him more aware of the currents of his time than has that of his more orthodox colleagues.

It would be a poor compliment to the Supreme Court to suggest that it is the relatively superficial arts of persuasion that have led to the ultimate vindication of so many of Judge Edgerton's opinions. Far more important are his careful and complete exposition of the grounds for his decision and his ability to penetrate to the underlying social and human realities of a case and recognize when the old rules of law no longer meet modern needs or conform to modern knowledge. Perhaps most important of all is the fact that his opinions are infused with the moral sense without which the law cannot reach its desired end of justice.

Judge Edgerton, in his article on Judge Pound, says that "a judge's emotions and point of view give direction to his work" and will be taken into account when it is evaluated. His own passion is for the preservation of a free society with all that that implies. When he weighs values, he does not think in terms of private versus public rights, nor does he find an inevitable conflict between the demands of individual liberty and national security. On his scales it is freedom that tips the balance.

I

Freedom of Religion, Speech, and the Press

Merchants of Religion

In the thirties and forties of this century a fundamentalist religious group called Jehovah's Witnesses embarked upon a course of aggressive evangelism, one of the most important results of which was the rapid development, along a zigzag course, of the meaning of the constitutional guarantee of freedom of religion, speech, and the press. Both the doctrines and the methods of this sect were highly unpopular. They attacked all organized religion, especially the Roman Catholic Church, refused to permit their children to participate in the flag-salute ceremonies required in the public schools, were militant pacifists, and in the war years claimed exemption from any form of military service on the ground that their members were ministers of the gospel or, in their terminology, "publishers." In their missionary zeal they claimed the right to invade homes in order to distribute their publications and to play their records attacking the Roman Catholic religion. The most innocuous of their activities was the distribution on city streets of their two religious publications—the

Sentinel and the *Watchtower*—but they refused to comply with existing licensing laws relating to peddlers, street vendors, and other users of the public streets. When convicted of violation of law, they fought their cases all the way to the Supreme Court, claiming that to apply a licensing requirement to their religious activities infringed the right of free speech and religion guaranteed by the First Amendment.

In 1938 in the first case involving this issue to reach the Supreme Court, *Lovell v. Griffin*, 303 U.S. 444, the ordinance in question gave unregulated discretion to the City Manager to permit or forbid the distribution of handbills. The Court held that this amounted to unconstitutional censorship of the press. In 1940 in *Cantwell v. Connecticut*, 310 U.S. 296, it found that a state law that required approval by the Secretary of State of solicitation for philanthropic and religious causes amounted to censorship of religion. In that same session, however, in *Minersville School District v. Gobitis*, 310 U.S. 586, the Court sustained the compulsory flag salute in public schools which the Witnesses believed to involve a violation of the First Commandment. In 1941 in *Cox v. New Hampshire*, 312 U.S. 569, the Supreme Court found that a fee that was calculated simply to cover the costs of policing a parade for religious purposes was reasonable, and in 1942 in three cases heard together—*Jones v. Opelika, Bowden v. Ft. Smith*, and *Jobin v. Arizona*, 316 U.S. 584—it upheld, in a 5 to 4 decision, a simple license tax for the distribution of literature, handbills, etc., that involved no discrimination and had no element of censorship.

In 1943 the trend of the decisions altered again, this time in favor of the Witnesses. In *West Virginia State Board of Education v. Barnette*, 319 U.S. 464, the Court overruled its earlier decision as to the constitutionality of the compulsory flag salute when refused because of religious scruples. In the second case of *Jones v. Opelika*, 319 U.S. 103, and in *Murdock v. Pennsylvania*, 319 U.S. 109, it reversed itself on the issue of a simple license tax when applied to the distribution of religious literature and in *Martin* v. *Struthers*, 319 U.S. 141, ruled that a city ordinance forbidding doorbell ringing to distribute handbills, etc., violated the guarantees of freedom of speech and the press. In the *Murdock* case the Court enunciated a new doctrine, namely, that "freedom of the press, freedom of speech, freedom of religion are in a preferred position."

David Busey and Orville J. Richie

v.

District of Columbia

Decided November 8, 1943

Before Groner, *Chief Judge*, and Miller and Edgerton, *JJ.*

David Busey and Orville J. Richie were two Jehovah's Witnesses who in 1941, the year of the first decision in *Jones* v. *Opelika*, undertook to distribute *Consolation* and the *Watchtower* on the streets of Washington, D.C., at an advertised price of five cents each. They had not paid the five-dollar licensing tax required of all street vendors and were both convicted and fined five dollars for violating the licensing law of the District of Columbia. At their trial they contended that they were proclaiming the gospel, not engaging in the business of selling magazines and so were not subject to the licensing tax. They appealed from their conviction on the ground that the license requirement when applied to them impaired freedom of the press and of religion. Believing itself to be bound by the recent decisions of the Supreme Court, the Court of Appeals sustained the conviction. The case was appealed to the Supreme Court and reached it after the decisions in the second case of *Jones* v. *Opelika* and in *Murdock* v. *Pennsylvania*. The Supreme Court remanded the case to the Court of Appeals for reconsideration in the light of its later decisions.

EDGERTON, *J.:* Appellants were convicted of selling copies of Consolation and Watch Tower, magazines published by Jehovah's Witnesses, on the streets of the District of Columbia without paying a license "tax" or fee and in other respects complying with the license law. Each appellant was sentenced to a fine of $5, or one day in jail.

The appeal has been here before. When we decided it in April, 1942, the majority of this court thought that decisions of the Supreme Court required us to hold the statute valid. In cases from other jurisdictions which it decided two months later, the Supreme Court not only confirmed that view but went beyond it, by upholding larger license taxes imposed merely for revenue purposes upon the sale of much the same literature in much smaller communities. But the Chief Justice and three Associate Justices dissented in those cases, and upon a change in the Court's membership in February, 1943, it granted rehearings in them. Though no member of the Court changed his position, the Court afterwards adopted the dissenting opinions which had previously been filed and reversed the state court judgments which had previously been affirmed. The Court then granted certiorari in the present case, heard argument, and remanded the case to enable us to re-examine our rulings on the construction and validity of the statute in the light of the Court's recent *Opelika* and *Murdock* decisions.

Construction. The District of Columbia license law provides: "No person shall sell any article of merchandise, or anything whatever, excepting newspapers sold at large and not from a fixed location, upon the public streets . . . without a license first having been obtained under this section." It requires a licensee to wear a numbered badge and to pay for his license at the rate of $12 a year or $1 a month, with a minimum of $5. The cost of a license to each appellant would have been $5. A violator of the license law may be fined not more than $300 or imprisoned not more than 90 days.

As we pointed out in our former opinion, the license law is a police or regulatory measure. Its aim is not to impose a "tax" for general revenue purposes but to provide a "fee . . . commensurate with the cost . . . of . . . inspection, supervision, or regulation."

Appellants stood on a street-corner and, by signs which they carried, offered magazines to the public at five cents each. Each appellant handed a magazine to the prosecuting witness and collected five cents. When this case was here before, appellants' counsel conceded that appellants "did sell" these two magazines. We held that their acts were within the meaning of the statute even if inferences not required by the record were drawn in their favor, *viz.*, that they were not engaged in a business or calling, that they acted from religious motives, and that they neither derived nor sought a profit from their sales. For the reasons which we stated in our former opinion, we now reach the same conclusion on this point. . . .

The *Murdock* opinion is more closely related to this question than the *Opelika* opinion. It does not call for a different answer. In the first place, *Murdock* involved a tax for general revenue purposes while the present case involves a fee for regulatory purposes. Second, the conduct of the Witnesses in that case and in this was different. There they engaged in house-to-house solicitation, including alleged "sales" of books and pamphlets. The Supreme Court said: "There was evidence that it was their practice in making these solicitations to request a 'contribution' of twenty-five cents each for the books and five cents each for the pamphlets . . ." The present appellants, on the other hand, displayed printed signs which read "Five cents per copy." As we have said, on the former hearing their counsel admitted that they made sales. Finally, the Supreme Court did not hold or say that the Witnesses made no sales in the *Murdock* case. While the Court thought it "a distortion of the facts of record to describe their activities as the occupation of selling books and pamphlets," in that statement the word "occupation" appears to be critical. For the Court went on to speak of the "selling activities" of the defendants, as being incidental to the object of propagating their doctrines.

Validity. The validity of the District of Columbia statute in the light of the *Opelika* and *Murdock* decisions is a harder question than its construction. While *Murdock* and the two cases decided with *Opelika* involved house-to-house sales, *Opelika* itself involved street sales similar to those which appellants made. The Supreme Court held that sales for propaganda purposes could not be subjected to taxation for general revenue purposes. Such taxation, the Court held, violated the constitutional freedoms of speech, press, and religion. But the Court emphasized the fact that it was dealing with "a flat tax, more than a nominal fee to defray the expenses of a regulatory license." In his dissenting opinion in the first *Opelika* case, which has now been adopted by the Court, the Chief Justice pointed out that the ordinances "on their face purport to be an exercise of the municipality's taxing power. In none is there the slightest pretense by the taxing authority, or the slightest suggestion by the state court, that the 'fee' is to defray expenses of the licensing system. . . . The controversy has been one solely relating to the power to tax, and not the power to collect a 'fee' to support a licensing system . . . This Court has often had occasion to point out that where the State may, as a regulatory measure, license activities which it is without constitutional authority to tax, it may charge a small or nominal fee sufficient to defray the expense of licensing . . ." *Jones* v. *Opelika*, 316 U.S. 584, 604–605. The Court used similar language in the *Murdock* case.

Since the fee in the present case is intended merely to defray the expenses of licensing and regulation, the rulings, as distinguished from the argument, in *Opelika* and *Murdock* do not apply here. But the argument which we have just quoted and which we take as our guide implies that if a fee so intended is in fact more than adequate to defray those expenses, or is more than "small or nominal," its enforcement against street sellers of religious propaganda would violate the constitutional freedoms of speech, press, and religion.

The record does not show what the expenses of licensing and regulation are. We must therefore determine who had the burden of proving them. When state taxes on the use of highways by motor vehicles have been attacked as interferences with interstate commerce the Supreme Court has held, in accordance with the general principle that legislation is to be presumed constitutional until the contrary is shown, that the taxpayer has the burden of showing that the tax exceeds the expenses incurred by the taxing authority.

It does not necessarily follow that the present appellants have the burden of proving that the license fees which the District of Columbia imposes on their sales exceed the expenses of licensing and regulation.

Freedoms of speech, press, and religion are entitled to a preferred constitutional position because they are "of the very essence of a scheme of ordered liberty." *Palko* v. *Connecticut*, 302 U.S. 319, 325. They are essential not only to the persons or groups directly concerned but to the entire community. Our whole political and social system depends upon them. Any interference with them is not only an abuse but an obstacle to the correction of other abuses. Because they are essential, the guarantees of free speech, press, and religion in the First Amendment, though not all constitutional guarantees, are within the "liberty" which is protected by the due process clause of the Fourteenth Amendment. And in the recent flag salute case the Supreme Court said: "The right of a state to regulate, for example, a public utility may well include, so far as the due process test is concerned, power to impose all of the restrictions which a legislature may have a 'rational basis' for adopting. But freedoms of speech and of press, of assembly, and of worship may not be infringed on such slender grounds." *The West Virginia State Board of Education v. Barnette,* 319 U.S. 624. The Supreme Court has specifically suggested that these freedoms may be entitled to special treatment in respect to the proof of facts on which the constitutionality of legislation depends. In sustaining a purely commercial regulation, the Court said: "The existence of facts supporting the legislative judgment is to be presumed, for regulatory legislation affecting ordinary commercial transactions is not to be pronounced unconstitutional unless in the light of the facts made known or generally assumed it is of such a character as to preclude the assumption that it rests upon some rational basis . . . There may be narrower scope for operation of the presumption of constitutionality when legislation appears on its face to be within a specific prohibition of the Constitution, such as those of the first ten amendments, which are deemed equally specific when held to be embraced within the Fourteenth." *United States v. Carolene Products Co.,* 304 U.S. 144, 152.

We think we may now hold that when legislation appears on its face to affect the use of speech, press, or religion, and when its validity depends upon the existence of facts which are not proved, their existence should not be presumed; at least when their existence is hardly more probable than improbable, and particularly when proof concerning them is more readily available to the government than to the citizen. The burden of proof in such a case should be upon those who deny that these freedoms are invaded. In many contexts it is both rational and convenient to presume "the existence of facts supporting the legislative judgment." But it would be neither rational nor convenient to presume that the uniform fee by which Congress sought to cover the cost of policing all sorts of street sales happens not to exceed the cost of policing the particular sort involved here.

The case comes to this. The argument in *Opelika* and *Murdock* implies that a regulatory license fee which exceeds the cost

of policing sales of religious propaganda is a prohibited interference with the freedoms of speech, press, and religion. There
is no evidence, and no clear probability, that the District of
Columbia license fee does not exceed the cost of policing these
sales. No presumption which lacks a probable basis in fact should
be permitted to conceal an interference with essential freedoms.
It follows that § 47-2336 of the license law appears on this record
to be invalid as against the appellants, and their convictions
should be reversed. We need not consider whether the fee which
each of these appellants would have had to pay in order to obtain
a license was "small or nominal."

The Right to Know

Martin L. Sweeney

v.

Eleanor M. Patterson

Decided May 25, 1942

Before Miller, Vinson, and Edgerton, *JJ*.

Edgerton, *J.*: This is one of a series of libel suits which appellant brought, in various courts and against various defendants, because of an article which was written by appellees Pearson
and Allen and published in appellee Patterson's newspaper,
among others. The complaint states that appellant is a member
of Congress from Ohio and a member of the Ohio bar. It alleges,
in the usual language of libel suits, that appellees intended to and
did injure his reputation; but it alleges no special damage. Appellees, in their answers, defended on grounds of privilege and truth.

This appeal is from an order granting appellees' motion for judgment on the pleadings.

The article follows. We italicize those sentences which appellant says are false:

"*A hot behind-the-scenes fight is raging in Democratic congressional ranks over the effort of Father Coughlin to prevent the appointment of a Jewish judge in Cleveland.* The proposed appointee is Emerich Burt Freed, U.S. District Attorney in Cleveland and former law partner of Senator Bulkley, who is on the verge of being elevated to the U.S. District Court. *This has aroused the violent opposition of Representative Martin L. Sweeney, Democrat of Cleveland, known as the chief congressional spokesman of Father Coughlin. Basis of the Sweeney-Coughlin opposition is the fact that Freed is a Jew, and one not born in the United States.* Born in Hungary in 1897, Freed was brought to the United States at the age of 13, was naturalized 10 years later. Justice Department officials say he has made an excellent record as U.S. Attorney, is able, progressive, and was second on the list of judicial candidates submitted by the executive committee of the Cleveland Bar Association. First on the list was Carl Friebolin, whom Justice Department officials say they would have gladly appointed despite his age of 60, had he not eliminated himself voluntarily for physical reasons. Two others on the Bar Association's list, Walter Kinder and Harry Brainard, were eliminated because of big business or reactionary connections. Last on the list was Dan B. Cull, a former Common Pleas Court judge, and an excellent appointment except that he happened to be a Catholic and the last two judicial appointments in Ohio have been Catholics. So the Justice Department returned to the No. 2 man on the list, a Jew. *Irate, Representative Sweeney is endeavoring to call a caucus of Ohio Representatives December 28 to protest against Freed's appointment.*"

Even if the italicized statements are false, appellant has stated no claim on which relief can be granted. The cases are in conflict, but in our view it is not actionable to publish erroneous and injurious statements of fact and injurious comment or opinion regarding the political conduct and views of public officials, so long as no charge of crime, corruption, gross immorality or gross incompetence is made and no special damage results. Such a publication is not "libelous per se." We need not consider whether it is privileged. Appellant might be entitled to relief if he had lost his seat in Congress, or had lost employment, as a lawyer or otherwise, or had been put to expense, or had suffered any other economic injury, by reason of appellees' statements. We do not decide that question, since it is not before us. Appellant alleges no such injury.

Cases which impose liability for erroneous reports of the political conduct of officials reflect the obsolete doctrine that the governed must not criticize their governors. Since Congress governs the country, all inhabitants, and not merely the constituents of particular members, are vitally concerned in the political conduct and views of every member of Congress. Everyone, including appellees and their readers, has an interest to defend, and any one may find means of defending it. The interest of the public here outweighs the interest of appellant or any other individual. The protection of the public requires not merely discussion, but information. Political conduct and views which some respectable people approve, and others condemn, are constantly imputed to Congressmen. Errors of fact, particularly in regard to a man's mental states and processes, are inevitable. Information and discussion will be discouraged, and the public interest in public knowledge of important facts will be poorly defended, if error subjects its author to a libel suit without even a showing of economic loss. Whatever is added to the field of libel is taken from the field of free debate. If other public interests are thought to outweigh, in respect to some utterances, the public interest in knowledge and debate, they call for legislative changes in public law rather than judicial changes in the law of libel. . . .

The Unwilling Listener

FRANKLIN POLLAK and GUY MARTIN

v.

PUBLIC UTILITIES COMMISSION OF THE DISTRICT OF COLUMBIA

Decided June 1, 1951

Before EDGERTON, BAZELON, and FAHY, *Circuit Judges*

In the late 1940's the street railway systems in some twelve cities, among them Washington, D.C., sought to increase their falling revenues by installing radios in streetcars and buses. The innovation was euphemistically called "Music As You Ride," but the programs, which, in the District of Columbia, were operated twelve hours a day, included commercials about every five minutes and various announcements. There was no way in which an objecting rider could turn off the programs or reduce their volume. In the District of Columbia the majority of riders were either pleased by or indifferent to the practice. A minority, estimated by the Public Utilities Commission as 3 per cent, composed of those who were sensitive to noise or musically educated, found that the broadcasts, especially at the end of a long, tiring day's work, amounted to a kind of torture. These riders protested vigorously against the practice and appealed to the Public Utilities Commission to stop it. The Commission refused to do so, the District Court sustained the Commission, and the protesting riders appealed. The American Civil Liberties Union was

permitted to file a brief *amicus curiae* supporting the protest. Judge
Edgerton wrote the opinion of the court, ruling against the Public
Utilities Commission.

The Public Utilities Commission and the Transit Company in turn
appealed from the adverse ruling of the Court of Appeals to the
Supreme Court, which agreed to hear the case. In a 6 to 1 decision,
343 U.S. 451, the Supreme Court reversed the Court of Appeals.
Justice Frankfurter did not participate in the case because he was
"too bitterly offended by the practice." The Court agreed that the
action of the Transit Company, which derived its powers from a
franchise granted by the Congress, amounted to "state action" in
the constitutional sense, but they found that neither the First nor the
Fifth Amendment was violated by radio broadcasts that were not
used for propaganda and did not prevent conversation. Justice
Black thought that there was nothing unconstitutional in the practice of broadcasting music, but that forced listening to broadcasting
of public speeches and propaganda would be a violation of the First
Amendment. Justice Douglas dissented from the majority opinion.

EDGERTON, *Circuit Judge:* Appellee Capital Transit Company
(Transit) operates streetcars and buses in the District of Columbia. In 1948 Transit made a contract with appellee Washington
Transit Radio, Inc., (Radio) by which Radio was to install and
maintain loudspeakers in Transit vehicles and provide broadcasts
at least 8 hours daily except Sunday. In October, 1949, loudspeakers were in operation in 212 vehicles and it was planned to
increase the number to 1,500.

Though Transit and Radio call the broadcasts "music as you
ride," they include not only music but also "commercials, announcements, and time signals." The contract permits six minutes of "commercial announcements" per hour. These vary from
15 to 35 seconds in length and are usually scheduled about once
in five minutes, though the interval varies.

Appellee Public Utilities Commission received protests against
Transit's use of radio. It ordered an investigation and held a

hearing "to determine whether or not the installation and use of radio receivers on the street cars and busses of Capital Transit Company is consistent with public convenience, comfort and safety . . ." Appellants, who ride Transit vehicles, and other persons and organizations were allowed to intervene and took part in the hearing. The Commission found that transit radio does not reduce safety, "tends to improve the conditions under which the public rides," and "is not inconsistent with public convenience, comfort and safety." The Commission's final order "dismissed" its investigation.

Appellants and others appealed to the District Court from the Commission's order. Appellants' petition of appeal states that appellants are "obliged to use the street cars and busses of Capital Transit Company in connection with the practice of their pro-fession and on other occasions and are thereby subjected against their will to the broadcasts in issue. These broadcasts make it difficult for petitioners to read and converse . . ." Each of the appellees, i.e. the Commission, Transit, and Radio, moved to dismiss the petitions of appeal as not stating claims on which relief could be granted and as not within the court's jurisdiction. The court dismissed the petitions on the ground that "no legal right of the petitioners . . . has been invaded . . ." This appeal followed.

Appellants' chief contention is that Transit radio deprives them of liberty without due process of law in violation of the Fifth Amendment of the Constitution. . . .

2. Transit passengers commonly have to hear the broadcasts whether they want to or not. The Commission made no finding on this point but the fact is well known. It was proved by many witnesses. It is in legal effect admitted by appellees' motions to dismiss the petition of appeal, since the petition states that appel-lants "are subjected against their will to the broadcasts in issue. These broadcasts make it difficult for petitioners to read and converse . . ." The brief of appellee Radio admits the fact in

these terms: "it is impossible to give effect to this alleged right [not to listen] without frustrating the desire of other passengers to listen . . ." Appellee Transit says in its brief: "The record shows that *every precaution is taken* in the installation of the equipment and its maintenance *to minimize the sound level at the operators' position* and to distribute sound evenly throughout the public spaces in the vehicle . . ." WWDC-FM, the transmitting station, advertised in 1949 that Transit Radio was "delivering a guaranteed audience." The passengers are known in the industry as a "captive audience." Formerly they were free to read, talk, meditate, or relax. The broadcasts have replaced freedom of attention with forced listening.

Most people have to use mass transportation. In the District of Columbia this means they have to use Transit and hear the broadcasts. Even as between the District and the adjoining Pentagon region in Virginia the Supreme Court has said: ". . . most government employees, in going to and returning from their work, were compelled to begin or complete their trips by utilizing buses or streetcars of Capital Transit." *United States* v. *Capital Transit Co.,* 325 U.S. 357, 359.

3. Though statutes and the law of torts forbid invasions of liberty by private individuals, the constitutional guarantees of liberty are directed against government action. But acts of individuals are beyond the reach of these guarantees only when they are "unsupported by State authority in the shape of laws, customs, or judicial or executive proceedings." . . . A private corporation that owns the streets of a town may no more abridge the freedoms of press and religion than a municipality regularly organized. *Marsh* v. *Alabama,* 326 U.S. 501, 506. The Supreme Court has recently said: "When authority derives in part from Government's thumb on the scales, the exercise of that power by private persons becomes closely akin, in some respects, to its exercise by Government itself." *American Communications Ass'n* v. *Douds,* 339 U.S. 382, 401.

The forced listening imposed on Transit passengers results from government action. By authorizing Transit and forbidding others to operate local streetcars and buses, Congress made it necessary to ride the vehicles in which Transit makes it necessary to hear the broadcasts. Streetcars and buses cannot operate in city streets without a franchise. Congress has given Transit not only a franchise but a virtual monopoly of the entire local business of mass transportation of passengers in the District of Columbia.

Furthermore the forced listening has been sanctioned by the governmental action of the Commission. If the Commission had found it contrary to public comfort or convenience, or unreasonable, it would have stopped. Because the Commission decided otherwise it continues. To suggest that a "negative" order cannot be the final step in a misuse of government power is to assert a distinction the Supreme Court has repudiated. . . . Even failure to enter any order may be a denial of constitutional rights. *Smith* v. *Illinois Bell Tel. Co.*, 270 U.S. 587. By dismissing its investigation the Commission declined to prevent valid action of Congress from having an unintended and unnecessary result.

4. No occasion had arisen until now to give effect to freedom from forced listening as a constitutional right. Short of imprisonment, the only way to compel a man's attention for many minutes is to bombard him with sound that he cannot ignore in a place where he must be. The law of nuisance protects him at home. At home or at work, the constitutional question has not arisen because the government has taken no part in forcing people to listen. Until radio was developed and someone realized that the passengers of a transportation monopoly are a captive audience, there was no profitable way of forcing people to listen while they travel between home and work or on necessary errands. Exploitation of this audience through assault on the unavertible sense of hearing is a new phenomenon. It raises "issues that were not implied in the means of communication known or

contemplated by Franklin and Jefferson and Madison." Mr. Justice Frankfurter, concurring, in *Kovacs* v. *Cooper*, 336 U.S. 77, 96. But the Bill of Rights, as appellants say in their brief, can keep up with anything an advertising man or an electronics engineer can think of. . . .

If Transit obliged its passengers to read what it liked or get off the car, invasion of their freedom would be obvious. Transit obliges them to hear what it likes or get off the car. Freedom of attention, which forced listening destroys, is a part of liberty essential to individuals and to society. The Supreme Court has said that the constitutional guarantee of liberty "embraces not only the right of a person to be free from physical restraint, but the right to be free in the enjoyment of all his faculties . . ." *Grosjean* v. *American Press Co.*, 297 U.S. 233, 244. One who is subjected to forced listening is not free in the enjoyment of all his faculties.

Both the decision and the opinions in *Kovacs* v. *Cooper*, 336 U.S. 77, give great weight to the public interest in freedom from forced listening. The Supreme Court upheld a municipal ordinance prohibiting loud and raucous sound trucks in public streets. . . . The Supreme Court's decision upholding the ordinance means that the public interest in freedom from forced listening is so important as to outweigh even the public interest in making more effective, by amplifying, a communication protected by the First Amendment. It would seem to follow that the public interest in freedom from forced listening outweighs the private interest in making more effective, by amplifying, a communication not protected by the First Amendment. The Amendment does not protect commercial advertising. *Valentine* v. *Chrestensen*, 316 U.S. 52.

Validation of the forced listening involved here would result in this curious paradox. Although a municipality may forbid speech protected by the First Amendment from being broadcast in a street, where no one need hear it more than a few minutes, speech not protected by the First Amendment may be broadcast in a streetcar where passengers must hear it for a substantial time.

Of course freedom from forced listening, like other freedoms, is not absolute. No doubt the government may compel attention, as it may forbid speech, in exceptional circumstances. But deprivation of liberty to which the government is a party is unconstitutional when it is "arbitrary or without reasonable relation to some purpose within the competency of the State to effect." *Meyer* v. *Nebraska*, 262 U.S. 390, 400. Forcing Transit passengers to hear these broadcasts has no reasonable relation to any such purpose. Some discomforts may perhaps be inevitable incidents of mass transportation, but forced listening is neither incidental nor inevitable. It deprives the appellants and other passengers who object to the broadcasts of their liberty for the private use of Transit, Radio, and passengers who like the broadcasts. This loss of freedom of attention is the more serious because many people have little time to read, consider, or discuss what they like, or to relax. The record makes it plain that the loss is a serious injury to many passengers. They suffer not only the discomfort of hearing what they dislike but a sense of outrage at being compelled to hear whatever Transit and Radio choose.

Willing hearers are entertained by the broadcasts. But the profit of Transit and Radio and the entertainment of one group of passengers cannot justify depriving another group of passengers of their liberty. The interest of some in hearing what they like is not a right to make others hear the same thing. Even if an impartial survey had shown that most passengers liked the broadcasts or were willing to tolerate them on the supposed chance of a money benefit, that would not be important, since the will of a majority cannot abrogate the constitutional rights of a minority. Moreover there is no evidence that any large group of passengers actually wish to go on being entertained by broadcasts forced upon other passengers at the cost of their comfort and freedom.[1]

[1] An organization employed by appellees Transit and Radio to make a survey of passenger sentiment failed to ask persons who said they favored

5. It has been argued that when freedom of attention is abridged freedom of speech and press are abridged, and that when Transit sells the forced attention of its passengers to Radio for advertising purposes it deprives them of property as well as liberty. Also, it may well be doubted whether Transit can perform its statutory duty of providing comfortable service for all by giving more than comfortable service to some and less than comfortable service to others. But we need not consider these issues. In our opinion Transit's broadcasts deprive objecting passengers of liberty without due process of law. Service that violates constitutional rights is not reasonable service. It follows that the Commission erred as a matter of law in finding that Transit's broadcasts are not inconsistent with public convenience, in failing to find that they are unreasonable, and in failing to stop them.

This decision applies to "commercials" and to "announcements." We are not now called upon to decide whether occasional broadcasts of music alone would infringe constitutional rights. . . .

---

transit radio whether they would still favor it if they knew it caused serious annoyance to a substantial number of passengers. Yet this survey did ask persons who said they opposed transit radio whether they would still object if the majority approved. To investigate the altruism of the objecting group and not that of the approving group reflects bias and produces a biased result. Moreover the survey did not inquire into the intensity of likes and dislikes. It ignored the question how many persons have been induced by the broadcasts to use Transit less, or more, than formerly.

All persons interviewed were passengers on radio-equipped vehicles. According to the report 76.3% said they favored radio, 13.9% did not care, 3.2% "didn't know," and 6.6% objected but 3.6% said they would not oppose the majority will. An unbiased inquiry which did not claim to be scientific produced a different result. On November 6, 1949 the Washington Post printed two "ballots," one reading "Yes I favor radio broadcasts in streetcars and buses" and the other "No I do not favor radio broadcasts in streetcars and buses." On November 13, 1949 the Post reported that of the 5,402 ballots returned, 2,387 favored the broadcasts and 3,015, or 55.8%, did not.

II

The "Informing Function" of Congress

Although the Constitution is silent on the point, Congress from the first days of the Republic has asserted the right to conduct investigations, to summon witnesses to testify, and to discipline those who refuse to answer the questions put to them. As Professor Robert K. Carr has pointed out, public approval or disapproval of a particular investigation has often depended upon agreement or disagreement with the political color of Congress or its committees, but the basic power, "the informing function" as Woodrow Wilson has called it, has generally been recognized as necessary to the intelligent exercise of the legislative powers of Congress and also as a legitimate and important instrument of public education. False testimony before congressional committees has always subjected a witness to prosecution for perjury provided the falsehood is deliberate and related to a matter material to the inquiry.

Until the middle of the nineteenth century the merely recalcitrant witness was summoned to the bar of the House and if necessary imprisoned until he agreed to testify or until Congress adjourned, when he had to be released. In 1857 Congress pro-

vided for more uniform punishment for those guilty of this form
of contempt of its processes. It passed a law making it a misdemeanor to refuse to answer "pertinent" questions in connection with any matter "properly under consideration by either
house." Since then, although the old power of punishment by
Congress itself still exists, witnesses in contempt of investigating
committees have been prosecuted in the courts.

For many years the right of congressional committees to question the witnesses before them was rarely challenged, and by
1948 only three cases involving the scope of the congressional
power of investigation had reached the Supreme Court. In them
the Court had found that the right to investigate is a necessary
aspect of legislative power but must be used only for a proper
legislative purpose—a term that includes investigation of the
activities of government officials and the disposition of government properties but does not extend to investigation of private
affairs. It further ruled that the Court may review the exercise of
the power by Congress. Justice Brandeis thought that this right
of judicial review would prevent abuse of the congressional
power. These cases gave very little guidance to the lower courts
when later they had to deal with a spate of cases in which reluc-
tant witnesses contended that the activities of investigating committees had violated the provisions of the Bill of Rights.

In 1938 a new era of congressional investigations began in
which the questions put to witnesses by certain committees dealt
primarily with their economic or political beliefs and their or-
ganizational associations. In that year Congressman Martin Dies
of Texas introduced the resolution that created the first Un-
American Activities Committee and authorized it to investigate:

> 1) The extent, character, and objects of un-American propa-
> ganda activities in the United States, 2) the diffusion within
> the United States of subversive and un-American propaganda
> that is instigated from foreign countries or of a domestic origin
> and attacks the principle of the form of government as guaran-

teed by our Constitution, 3) all other questions in relation thereto that would aid Congress in any necessary remedial action.

Speaking in support of this resolution, the Congressman said:

> I am not in a position to know whether we can legislate effectively in reference to this matter, but I do know that exposure in a democracy of subversive activities is the most effective weapon that we have in our possession. Always we must keep in mind that in any legislative attempt to prevent un-American activities, we may jeopardize fundamental rights far more precious than the objective we seek but when these activities are exposed, when the light of day is brought to bear upon them, we can trust public sentiment in this country to do the rest.

The life of this temporary committee, popularly known as the Dies Committee, was extended by resolution in each succeeding Congress until in 1945 it was made a permanent standing committee, a status that was confirmed by the Legislative Reorganization Act of 1946.

Mr. Dies forecast accurately the work of his Committee and its successors. It was not until 1947 that problems of legislation constituted any substantial part of the Committee's activities. Its hearings were devoted for the most part to the exposure of organizations allegedly Communist and of individuals accused by it of Communist associations. The Committee has continued to assert from time to time that exposure is "its job." Its publications consist largely of the listing of names of persons and organizations allegedly Communist, and it has issued pamphlets based solely on staff investigations without the benefit of hearings or even of notice to those involved.

In 1950 the Senate entered the same area of investigation. It established a subcommittee of the Judiciary Committee to serve as a watchdog over the administration of the new Internal Security Act and related legislation. When in 1952 Senator McCarthy took over the chairmanship of the Subcommittee on

Investigations of the Government Operations Committee, he proceeded to devote his monstrous energies and inventiveness almost entirely to questioning the beliefs and associations of individuals both in and out of the government service.

In 1946 and 1947 the Un-American Activities Committee found itself dealing with a number of recalcitrant witnesses, many of whom, the record shows, were plainly guilty of contempt in the ordinary sense of the word. Dr. Barsky, the president, and fifteen officers of an organization called the Joint Anti-Fascist Refugee Committee refused to honor a subpoena requiring them to produce the books and papers of their Committee and to name its members. A little later the chairman of the National Federation for Constitutional Liberties and the executive secretary of the National Council of American-Soviet Friendship took a similar position before the Un-American Activities Committee. In stormy sessions Gerhard Eisler and Leon Josephson, two prominent Communists, refused to be sworn when they appeared before the Committee, and Eugene Dennis, the chairman of the Communist Party, at first demanded to be heard and when the demand was granted refused to appear, submitting instead a statement in which he said, "In the name of the American people, I hold this Committee in contempt." In Washington in the course of spectacular hearings on communism in Hollywood ten turbulent witnesses refused to answer the question, "Are you now or have you ever been a Communist?" All these persons were promptly cited for contempt of Congress and were indicted, tried, and convicted in the district courts of the United States where their constitutional objections to the power of the Committee received short shrift.

In the Second Circuit and in the District of Columbia the appellate courts took the position that they were balancing private right against public security and in 2 to 1 decisions ruled in favor of the latter. The Supreme Court refused to review the cases. Thereafter until the decision in the *Watkins* case in 1957, the courts of the District of Columbia were bound by the first decision of the Court of Appeals.

Judicial sanction having been received, the hearings of the congressional committees investigating subversion became increasingly spectacular and the tactics of the investigators increasingly brutal. Other committees began to adopt some of their methods. After the conviction of the Communist leaders in 1949 for seditious conspiracy the view that members of the Communist Party are participants in an international conspiracy to overthrow the government was widely accepted. The whole area of investigation became affected with the taint of criminality. Hearings in both houses took on many of the aspects of a criminal trial in which the committee members were the accusers, the prosecutors, and the judges and in which there were no rules to protect the accused. Their effect, if not their purpose, was not only exposure but extralegal punishment including the denial of employment either in or out of government to those accused of Communist associations past or present. Congress also showed an increasing disposition to inflict legal punishment by referring cases to the Department of Justice for prosecution under either the perjury or the contempt statute.

In spite of these mounting pressures witnesses continued to refuse to answer certain questions, to appeal their convictions for contempt of Congress, and to assert among other things that their constitutional rights had been violated. After the first decisions the courts dealt with these cases in terms of statutory interpretation or acted on other relatively narrow grounds. Basically they were still weighing the imponderables, and opinion among the judges was still divided. Gradually the courts began to share the "wide concern both in and out of Congress over some aspects of the exercise of Congressional power of investigation," and the presumption that had equated congressional power with public interest and had brought the scales down on the side of the investigating committees began to be weakened.

In 1950 Mr. Edward A. Rumely, the executive secretary of a right-wing organization admittedly concerned with influencing legislation, was summoned before a special committee investigating lobbying. His organization was suspected of evading the Lobbying Act by the device of selling and distributing its publications instead of asking for contributions for lobbying purposes. Like Dr. Barsky, Mr. Rumely refused to give the Committee the names of contributors and subscribers to its publications on the ground that the request violated the First Amendment. His subsequent conviction for contempt was overturned by the Court of Appeals when Judge Prettyman distinguished Mr. Rumely's case from that of Dr. Barsky on the ground that the former involved no question of a recognized threat to our Government. The Government appealed, and the Supreme Court affirmed the judgment of the lower court. It deliberately refused, however, to consider the question of the impact of the First Amendment on the investigative power of Congress and simply found that the term "lobbying" in the Committee's authorizing resolution did not cover the activities in question.

In April, 1956, Judge Keech of the District Court for the District of Columbia had before him the records of a special investigating committee and the testimony of its chairman that showed that the Committee had summoned Aldo Lorenzo Icardi before it for the express purpose of laying the foundation for a perjury prosecution. Icardi had denied the accusation that he had murdered an American major in Italy. Judge Keech threw out the resulting indictment for perjury on the ground that when the Committee questioned Icardi it was acting as a committing magistrate, not as a legislative body. He stated that questions relating simply to guilt or innocence are not material to any legislative purpose.

In several cases the courts ruled that Senator McCarthy's Subcommittee on Government Operations was not authorized to question persons wholly unconnected with the Government as to their opinions and associations, and in three cases the Supreme Court sustained the right of witnesses before congressional committees to invoke the privilege against self-incrimination.

Finally, in 1957, the Supreme Court dealt directly with two of the more important constitutional issues. It reviewed a decision of the Court of Appeals, sustaining the conviction in the District Court of John T. Watkins for contempt of Congress in politely refusing to identify as Communists associates in Communist-front activities of some fifteen years ago, and reversed the judgment of the lower courts. Speaking for the Court, Chief Justice Warren discussed at some length the scope and limitations of the investigative power of Congress. "It encompasses," he said, "inquiries concerning the administration of existing laws as well as proposed or possibly needed statutes. It includes surveys of defects in our social, economic or political system for the purpose of enabling Congress to remedy them. It comprehends probes into the departments of the Federal Government to expose corruption, inefficiency or waste." The Chief Justice also listed the areas that are off bounds for congressional investigators. Congress, he declared, may not act as a law enforcement or trial agency, may not inquire into private affairs or make exposure an end in itself, unrelated to a legitimate legislative purpose, may not conduct investigations for the purpose of personal aggrandizement or the punishment of the individuals summoned before it. Furthermore, the power to investigate is subject to the limitations of the Bill of Rights, including the First Amendment. He then ruled that when Congress turns to the courts to enforce its powers through a criminal prosecution it is subject to the provision of due process that requires that a crime be clearly defined. The Committee when questioning Watkins had failed to meet this standard.

On the same day that it decided the *Watkins* case the Supreme Court also reversed the judgment of the Supreme Court of New Hampshire that sustained the conviction of Paul M. Sweezy for contempt committed in the course of a state legislative investiga-

tion of subversive activities within its borders. Sweezy had been
questioned as to the content of a lecture given by him at the
University of New Hampshire. The Court stated in this case that
there can be no doubt that such investigations may encroach upon
the constitutional liberties of individuals, and it appeared to take
the position that academic freedom and the privacy of political
belief are so important to a free society that they may not be
impaired by legislative investigations except in accordance with a
clear legislative mandate based upon compelling reasons of self-
protection for the state.

These two decisions aroused considerable hostility in Congress
and with the general public. The opinions in both cases were
somewhat obscure, and they were believed to go far beyond the
position which the Court later showed that it was prepared to
take. On June 8, 1959, the Court handed down two decisions,
Barenblatt v. *United States* and *Uphaus* v. *Wyman*, that limited
and, to that extent, clarified the earlier decisions. In both cases
it sustained convictions for contempt in refusing to answer questions put in the course of legislative investigations. The one
involved an inquiry by the Un-American Activities Committee
into communism in education; the other, the same investigation
as to the presence of "subversive persons" in the State of New
Hampshire that had been discussed in the *Sweezy* case. Barenblatt was questioned as to his past Communist membership and
activities. Uphaus was ordered to produce the list of guests at
the summer camp of an organization suspected of some Communist connections. The Court found that in each case the investigating body was pursuing a legitimate legislative purpose and
that the necessary clear mandate to ask the particular questions
could be found in their respective legislative histories. In the
Barenblatt case it stated that the field of education is not exempt
from such inquiry and that when Congress is pursuing a legitimate legislative purpose the Court has no authority to inquire as

to whether it is acting from ulterior motives such as exposure or punishment.

EDWARD K. BARSKY *et al.*

v.

UNITED STATES OF AMERICA

Decided March 18, 1948

Before EDGERTON, CLARK, and PRETTYMAN,
Associate Justices

The *Barsky* case was the second one to reach an appellate court in which an investigation by the Un-American Activities Committee was challenged on constitutional grounds. The first case had been heard shortly before in the Second Circuit and decided adversely to the appellant, Leon Josephson, by a divided court.

Dr. Edward K. Barsky and the other appellants were, respectively, the chairman and the members of the executive board of the Joint Anti-Fascist Refugee Committee, a private organization, the purpose of which was said to be to help Spanish Loyalists and German Communists who were refugees from Nazi and Fascist persecution. In 1946 the Un-American Activities Committee received complaints that the organization was in fact a Communist front, using the funds it collected for political propaganda instead of for relief. The Committee initiated an investigation of these charges. Dr. Barsky was subpoenaed and ordered to bring with him the books, records, and foreign correspondence of the organization. He appeared before the Committee, but, on advice of counsel, refused to produce the books and records on the ground that his executive board had instructed him not to do so. The Committee then issued subpoenas to all the other officers and members of the executive board. On April 4 they appeared before the Committee in executive session. There then began what Professor Robert K. Carr has called a game of "Button, button, who's got the button?" Each officer and board member, except Helen R. Bryan, the executive secretary, claimed that he could not produce the records because they were in the custody of Miss Bryan. She refused to produce them on the ground that the subpoena was invalid. All those involved were promptly cited for contempt of Congress. They were indicted and all but Miss Bryan and Miss Ernestina G. Fleischman were tried together in the District Court for the District of Columbia and convicted. They appealed, contending that the resolution establishing the Un-American Activities Committee was unconstitutional because it authorized the Committee to inquire into political opinion and expression and was so vague as to violate the Sixth Amendment. The appellate court overruled these contentions in a 2 to 1 decision, Judge Edgerton dissenting.

Judge Prettyman wrote the majority opinion in which he stated as his major premise that the problem is "the relative necessity of the public interest as against private rights." He was willing to assume that to compel a witness to reveal publicly his Communist beliefs or activities would be an interference with freedom of speech, but "unless democratic government (by which we mean government premised upon individual human rights) can protect itself by means commensurate with danger, it is doomed."

Speaking for the court, Judge Prettyman found not only that Congress has the right to investigate in any area in which it may legislate, regardless of any immediate legislative purpose, but that where there is a potential threat to the government itself it has both an independent right and a duty to inquire into that threat in order to preserve the government for the people and to fulfill the constitutional guarantee to the States of a republican form of government. He found that in view of the opinions of respectable authorities, both judicial and lay, and of statements of the President and the Secretaries of State, Congress was justified in treating communism as such a threat. He thought it absurd to apply the "clear and present danger" doctrine to inquiry as distinguished from action and said, "If Congress has power to inquire into the subjects of Communism and the Communist Party it has power to identify the individuals who believe in Communism. . . . Personnel is part of the problem."

Judge Prettyman also rejected the contention that the resolution creating the Committee was too vague to be valid and found that the vague phrase "Un-American activities" was sufficiently clarified by the clause "subversive and un-American propaganda that attacks the principles of the form of government as guaranteed by our Constitution" and that in any case the authorization for an investigation need not be as specific as the definition of a crime. The particular question put to the defendants, which, he said, was to account for funds not to elicit opinions, was clearly pertinent to the Committee's purposes.

Judge Prettyman's opinion and Judge Edgerton's dissent remain the classic statements of the opposing views as to the relation between the investigative power of Congress and the Bill of Rights.

Miss Bryan, the executive secretary, was indicted separately, and she and Miss Fleischman were each tried separately and convicted. The Court of Appeals did not deal with the constitutional issues in either case. In the *Bryan* case it found that the judge below had erred when he ruled as a matter of law that a quorum of the Committee was present at the hearing, whereas the question was one of fact for the jury, not for the judge. In speaking for the court in the *Fleischman* case Judge Edgerton said:

> A will or desire or intention that has no practical consequences has no legal consequences. . . . Our system of law does not take the will for the deed. . . . Since a bad intention and a prohibited event do not make a crime proof of them does not make a case. *Fleischman v. United States,* 174 F. 2d 519, 520.

The Supreme Court agreed to hear these cases and reversed the Court of Appeals in both of them.

Dr. Barsky served a prison term, as did defendants similarly convicted of contempt of Congress. Later Dr. Barsky suffered a further penalty. His license to practice medicine in the State of New York was suspended for six months on the ground that he had been convicted of a crime.

Nine years later Judge Edgerton's contention that the Committee's enabling resolution was so vague and indefinite that it did not establish the clear standard of criminality required by the Due Process Clause was sustained by the Supreme Court in the case of *Watkins* v. *United States.* Whether the *Watkins* decision would have governed in the *Barsky* case is not clear.

EDGERTON, *J., dissenting:* In my opinion the House Committee's investigation abridges freedom of speech and inflicts punishment without trial; and the statute the appellants are convicted of violating provides no ascertainable standard of guilt. It follows that the convictions should be reversed on constitutional grounds.

I

The First Amendment forbids Congress to make any law "abridging the freedom of speech, or of the press." If this "is to mean anything, it must restrict powers which are . . . granted by the Constitution to Congress." Zachariah Chafee, *Free Speech in the United States* (Harvard University Press, 1940), 30–31. Legislation abridging the freedoms guaranteed by the First Amendment is not made valid by the fact that it would be valid if it did not abridge them.

The *Murdock, Opelika,* and *Busey* cases make this plain. . . . It was not the weakness of the taxing power but the strength of the First Amendment that made the *Murdock* and *Opelika* taxes unconstitutional. Yet this court now holds that the first Amendment, which restricts the express power of taxation, does not restrict the implied power of investigation. Investigation in general, and this investigation in particular, is not more necessary than taxation. There is no basis in authority, policy, or logic for holding that it is entitled to a preferred constitutional position. "Freedoms of speech, press, and religion are entitled to a preferred constitutional position." *Busey* v. *District of Columbia,* 78 U.S. App. D.C. 189, 192. The power of investigation, like the power of taxation, stops short of restricting the freedoms protected by the First Amendment.

Quite as clearly as the taxes in the *Murdock, Opelika,* and

Busey cases, the House Committee's investigation is on its "face
. . . a restriction of the free exercise of those freedoms." It actually restricts them and puts a substantial clog upon them. It is
therefore more clearly unconstitutional than the taxes.

The investigation restricts the freedom of speech by uncover-
ing and advertising expressions of unpopular views. The Committee gives wide publicity to its proceedings. This exposes the
men and women whose views are advertised to risks of insult,
ostracism, and lasting loss of employment. Persons disposed to
express unpopular views privately or to a selected group are often
not disposed to risk the consequences to themselves and their
families that publication may entail. The Committee's practice of
discovering and advertising unpopular views is therefore a strong
deterrent to any expression, however private, of such views.

The investigation restricts the freedom of speech by forcing
people to express views. Freedom of speech is freedom in respect
to speech and includes freedom not to speak. "To force an
American citizen publicly to profess any statement of belief" is
to violate the First Amendment. "If there is any fixed star in our
constitutional constellation, it is that no official, high or petty,
can prescribe what shall be orthodox in politics, nationalism, religion, or other matters of opinion or force citizens to confess
by word or act their faith therein." That is the rule of the
Barnette case, which involved pressure on school children to
profess approved beliefs. *West Virginia State Board of Education* v. *Barnette*, 319 U.S. 624, 634, 642. Witnesses before
the House Committee are under pressure to profess approved beliefs. They cannot express others without exposing themselves
to disastrous consequences. Yet if they have previously expressed
others they cannot creditably or credibly profess those that are
approved. If they decline "publicly to profess any statement of
belief" they invite punishment for contempt. The privilege of
choosing between speech that means ostracism and speech that
means perjury is not freedom of speech.

"Under our traditions beliefs are personal and not a matter

of mere association." *Schneiderman* v. *United States*, 320 U.S. 118, 136. Yet the House Committee attributes unpopular and "communistic" beliefs to persons and groups on the basis of mere association with other persons and groups. By this device it greatly extends the restraining effect of its investigation. . . . It further extends the restraining effect of its investigation by stigmatizing a remarkably wide range of beliefs as un-American.

That the Committee's investigation does in fact restrict speech is too clear for dispute. The prosecution does not deny it and the court concedes it. The effect is not limited to the people whom the Committee stigmatizes or calls before it, but extends to others who hold similar views and to still others who might be disposed to adopt them. It is not prudent to hold views or to join groups that the Committee has condemned. People have grown wary of expressing any unorthodox opinions. No one can measure the inroad the Committee has made in the American sense of freedom to speak. There has been some suggestion that it restrains only timid people. I think it nearer the truth to say that, among the more articulate, it affects in one degree or another all but the very courageous, the very orthodox, and the very secure. But nothing turns on this question of fact. The views of timid people are not necessarily worthless to society. No one needs self-expression more. The Constitution protects them as it protects others. If it be true that the Committee's investigation would not restrain a determined man, this matters no more than the fact that the taxes in the *Murdock* and *Opelika* cases would not restrain a rich man.

The case is stronger than *Murdock* and *Opelika* not only because the investigation actually and greatly restrains speech but in other respects as well. In the *Murdock* and *Opelika* cases there was no purpose to restrain and no singling out of propaganda for special treatment. License taxes on sales, imposed in general terms and for the legitimate purpose of raising revenue, were unconstitutional in failing to exempt sales of propaganda not made for profit. The mere incidental inclusion of propaganda among activities burdened only incidentally to a proper legislative purpose was bad. But in the present case neither the inclusion nor the burdening of propaganda is incidental. The House Committee's enabling Act concerns, specifically and exclusively, "propaganda activities," and the Committee's principal purpose is to restrain them. Its purpose is shown clearly by its acts and conclusively by its statements. The Committee and its members have repeatedly said in terms or in effect that its main purpose is to do by exposure and publicity what it believes may not validly be done by legislation. This is as much as to say that its purpose is to punish or burden propaganda. The Committee has "embarked upon a systematic campaign to suppress freedom of political and economic opinion." Robert E. Cushman, "Civil Liberty and Public Opinion," in *Safeguarding Civil Liberty Today*, Bernays lectures of 1944 at Cornell University, 100.

What Congress may not restrain, Congress may not restrain by exposure and publicity. If it be thought that the Committee's purpose does not include "punishment, in the ordinary sense," this is immaterial to the present point. The First Amendment forbids Congress purposely to burden forms of expression that it may not punish.

It is said that Congress may punish propaganda that advocates overthrow of the government by force or violence; that it may therefore investigate to determine whether such legislation is necessary; and that it may do this even if the investigation burdens such propaganda and is intended to do so. To this there are at least three answers.

(1) Investigation of possible need for legislation making it unlawful to advocate overthrow of the government by force or violence has not been among the purposes of Congress or of the House Committee at any time since 1940. The broadest possible legislation of that sort was passed in that year and is still on the books.

(2) The Committee's enabling Act says nothing about force or violence or overthrow of the government. It is broad enough to include investigation of propaganda advocating such things, but it is not by any means limited to such propaganda, and neither is the Committee's actual investigation. Though the Committee has concerned itself largely with communism, and formerly with fascism, it has also concerned itself with propaganda unrelated to any possible overthrow of the government by force and plainly beyond any power of Congress to burden or restrain. "In the course of its inquiries such diverse groups have come under its scrutiny as the American Civil Liberties Union, the C.I.O., the National Catholic Welfare Conference, . . . the Farmer-Labor party, sit-down strikes, the Federal Theatre Project, consumers' organizations . . . the magazine Time." Among various "other criteria which the Committee or its agents have from time to time suggested as indicative of activity within the scope of its inquiries are: opposition to 'the American system of checks and balances,' opposition to the protection of property rights, belief in dictatorship, opposition to the Franco government of Spain, opposition to General MacArthur, advocacy of a world state, advocacy of the dissolution of the British Empire, criticism of members of Congress, and criticism of the Committee on Un-American Activities." "Constitutional Limitations on the Un-American Activities Committee," 47 *Columbia Law Review* 418, 422–423. Obviously there could be no necessity for many of the Committee's activities, and no excuse for the restraints they impose, even if the Act of 1940 were not on the books.

Legislative action that restrains constitutionally protected speech along with other speech cannot be enforced against either. Legislation is unconstitutional as a whole if it "does not aim specifically at evils within the allowable area of state control but . . . sweeps within its ambit other activities that in ordinary circumstances constitute an exercise of freedom of

speech or of the press. The existence of such a statute . . . results in a continuous and pervasive restraint on all freedom of
discussion that might reasonably be regarded as within its pur-
view. . . . An accused, after arrest and conviction under such
a statute, does not have to sustain the burden of demonstrating
that the State could not constitutionally have written a different
and specific statute covering his activities as disclosed by the
charge and the evidence introduced against him. . . . Where
regulations of the liberty of free discussion are concerned, there
are special reasons for observing the rule that it is the statute, and
not the accusation or the evidence under it, which prescribes
the limits of permissible conduct and warns against transgres-
sion." *Thornhill* v. *Alabama*, 310 U.S. 88, 97–98.

Even if the views the House Committee sought to elicit from
these appellants had been of a sort that Congress might properly
restrain, by investigative or other action aimed specifically at
such views, the appealed convictions would have to be reversed. . . .

(3) The problem is not, as the court suggests, that of balancing public or social interests against private interests. "The
principle on which speech is classified as lawful or unlawful
involves the balancing against each other of two very important
social interests, in public safety and in the search for truth.
. . . Imprisonment of 'half-baked' agitators for 'foolish talk'
may often discourage wise men from publishing valuable criticism of governmental policies. . . . The great interest in free
speech should be sacrificed only when the interest in public
safety is really imperiled . . . The American policy is to meet
force by force, and talk by talk." Chafee, *op. cit.*, at 35, ix,
180. . . .

There is no evidence in the record that propaganda has created danger, clear and present or obscure and remote, that the
government of the United States or any government in the
United States will be overthrown by force or violence. "When

legislation appears on its face to affect the use of speech, press, or religion, and when its validity depends upon the existence of facts which are not proved, their existence should not be presumed . . ." *Busey* v. *District of Columbia, supra,* at 192. "The usual presumption supporting legislation is balanced by the preferred place given in our scheme to the great, the indispensable democratic freedoms secured by the First Amendment." *Thomas* v. *Collins,* 323 U.S. 516, 529–530.

The court asks "How, except upon inquiry, would the Congress know whether the danger is clear and present?" The context shows that this means "How, except upon *congressional* inquiry . . . ?" The answer is: through the Department of Justice, whose duty it is, if clear and present danger can be discovered, to enforce the law of 1940 which makes it a crime to advocate overthrow of the government by force; through the intelligence services; and through any new agency that Congress may think it useful to create. As the House Committee's history shows, no dangerous propaganda that eludes other agencies is likely to be discovered by a congressional inquiry. But a congressional inquiry, however superfluous, to discover whether there is clear and present danger, could be authorized and could be conducted without violating the First Amendment. The premise that the government must have power to protect itself by discovering whether it is in clear and present danger of overthrow by violence is sound. But it does not support the conclusion that Congress may compel men to disclose their personal opinions, to a committee and also to the world, on topics ranging from communism, however remotely and peaceably achieved, to the "American system of checks and balances," the British Empire, and the Franco government of Spain. Since the premise does not support this conclusion it has nothing to do with this case. There is no necessity for the House Committee's investigation. It actually weakens the government by warning the unorthodox, some of whom are conspicuous for ability and patriotism, to avoid government service.

The free speech point comes to this. Congressional action that is either intended or likely to restrict expression of opinion that Congress may not prohibit violates the First Amendment. Congressional action in the nature of investigation is no exception. Civil liberties may not be abridged in order to determine whether they should be abridged. The House Committee's investigation is both intended and likely to restrict expression of opinion that Congress may not prohibit. That it actually does so is clear and undisputed. If all this were otherwise the investigation might perhaps be within legislative power. But that is immaterial, like the fact that a tax restricting non-profit sales of propaganda, or intended to restrict circulation of newspapers, would be within legislative power if it had no such effect or purpose.

Congress has ratified the Committee's course by renewing its appropriations and extending its life. However, the question is whether the Committee's investigation is constitutional, not whether it is authorized as between the Committee and Congress. Since Congress could not authorize it, whether or when Congress intended to do so is immaterial. "In passing upon constitutional questions . . . the statute must be tested by its operation and effect." *Near* v. *Minnesota,* 283 U.S. 697, 708. The case is as if the enabling Act read "The Committee shall expose unorthodox propaganda in order to restrain and punish it." The issue is whether Americans may be fined and imprisoned for passive resistance to this inquest into their political and economic views. No one denies that the inquest is an effective instrument of restraint. I hope the last word has not been said on the question whether it is a legal one.

II

"An act of Congress which proposed to adjudge a man guilty of a crime and inflict the punishment, would be conceded by all thinking men to be unauthorized by anything in the Constitution." *Kilbourn* v. *Thompson*, 103 U.S. 168, 182. "Legislative acts, no matter what their form, that apply either to named individuals or to easily ascertainable members of a group in such a way as to inflict punishment on them without a judicial trial are bills of attainder prohibited by the Constitution." *United States* v. *Lovett*, 328 U.S. 303, 315–316. A punitive statute is no better if it creates the offense, or authorizes a committee to create it; delegates to the committee the ascertainment of individuals to be punished and the infliction of punishment; provides no standard of guilt; compels the individual, in the committee's discretion, to testify against himself; deprives him of the right to testify in his own defense; and deprives him also of the right to counsel, the right to call witnesses, and the right to cross-examine opposing witnesses. The House Committee's enabling Act, as the Committee has construed and applied it, does all that.

Punishment is harm intentionally inflicted because of conduct. Intentionally inflicted loss of employment is punishment, as the Court held in the *Lovett* case. Sometimes, as in that case, the Committee intentionally inflicts dismissal from employment. It intentionally and directly inflicts publicity and opprobrium. That these may be damaging is both obvious and recognized by law, including the law of libel. Publicity and opprobrium that are intended as an "effective weapon" against activities that cannot be reached by legislation are intended to inflict damage. They are damaging in fact as well as intention. The Court implied in the *Lovett* case that no "congressional action, aimed at . . . named individuals, which stigmatized their reputation and seriously impaired their chance to earn a living" can be sustained. The Committee takes such action. Even courts, to which the Constitution entrusted the function of punishment, "were commanded to stay their hands until and unless certain tested safeguards were observed. An accused in court must be tried by an impartial jury, has a right to be represented by counsel, he must be clearly informed of the charge against him, the law which he is charged with violating must have been passed before he committed the act charged, he must be confronted by the witnesses against him, he must not be compelled to incriminate himself . . ." *United States* v. *Lovett, supra,* at 314, 317. The Committee inflicts punishment for unorthodox opinions or associations without any of these safeguards. To say that it may do so because it is not a court is to say that many vital constitutional rights may be denied because another and a most vital one is also denied.

III

"Statutes defining crimes may fail of their purpose if they do not provide some reasonable standards of guilt . . . Legislation may run afoul of the Due Process Clause because it fails to give adequate guidance to those who would be law-abiding, to advise defendants of the nature of the offense with which they are charged, or to guide courts in trying those who are accused." On these grounds the Supreme Court, in the recent *Musser* case, vacated a conviction under a Utah statute punishing conspiracy "to commit any act injurious to the public health, to public morals, or to trade or commerce, or for the perversion or obstruction of justice or the due administration of the laws . . ." Unlimited by its context or by judicial construction, the Court found this statute so indefinite as to cover "agreement to do almost any act which a judge and jury might find at the moment contrary to his or its notions of what was good for health, morals, trade, commerce, justice or order." *Musser* v. *Utah,* 333 U.S. 95. Since such notions are highly various, the statute is too vague to support a criminal conviction.

It would be hard to find a clearer instance of this principle than the one before us. The Act under which appellants were convicted makes it a misdemeanor to fail to produce papers "upon any matter under inquiry" before a congressional committee. "A witness rightfully may refuse to answer where . . . the questions are not pertinent to the matter under inquiry." *McGrain* v. *Daugherty*, 273 U.S. 135, 176. The matter under inquiry before the House Committee is thus described in its enabling Act and in earlier resolutions: "(i) the extent, character, and objects of *un-American propaganda* activities in the United States, (ii) the diffusion within the United States of *subversive* and *un-American propaganda* that is instigated from foreign countries or of a domestic origin and *attacks* the *principle of the form of government as guaranteed by our Constitution*, and (iii) all other *questions in relation thereto* that would aid Congress in any necessary remedial legislation." Under each of these three clauses, the matter under inquiry is limited by the term "un-American." If that term is so indefinite as to cover "almost any act which a judge and jury [or the Committee] might find at the moment contrary to his or its notions of what was good . . ." the *Musser* case requires reversal of the present convictions. For then the matter under inquiry is similarly indefinite; a witness before the Committee cannot know whether a question or demand is "pertinent to the matter under inquiry"; and he cannot know whether or not he will be committing a crime if he fails to respond.

The term un-American is completely indefinite. Government counsel do not attempt to define it and concede that they cannot define it. In effect, though not in purpose, they thereby confess error.

In a literal sense whatever occurs in America is American. The President's Advisory Committee on Universal Training, in response to the contention that universal military training was un-American, said "An epithet is not an argument. 'Un-American' means simply that it has not been done before in America." *A Program for National Security*, Report of the President's Advisory Committee on Universal Training (1947), 39. But obviously Congress employed a different usage, and meant the

term un-American to connote some propaganda that does occur
in America. Just as obviously Congress did not mean it to cover
all propaganda that occurs here, including *e.g.* the usual campaign literature of the major parties. The question is, what line
did Congress draw? Congress drew none.

Once the literal sense, which Congress plainly did *not* intend,
is left behind, the term un-American is one of the vaguest in the
language. It may suggest what is not customary or popular here.
But different persons have very different ideas of what is not
customary or popular. It seems probable that Congress used the
term in some undisclosed sense that includes only some unidentified part of this field and is therefore even more indefinite. The
House Committee may perhaps be said to have interpreted the
term in practice as including, though not always limited to, (1)
"communistic" (and, formerly, "fascistic") ideas, (2) ideas
commonly called radical, and (3) ideas commonly called liberal.
The Committee's practice has made this usage somewhat familiar.
But in a different usage that is at least as familiar the term un-
American includes, without being limited to, ideas commonly
called undemocratic. And even if it were conceded that Congress intended the suggested interpretation of the Committee's
interpretation, the term un-American would still be too vague
for criminal purposes because (a) nothing in the enabling Act
informs the public that such an interpretation is intended, (b)
the words communistic, fascistic, radical, and liberal are themselves too vague for criminal purposes, and (c) the suggested
interpretation is not limited to those words.

This does not begin to exhaust the ordinary varieties of usage
of the term un-American. Since some connotation of odium is
common to most of them, "un-American propaganda" might
perhaps be said to mean "odious propaganda." But this again
would not do for criminal purposes. Witnesses before the Committee cannot be required to decide whether or not demanded
evidence relates to propaganda that is odious, on pain of criminal punishment if they think it does not and a court thinks it

does. And the basic question, whether demanded evidence relates to propaganda that is un-American, is vaguer still, since the answer depends not only upon applying but also upon selecting one of the vague and various meanings of un-American.

The enabling Act uses the word "subversive," the word "attacks," and the words "the principle of the form of government as guaranteed by our Constitution," but it uses none of them independently of the word un-American. Moreover, the quoted words themselves have no reasonably clear meaning. Does "the principle of the form of government" here mean the republican or democratic principle only, or does it include *e.g.* the constitutional duty of courts not to enforce unconstitutional legislation? This court puts a plural where Congress put a singular, and says "the principles . . . are obvious." To me it is not obvious how much Congress meant by "the principle," or how much the court means by "the principles," or that the two meanings are identical. Both because "the principle" is vague and because "attacks" is vague, I do not know whether propaganda "attacks the principle" if, *e.g.*, it advocates a constitutional amendment replacing the American principle of judicial review by the British principle of legislative supremacy. Neither do I know whether the kind of propaganda with which the House Committee undertook to connect the appellants through their records "attacks the principle." A member of the Communist Party who advocates sweeping constitutional changes may, in the Supreme Court's view, be "attached to the principles of the Constitution" within the meaning of those words in a naturalization act: "As Justice Holmes said, 'Surely it cannot show lack of attachment to the principles of the Constitution that . . . [one] thinks it can be improved. . . . If there is any principle of the Constitution that more imperatively calls for attachment than any other it is the principle of free thought—not free thought for those who agree with us, but freedom for the thought that we hate.' " *Schneiderman* v. *United States,* 320 U.S. 118, 136. But we do not know that Congress intended the House Committee's enabling Act to be interpreted in accordance with that view. The Committee interprets it differently.

Apparently Congress did not even intend to give the Committee a definite function. "The purpose seems to have been to give the Committee a roving commission to inquire into any propaganda activities which a majority of the Committee thought warranted investigation." At all events the statutory language, like that held bad in the *Musser* case, covers "almost any act which a judge and jury [or the Committee] might find at the moment contrary to his or its notions of what was good . . ." A court might as well be asked to enforce "a statute which in terms merely penalized and punished all acts detrimental to the public interest . . . So vague and indeterminate are the boundaries thus set to the freedom of speech . . . that the law necessarily violates the guarantees of liberty . . ." *Herndon* v. *Lowry,* 301 U.S. 242, 263, 264. In so ruling in the *Herndon* case the Court did not add: "unless the defendant's act seems to the Court clearly on the penalized side of the vague and indeterminate boundaries." I understand this court to hold that the Committee's demand for appellants' records was clearly within the limits, however vague, of the enabling Act, and that appellants are therefore punishable for not producing them. I have tried to show that the court's premise is erroneous. The *Musser* and *Herndon* cases show that it does not support the court's conclusion.

IV

Appellants appeared and testified before the Committee but did not produce the demanded records. The court says "These appellants were not asked to state their political opinions. They were asked to account for funds." This distinction merely makes any possible pertinence to the Committee's investigation the more remote. The appellants were asked to account for funds in order to reveal their political opinions. Accordingly the court says: "We are considering a specific question only, which is whether this Congressional Committee may inquire whether an individual is or is not a believer in Communism or a member of the Communist Party." That specific question is before us, if at all, as an aspect of the larger question whether courts may punish individuals for not responding to an inquiry by this Committee into their political opinions. My answer to both questions is no. The Committee's specific inquiry abridged appellants' freedom of speech and attempted to inflict punishment without trial. The Committee's entire investigation was unconstitutional both as abridging freedom of speech and as attempting to punish without trial; and there is no duty to respond to inquiries in an unconstitutional proceeding. The statute appellants are convicted of violating provides no ascertainable standard of guilt.

I do not consider other alleged errors. For the same reasons that make it an exception to the principle that constitutionality is presumed, legislation restraining speech should be an exception to the principle that unconstitutionality is not declared when a case can be decided on other grounds.

UNITED STATES OF AMERICA

v.

OWEN LATTIMORE

Decided July 8, 1954

Heard in banc

On February 9, 1950, Senator McCarthy made his now-famous speech at Wheeling, West Virginia, in which he declared that he had a list of 205 Communists who were working in and shaping policy in the State Department. Following this speech and one on the floor of the Senate in which he described 81 specific cases, identified by number, the Senate Committee on Foreign Relations established a subcommittee to determine the truth or falsehood of the charges. The Senator appeared as the first witness before the Subcommittee, popularly known as the Tydings Committee. In his testimony he named Owen Lattimore as "one of the principal architects of our Far Eastern policy," who has "a long pro-Communist record" and who "by any yard-stick of loyalty could not possibly be a good security risk." The Senator then held a press conference at which he stated that Lattimore was one of the top Communist agents in this country.

Since 1941 Owen Lattimore had been a University professor and the head of the Walter Hines School of International Relations at Johns Hopkins University in Baltimore. As a young man he had engaged in business in China, where he had traveled widely and was one of the few Americans to explore the remote and then almost unknown areas of northwestern China. He became a prolific writer on the problems of the Far East, especially of China, and was recognized as an expert in that field. In the thirties he was connected with the Institute of Pacific Relations in various capacities and for a while was editor of its magazine *Pacific Affairs*. During World War II he served for a year as political adviser to Chiang Kai-shek, was Director of Pacific Operations for the Office of War Information, and later was a member of the Pauley Reparations Commission Mission to Japan. In 1950 Lattimore was in Afghanistan with a United Nations Mission to explore the possibilities of technical aid.

As soon as Lattimore heard of the charges against him, he hurried home to defend himself. He appeared at his own request before the Tydings Committee and was cross-examined for three days. Later in the hearings Louis Budenz testified that Lattimore had been a member of a Communist cell in the Institute of Pacific Relations and that he, Budenz, had received orders "to treat Lattimore as a Communist when the latter accompanied Henry Wallace on a trip to China." Lattimore was again questioned by the Subcommittee for two days. After this the Committee reported that Lattimore was "not the architect of our Far Eastern policy," "not a spy," and not an employee of the State Department. It reported further that there was no legal evidence to support the charge that he had a long record of procommunism.

In 1951 the newly established Senate Subcommittee on Internal Security began an investigation of the Institute of Pacific Relations, and it opened hearings on that subject in July, 1952. During the course of these hearings Owen Lattimore was the subject of unfavorable testimony. Again he asked for an opportunity to refute the charges against him publicly. He was first heard in executive session, and on February 26, 1952, he appeared before the Committee in open session. He was permitted to read an opening statement, already given out to the press, in which he vigorously attacked the Committee's methods and motives in the present investigation. Thereafter he was grilled for thirteen days.

The previous summer the committee staff had examined all the old records and papers of the Institute of Pacific Relations. In the course of examination, Lattimore found himself confronted with a written record of events that had taken place some fifteen years ago that conflicted with some of his own testimony. He vigorously denied all charges of pro-Communist sympathy or activity and at one point said heatedly, "I am not and never have been a Communist, a Soviet agent, sympathizer or any other kind of a promoter of Communism or Communist interests and all of these are nonsense."

When the Committee issued its report, it stated that Owen Lattimore had from sometime in the 1930's been "a conscious and articulate instrument of the Soviet conspiracy," that he testified falsely before the Subcommittee at least five separate times, and that he had "influenced United States policy favorable to the Chinese Communists." The Committee recommended that the Department of Justice prosecute him for perjury. When the name of James McGranery was submitted to the Senate for confirmation as Attorney General, he was questioned as to his intentions in the Lattimore case. Thereafter a special prosecutor was appointed to handle the case and on December 16, 1952, Lattimore was indicted in the District of Columbia for perjury on seven counts.

The indictment did not contain any reference to espionage or Communist membership. The first count charged that Lattimore had lied when he stated that he had never been "a sympathizer or any other kind of promoter of Communism or Communist interests." The other six counts related to relatively minor matters. Count Two charged that he testified falsely when he stated that he had no reason to believe that a certain Chinese was a Communist. Counts Three and Four related to his activities as editor of *Pacific Affairs* and alleged that he lied when he said that he did not know that a contributor to *Pacific Affairs*, who used the pen name Asiaticus, was a Communist and denied that he had published articles in that magazine by persons other than Russians whom he knew to be Communists. The remaining counts charged that he testified falsely when he said that a luncheon conference between him and the Russian Ambassador Oumansky took place after Hitler had invaded Russia, that he did not take care of Laughlin Currie's mail at the White House when Currie was out of the country, and that it was not necessary to get permission from the Communist authorities to cross a certain line of demarcation in order to go to Yenan, and he had not made prearrangements with the Communist Party for his trip to Yenan, the headquarters of the Chinese Communist Party.

Lattimore pleaded not guilty to all counts of the indictment and then moved that the whole indictment be dismissed. The motion for dismissal was argued before Judge Youngdahl of the District Court for the District of Columbia on March 31 and April 1, 1954. The judge found that the first count was fatally defective and in violation of the Sixth Amendment because of its vagueness. The phrase "sympathizer and promoter of Communism" was too nebulous to inform the defendant or the jury of the nature of the charges against him. Judge Youngdahl also found that the concept of "knowledge" in Courts Three and Four was too nebulous and that all three counts were in violation of the First Amendment to the Constitution in that they restricted freedom of belief and the press. He ruled that Count Seven was invalid because of a fatal inconsistency in the use of the terms "Communist authorities" and "Communist Party." Although the other three counts (Two, Five, and Six) appeared to the judge to be trivial, he sustained them on the ground that in the course of a trial they might prove to be material.

The case had been widely publicized, and by the time it reached the Court of Appeals it had become a *cause célèbre* and a hot political issue. The court sat in banc to hear Lattimore's appeal. There was no single issue on which all the judges agreed, and four separate opinions were written, Judge Prettyman speaking for the majority. With one dissent, the Court of Appeals sustained the District Court as to Counts One and Seven and reversed it, 5 to 4, as to Counts Three and Four. Judge Prettyman, in his majority opinion, agreed with Judge Youngdahl that the word "sympathizer" was too vague to sustain a perjury indictment. He also agreed as to the fatal variance between the terms "Communist authorities" and "Communist Party" in the last count, but he thought that the words "know" and "Communist" used in Counts Three and Four were sufficiently definite. He disposed of the argument based on the First Amendment by citing the *Barsky* case in support of the propriety of the general inquiry and by asserting that freedom of speech did not include freedom to lie under oath and that although Lattimore, as an editor of a publication, might have a right not to speak he did not have the right to speak falsely.

Judge Edgerton wrote a minority opinion, concurred in as a whole by Judges Bazelon and Clark and in part by Judge Miller, in which he dealt only with Counts Three and Four and upheld Judge Youngdahl's decision on those counts. The net result of the case was that Lattimore was now subject to trial on five counts but that the major count, to which the others were subordinate, had been thrown out.

In February, 1955, the Department of Justice obtained a new indictment that reinstated Count One in a different form. This count was then joined for trial with the valid counts of the old indictment. The Government had attempted to meet the court's objection to the old Count One by dropping the word "sympathizer" and substituting "promoter," a word that the court had not discussed in its opinion. It also split the count into two parts. The first again alleged that Lattimore lied when he denied that he was a follower of the Communist line and gave a long list of examples from his voluminous writings which were alleged to correspond with that line. The second part contained a similar and equally long bill of particulars. Again Lattimore moved to dismiss the indictment. His motion was scheduled to come before Judge Youngdahl. The Government then took an extraordinary step. It filed a certificate of prejudice asserting that in the earlier case the judge had shown that he was already convinced of Lattimore's innocence. The petition was rejected. Judge Youngdahl ruled that Count One in its new form was even vaguer than before. The Court of Appeals was not asked to rule on the second version. Since this count was the heart of the case, the Government formally asked that the indictment be dismissed, and the *Lattimore* case was at last closed.

EDGERTON, *Circuit Judge*, with whom *Circuit Judges* CLARK and BAZELON concur: We think all four counts were rightly dismissed. Accordingly we concur in this court's result as to Counts I and VII but dissent as to Counts III and IV.

Asiaticus was the pen name of a contributor to the magazine "Pacific Affairs" which Lattimore edited from 1934 to 1941. Count III says Lattimore testified falsely that he "didn't know," in the late 1930's, that Asiaticus was a "Communist." Count IV says Lattimore testified falsely that he never published, while he was editor, an article by a non-Russian whom he knew to be a "Communist." In our opinion these counts are void because they are vague and also because they concern immaterial matters.

Vagueness of Counts III and IV

Due process of law requires that a charge be definite enough so that a jury can understand it and the accused can prepare his defense. The Sixth Amendment requires that the accused "be informed of the nature and cause of the accusation." Counts III and IV do not meet these requirements.

Count III calls for a jury's opinion as to whether Lattimore's opinion "in the late 1930's," as he remembered it, regarding the opinions of Asiaticus, was such that he "well knew" he testified falsely in saying he "didn't know" in the late 1930's that Asiaticus was a "Communist."

Whether it is vague or definite to say one "knows" something depends on what one is said to know. That a watch cost $50, or was stolen, is definite enough. But a valid charge of perjury could not be framed on the theory that when a witness swore he did not know a watch was worth having, he did know it was worth having; or when he swore he did not know it was a long way from Washington to Baltimore, he did know it was a long way. The terms "worth having" and "a long way" are too vague.

Few terms are vaguer than "Communist." It may mean a member of the Communist Party, or a sympathizer and promoter of Communism and Communist interests, or a believer in dialectical materialism, or a radical, or an opponent of inherited wealth, or many other things. The court says, and we agree, that the term "sympathizer and promoter of Communism and Communist interests" in Count I makes that count void for vagueness. Since the word "Communist" incorporates that vagueness, and adds more, Count III is void for vagueness.

Count IV is like Count III in this respect.

Immateriality of Counts III and IV

Under the federal statute and also under the District of Columbia statute, perjury is "any material matter" falsely sworn before "a competent tribunal." 18 U.S.C. (1952 ed.) § 1621, 62 Stat. 773; D.C. Code (1951) § 22-2501, 31 Stat. 1329. "And the materiality of what is falsely sworn, when an element in the crime of perjury, is [a question] for the court." *Sinclair* v. *United States*, 279 U.S. 263, 298 (1929). When materiality is uncertain on the face of an indictment, the government may be able to prove materiality at a trial. But when on the face of the indictment it is plain that the testimony charged as perjury cannot be material, a demurrer should be sustained or the indictment dismissed. We think this applies to Counts III and IV. Because of the period of time to which they relate, and also because of the subject to which they relate, we think they cannot be material to the investigation that the Committee was authorized to conduct.

I. *Disparity in time.* Counts III and IV relate to the period between 1934 and 1941. But the Committee was authorized, at the end of 1950, to investigate current matters.

The Internal Security Act of 1950 became law September 23, 1950. 64 Stat. 987, 1031. Three months later, December 21, 1950, Senate Resolution 366, 81st Cong., 2d Sess., was passed. The Resolution recites that "continuous surveillance" is "vital to the internal security of the United States." It directs the Committee to make a "continuing study and investigation"— not a historical study and investigation—of "the administration, operation, and enforcement" of the internal security laws and of "the extent, nature, and effects of subversive activities in the United States . . . including . . . espionage, sabotage, and infiltration by persons who are or may be" Communist-dominated. The Resolution expresses no interest in persons who *were, or may have been,* Communist-dominated years ago, when Hitler, not Russia, was threatening the world and many people were Communist sympathizers who are now anti-Communists. The Committee is to study what goes on in the 1950's, not what went on in the 1930's. It is to be a watchman, not a historian.

If the Resolution left this point in doubt, legislative history would remove the doubt.

Senator Eastland introduced the Resolution on behalf of

Senators McCarran, O'Connor, Wiley, Ferguson, Jenner, and
Langer. He said: "we feel that the Committee on the Judiciary
. . . owes a duty to the Senate and to the people which cannot be fully discharged *unless the committee conducts a continuous study and investigation* of the operation of our laws relating to espionage, sabotage, and the protection of the internal
security of the United States . . . I am convinced that we are
confronted by a task which must be the subject of continuous
effort. If, Mr. President, it is sound for the Congress to set up
watch-dog committees to maintain a surveillance over the operation of our programs of expenditures at home and abroad, it
is equally sound to equip the Committee on the Judiciary to
maintain a watchful eye over our program to protect the internal
security of this country." Senator Eastland read a statement by
Senator McCarran which said: "*Over the course of many years
there have been accumulated by various committees of the Congress substantial quantities of information* respecting the scope
and nature of the Communist fifth column in the United States,
and the Congress has, from time to time, enacted laws which
were designed to meet this threat. *The purpose of the Senate
resolution is not to again marshal the factual material which has
already been assembled and which demonstrates conclusively the
deadly menace of the Communist fifth column* . . . One of the
elementary truths respecting communism in the United States
is that it is a dynamic movement which, with devilish cunning,
constantly seeks new avenues of expression and escape from de-
tection. . . . *We must be constantly alert to the new tactics
which are being devised to evade our best legislative efforts. It
is for this reason principally that the instant resolution has been
presented to the Senate, so that the Congress and the people
may constantly be informed of our progress in this fight.*"
(Emphasis added.) . . .

II. *Disparity in subject.* The particular subject to which

Counts III and IV relate—Lattimore's knowledge or ignorance of the views of other persons between 1934 and 1941—is not within the Committee's competence. Paraphrasing what we said in *Bowers*, we are unable to see how a "continuing study and investigation," conducted in the 1950's, of subversive activities and the operation of the security laws, would be furthered in any way by the Committee's knowledge of what an editor did or did not know between 1934 and 1941 about the views of authors whose work he then published. It is impossible to find in the Senate Resolution any suggestion of an intention to authorize inquiry into that subject.

Even today it is not illegal to publish an article by a known Communist. It was not illegal between 1934 and 1941. Therefore the question whether Lattimore did so between 1934 and 1941 has no connection with the clauses of the Resolution that concern "administration, operation, and enforcement" of laws. For several reasons, the question has no connection with the clause of the Resolution that concerns "subversive activities."

(1) In June 1941 Germany attacked Russia. In December of that year Germany's ally attacked Pearl Harbor and the United States joined Russia in the war against Germany. In January, 1942, President Roosevelt wrote to Admiral Land, "I am still terribly disturbed about the fact that an adequate number of ships are not available for Russia. . . . This Government has made a firm pledge to Russia and we simply cannot go back on it. . . . You simply must find some ships that can be diverted at once for this Russian business." The President "assured Stalin that there would be no relaxation of efforts to keep the shipments going to the Soviet Union." In February, 1942, on the occasion of the 24th anniversary of the foundation of the Red Army, General MacArthur sent a message from his headquarters in the Philippines in which he said: "The world situation at the present time indicates that the hopes of civilization rest upon

the worthy banners of the courageous Russian Army. . . ."
Quoted in Robert E. Sherwood, *Roosevelt and Hopkins* (1948),
pp. 496, 497.

During our alliance with the Communist world power, and
before that alliance, there could be nothing "subversive" in
publishing even articles showing sympathy for that power—
which the indictment does not allege that Lattimore did—to
say nothing of colorless articles whose authors happened to be
Communists. What might be "subversive" now has nothing to
do with the case. The prosecution cannot project the 1950's into
the 1930's.

(2) Even today, just as the fact that a picture was painted
by a known Communist would not make it subversive to ex-
hibit the picture, the fact that an article was written by a known
Communist would not make it subversive to publish the article.
If anything can make it "subversive" to publish an article it is
the article's content, not who wrote it. It cannot be subversive
to publish an innocuous article even if a known Communist
wrote it. Counts III and IV do not allege either that Lattimore
published, or that he denied publishing, subversive articles. If
these counts go to trial, and if the government offers to prove
that Lattimore did publish "subversive" articles and also that
their authors were Communists, it will remain immaterial
whether or not Lattimore knew they were Communists.

(3) Since Pacific Affairs was a scholarly journal, it was Lattimore's business as its editor to see that it presented a wide range
of expert opinion. Unbiased scholarship probably required and
certainly permitted the occasional inclusion of an article by a
known Communist expert among the 250 articles published between 1934 and 1941.

(4) Lattimore made clear to the Committee that articles by
Russian Communist experts were acceptable but hard to get. So
far as Count IV is concerned, therefore, his alleged false statement may be paraphrased; he did not know that some Com-

munists whose articles he published were non-Russians. But whether Communists were Russians or not, and whether Lattimore knew it or not, could have nothing to do with the question whether the articles themselves, and Lattimore's activity in publishing them, were innocuous or subversive.

Since an editor of any political views, or none, might well have published articles by known Communists between 1934 and 1941, Lattimore's knowledge or ignorance of authors' views has nothing to do, directly or indirectly, with the subject of subversive activities, then or later. No testimony concerning his knowledge or ignorance could have any value, even as a lead to other testimony. Suppose he had answered that he *did know* that Pacific Affairs had non-Russian Communist contributors and that Asiaticus was one of them. This would not have increased the Committee's knowledge about the contributors. Neither would it have thrown light on the political connections or tendencies of Lattimore, the Institute, or the magazine.

III. *Meaning of "material."* The court says the question whether an editor knew, in the 1930's, that a contributor was a Communist "Perhaps . . . was not important, but it was within the realm of materiality in so far as appears upon the face of the indictment."

The court overlooks the fact that in statutes, as well as in ordinary use, "material" means not only pertinent but also important in some substantial degree. The perjury statute, which uses the word "material" while the contempt statute uses the word "pertinent," is no exception. It is one thing to say that if a committee were authorized to investigate pneumonia, the lifelong clinical history of a man believed to have had pneumonia might be pertinent to the inquiry. It would be quite another thing to say that if he testified he had six colds in one winter ten years ago, whereas in fact he had only five, he could be indicted and punished for perjury. . . .

The reason why the law restricts the crime of perjury to

testimony of some importance before a "competent tribunal" is clear. Congress, the courts, and administrative bodies must not be misled, in their official action, by false testimony. But false testimony that is very unlikely to influence official action is little worse than ordinary lying.

IV. *Congressional power.* If there be doubt that Counts III and IV are void for the reasons we have discussed, the doubt should be resolved against the counts in order to avoid a grave constitutional question.

If we could not avoid the question, it might be hard to avoid the conclusion that a congressional inquiry into what an editor knew, between 1934 and 1941, about the views of the authors whose work he published, would abridge the freedom of the press guaranteed by the First Amendment. The Supreme Court's unanimous affirmance of our judgment in the *Rumely* case emphasizes the rule the Court established: that courts must not treat Congress as having meant to authorize a committee to ask questions that may invade First Amendment rights, unless Congress makes that meaning unmistakably clear. *United States* v. *Rumely,* 345 U.S. 41, 46 (1953). We have shown how far from clear it is that the Senate meant to authorize such an inquiry.

The Supreme Court said: "there is wide concern, both in and out of Congress, over some aspects of the exercise of the congressional power of investigation. . . . Surely it cannot be denied that giving the scope to the resolution for which the Government contends . . . raises doubts of constitutionality in view of the prohibition of the First Amendment." *United States* v. *Rumely,* 345 U.S. 41, 44, 46. Our court had held that Congress could not require Rumely, a publisher, to identify the purchasers of books: "To publicize or to report to the Congress the names and addresses of purchasers of books, pamphlets and periodicals is a realistic interference with the publication and sale of those writings." We pointed out that the "effect of public embarrassment is a powerful interference with the

free expression of views." *Rumely* v. *United States,* 90 U.S.
App. D.C. 382, 390, 197 F. 2d 166, 174 (D.C. Cir. 1952). In
the Supreme Court, likewise, Justice Douglas with whom Justice Black concurred held that Congress could not require a
publisher to identify the purchasers of books. No member of
the Supreme Court expressed a contrary view. But the majority
of the Court affirmed our judgment on the ground that it was
doubtful whether Congress could impose such a requirement and
that the Court should therefore adopt a "strained" (345 U.S.
at 47) construction of congressional language rather than find
that Congress undertook to impose it.

It is doubtful, to say the least, whether the Senate could require an editor to tell what he knew between 1934 and 1941
about the views of authors whose work he published. More
directly than the embarrassment of purchasers involved in the
Rumely case, embarrassment of editors interferes with freedom
of the press. It restricts not only reading but printing. And
unlike *Rumely,* no strained construction of congressional language is necessary to keep the constitutional issue out of this
case. On the contrary, a strained construction of congressional
language would be necessary to bring the constitutional issue
into the case; for, as we have shown, the ordinary meaning of
the Senate Resolution makes the matter in Counts III and IV
immaterial and the counts therefore void.

In *Rumely* we distinguished the *Barsky, Lawson,* and other
cases on the grounds that "Communism and the Communists are,
in the current world situation, potential threats to the security of
this country" and that Congress could, therefore, interfere with
freedom of expression in order to inquire into the subject. 90
U.S. App. D.C. at 389, 197 F. 2d at 173. For at least two reasons this distinction does not support Counts III and IV. First,
the questions in *Barsky, Lawson,* etc. concerned objective facts
and did not directly probe mental states. The *Barsky* defendants
"were not asked to state their political opinions. They were asked

to account for funds." The *Lawson* defendants were asked about membership in the Communist Party and in the Screen Writers Guild. Second, Counts III and IV relate exclusively to the time between 1934 and 1941, before the commencement of the "potential threats to the security of this country" with which Congress and the courts were concerned in *Barsky* and *Lawson*.

Nothing in the opinion of the Supreme Court, or in the concurring opinion, in *Rumely* suggests that the case turned or might have turned on evidence introduced at Rumely's trial. Neither opinion mentions his trial, except to say he was convicted under R.S. § 102 for refusal to testify and was sentenced to a fine of $1,000 and imprisonment for six months. As far as appears, everything in both opinions would have been equally apposite if the indictment had been before the Court on a motion to dismiss. In the present case it has been suggested that the government should be given an opportunity to prove, at a trial, that the matter in Counts III and IV is material. But we do not know that anyone has suggested what sort of testimony might possibly have that effect.

The court says: "freedom of speech . . . does not include freedom to lie under oath. Even if Lattimore, as the editor of a publication, had a right not to speak, he did not have a right to speak falsely. When he chose to speak under oath he was obliged to speak truly and was subject to the penalties of perjury if he lied on a material matter." The court overlooks the fact that what is not pertinent cannot be material and the *Rumely* rule that pertinence cannot be decided without regard to constitutional limits on congressional power. The court overlooks, also, the fact that perjury is limited to material matter falsely sworn before a "competent tribunal." Lying under oath before a tribunal that is not competent is not perjury. *Christoffel* v. *United States*, 338 U.S. 84 (1949). Within the limits of the Constitution and the Senate Resolution, the Committee was competent. But outside either limit, the Committee was no more "a competent tribunal" than the Tax Court of the United States would be competent to investigate an election.

MARY JANE KEENEY

v.

UNITED STATES OF AMERICA

Decided August 26, 1954

Before EDGERTON, PRETTYMAN, and DANAHER,
Circuit Judges

The name of Mary Jane Keeney was first brought to the attention of the public in the course of the trial of Judith Coplon for espionage. During the trial some FBI reports were introduced in evidence that contained allegations by several unidentified informants to the effect that Mary Jane Keeney had engaged in Communist activities on the West Coast, had had Communist associations, and on her return from Europe had delivered a manila envelope to a known Communist, which was thought to contain a will of an important Communist who had died in Germany. On the strength of these reports she was summoned to appear before the Un-American Activities Committee of the House of Representatives.

During the war years, Mary Jane Keeney had worked in various capacities for the Federal Government, but at the time she was summoned before the Committee, she was an employee of the United Nations. When she appeared before the Committee, she denied that she had ever been a member of the Communist Party or engaged in Communist activity and answered all the questions put to her, until she was asked through whom she had obtained employment with the United Nations. She then refused to answer, explaining that she had received explicit instructions from the officials of the United Nations that she must not answer any questions relating to matters of internal administration of the UN and that personnel matters fell in this category. The committee chairman refused to accept this theory of privilege, denied the right of the United Nations to give such instructions, and warned her that in refusing to answer she acted at her own peril. The Committee, however, took no further action in her case.

About two and a half years later, in the course of the investigation of the Institute of Pacific Relations, Mary Jane Keeney was summoned to appear before the Senate Subcommittee on Internal Security. At this time Mrs. Keeney had left the United Nations and was unemployed. Before the Senate Committee, she invoked the privilege against self-incrimination when she was questioned about membership in the Communist Party or in the Institute of Pacific Relations. She was then asked whether anyone in the State Department had helped her to get employment with the United Nations. She contended that under the rules of the United Nations she was still bound by the instructions that she had invoked before the House Committee. She was again warned that she acted at her peril, was ordered to answer, and when she continued to refuse was cited for contempt of Congress and indicted.

In the interval between the hearing and her trial she again consulted the officials of the United Nations who told her that she was free to disclose any information she might have that had not come from the files of the United Nations. Accordingly at the trial she testified that she did not know who had recommended her or whether anyone in the State Department had helped to get her a position with the United Nations. Her claim of privilege before the Committee was not sustained by the District Court, and she was convicted of contempt of Congress.

The judges of the division of the Court of Appeals that heard her case agreed that it should be remanded for a new trial because the jury had been permitted to hear highly prejudicial testimony as to her alleged Communist activities given by the prosecution in the course of an argument as to the pertinency of the question put to her by the Committee. Judge Prettyman and Judge Edgerton also thought that it was not clear that her refusal to answer was willful and that that question should be submitted to the jury. They agreed that it would be illegal for her to reveal information acquired as the result of her official position, but disagreed as to the scope of the privilege.

Mrs. Keeney has never been retried. The case as it stands adds the internal affairs of international organizations to the list of subjects that are beyond the power of congressional investigating committees.

EDGERTON, *Circuit Judge:* Appellant, a former employee of the United Nations, was a witness before a Subcommittee of the Committee on the Judiciary of the United States Senate. She was asked whether anyone in the State Department had aided her in obtaining employment with the United Nations. She did not answer, and asserted a privilege not to answer by reason of the Charter and the Staff Rules of the United Nations. On the theory that she had "refused" to answer, she was prosecuted for contempt of Congress. *Rev. Stat.* § 102, as amended, 52 Stat. 942, 2 U.S.C. § 192. The District Court overruled her claim of privilege and she was convicted. *United States* v. *Keeney*, 111 F. Supp. 233.

Appellant was not asked whether anyone in the State Department *told her he would try* to aid her. Perhaps it was a mistake not to ask her that question, but if so, the mistake was not hers. We need not speculate whether she would have answered that question if it had been asked, or whether she would have been punishable if she had not answered it. She was asked whether anyone in the State Department *did* aid her: "Did anyone in the State Department aid you in obtaining employment with the United Nations?" Whether she realized it or not, this was equivalent to asking her whether the United Nations officials who decided to appoint her had received and been influenced by communications from anyone in the State Department recommending that she be appointed.

Staff Rule 7 of the United Nations provides that "Staff members shall exercise the utmost discretion in regard to all matters of official business. They shall not communicate to any other person any unpublished information known to them by reason of their official position except in the course of their

duties or by authorization of the Secretary-General." In my
opinion both the first sentence and the second sentence of this
Rule support appellant's failure to answer. (1) Since the appointment of official personnel is official business, appellant
could not answer without violating her obligation to "exercise
the utmost discretion in regard to all matters of official business."
She could not, consistently with "the utmost discretion," even
answer that she did not know, for that would have meant that
her superiors had not told her. Whether officials do or do not
tell an employee who aided her in obtaining employment is a
matter of official policy and official business. (2) The question
related to "unpublished information." The United Nations does
not tell the world what recommendations underlie appointments
of staff members. The United Nations Administrative Manual
even defines "unpublished information" to include "the appointment . . . [of] or any other confidential information concerning" a staff member. I think it plain that staff members
would not have such unpublished and confidential information
unless it had been made "known to them by reason of their
official position."

The Charter of the United Nations supports Staff Rule 7.
The Charter provides:

> "Article 100.
> "1. In the performance of their duties, the Secretary-
> General and the Staff shall not seek or receive instructions
> from any government or from any other authority external
> to the Organization. They shall refrain from any action
> which might reflect on their position as international offi-
> cials responsible only to the Organization.
> "2. Each member of the United Nations undertakes to
> respect the exclusively international character of the re-
> sponsibilities of the Secretary-General and the staff and
> not to seek to influence them in the discharge of their re-
> sponsibilities. . . .

"Article 105.

"1. The Organization shall enjoy in the territory of each of its members such privileges and immunities as are necessary for the fulfillment of its purposes.

"2. Representatives of the members of the United Nations and officials of the Organization shall similarly enjoy such privileges and immunities as are necessary for the independent exercise of their functions in connection with the Organization." 59 Stat. 1052, 1053.

Compulsory disclosure of the persons who influence appointments to the staff of the United Nations would not be consistent with the independence of the Organization or "the exclusively international character of the responsibilities of the Secretary-General and the staff . . ." (Art. 100, Par. 2) And the prospect of such disclosure might influence staff members, in one degree or another, to regulate their official conduct with a view to avoiding embarrassment of sponsors. The privilege of non-disclosure is therefore "necessary for the independent exercise of their functions in connection with the Organization." (Art. 105, Par. 2)

Thus the Charter and the Staff Rules of the United Nations establish, in my opinion, the privilege on which appellant relied. And her failure to answer is within the spirit if not the letter of the International Organizations Immunities Act, which provides in § 7(b), 59 Stat. 672, 22 U.S.C. § 288d(b): "Representatives of foreign governments in or to international organizations and officers and employees of such organizations shall be immune from suit and legal process relating to acts performed by them in their official capacity and falling within their functions as such representatives, officers, or employees except insofar as such immunity may be waived by the foreign government or international organization concerned." . . .

I agree with Judge Prettyman that there was no obvious *refusal* to answer. In my opinion there was clearly no deliberate and intentional refusal. . . .

John T. Watkins

v.

United States of America
Decided April 23, 1956
On rehearing in banc

In pursuit of its avowed objective of exposing Communists, the Un-American Activities Committee has not limited itself to the original question, "Are you now or have you ever been a Communist?" Once a witness has admitted past Communist activities, the committee demands that he name his former associates. Other committees have adopted the same practice, and the question seems to have become the acid test of a witness's veracity and sincerity in denying present Communist connections.

For some witnesses the question poses a serious moral problem, especially in view of the social penalties inflicted upon those identified as Communists, past or present. Witnesses who have not themselves been very deeply involved in the movement often are not sure even of the extent of the past involvement of their former associates in unions or Communist-front organizations and know little or nothing of their present activities. They do not want to save themselves at the expense of others who may today be quite innocent of any taint of subversion. Some have mistakenly taken refuge in the Fifth Amendment. Recently several witnesses have instead respectfully claimed the right to refuse to answer the question. Among these persons was John T. Watkins, who was thereafter convicted of contempt and appealed.

Watkins invoked the familiar constitutional objections to the power of the Un-American Activities Committee and also contended that when a subcommittee of that body questioned him it was concerned only with the exposure of Communists, that exposure is not a legislative function, and that the questions put to him, therefore, were not pertinent to the purposes of the Committee.

On January 26, 1956, a division of the Circuit Court of Appeals, composed of Chief Judge Edgerton and Circuit Judges Bazelon and Bastian, reversed the District Court. Judge Edgerton wrote the majority opinion, agreeing with Watkins as to lack of pertinency, and Judge Bastian dissented.

The decision aroused a great deal of criticism and met with an angry reception from the chairman of the Committee, who publicly denounced the majority judges. The Department of Justice asked for a rehearing of the case in banc. The request was granted and on April 23, 1956, the earlier decision was reversed. This time Judge Bastian spoke for the majority, and Judges Edgerton and Bazelon were the sole dissenters.

The court now found that the purpose of the particular hearing was made sufficiently clear by the opening statement of the chairman to the effect that it was being held in connection with a proposed amendment to existing law relating to Communist dominated unions, that exposure is legitimate if it is incidental to a legislative function, and that the questions asked were pertinent. Judge Edgerton's dissenting opinion is a reaffirmation of his earlier opinion in the case.

The Supreme Court agreed to review the case "because of the very important questions of constitutional law involved," and on June 17, 1957, it handed down its decision reversing the lower courts and ordering the District Court to dismiss the indictment. It asserted that as a general proposition exposure is not a valid legislative purpose, but it refused to consider the motive of the Committee in questioning Watkins. In view of the history of the Committee's activities it disagreed both with the position taken by Judge Edgerton in the *Barsky* case that the vague terms of the Committee's authorizing resolution are clarified and limited by its reference to "subversive propaganda attacking our form of government" and with the conclusion of the majority of the Court of Appeals that the legislative purpose of the particular hearing was sufficiently established by the chairman's opening statement. It found that the terms of that resolution are so vague as to make it impossible for any court to determine whether or not a particular question is pertinent and that the pur-

pose of the particular inquiry was equally obscure. It ruled, therefore, that the requirement of the Due Process Clause that standards
of criminality must be clear was violated when Congress sought to
make that resolution the basis of a criminal prosecution.

Following the *Watkins* case, the indictments of several persons
who had refused to answer questions put to them by the Un-
American Activities Committee were dismissed. The District Court
for the District of Columbia also dismissed the indictment of a
witness who refused to comply with the demand of a Senate subcommittee that he identify as Communists persons he had known
in the period 1937–1942 on the ground that the Committee's mandate
to investigate subversive activities was also too vague to be made
the basis of a criminal prosecution.

The Court of Appeals scheduled a hearing in banc of eight cases,
decided one of them in favor of the appellant, but postponed the
others until the *Barenblatt* case (infra, p. 100) should be decided by
the Supreme Court.

EDGERTON, *Chief Judge,* with whom BAZELON, *Circuit Judge,*
joins, *dissenting:* The appellant has been convicted of refusing
to answer certain questions before a subcommittee of the Committee of the House of Representatives on Un-American Activities. He told the Committee he had co-operated with the
Communist Party from 1942 to 1947. He did not plead the
Fifth Amendment. Asked whether he knew certain persons as
Communists, he answered freely concerning all whom he believed to be Communists at the time of the hearing. He refused
to answer concerning other persons. As the District Court said
in sentencing him, he did not "attempt to impede the committee in any respect, other than his refusal to answer questions
dealing with persons who, to use his words, 'may in the past
have been Communist Party members or otherwise engaged in
Communist activities, but who to my best knowledge and belief have long since removed themselves from the Communist

movement.'" We have to decide whether his refusal to expose their past history was a crime.

Since 1953 he has been a United Automobile Workers organizer. From 1935 to 1953 he was employed by the International Harvester Company at East Moline, Illinois, but from 1942 to 1953 he was on leave and worked for the Farm Equipment Workers, CIO, and its successor. At a hearing of the Committee in 1952, one Spencer named him as having been a member of the Communist Party between 1943 and 1946. At a hearing of the Committee in Chicago in March 1954, one Rumsey testified that in 1942 or 1943 Watkins recruited him into the Party and collected his Party dues.

In April 1954, in response to a subpoena, Watkins appeared and testified before the Committee in Washington. He said: "I am not now nor have I ever been a card-carrying member of the Communist Party. Rumsey was wrong when he said I had recruited him into the party, that I had received his dues . . . Spencer was wrong when he termed any meetings which I attended as closed Communist Party meetings.

"I would like to make it clear that for a period of time from approximately 1942 to 1947 I cooperated with the Communist Party and participated in Communist activities to such a degree that some persons may honestly believe that I was a member of the Party. I have made contributions upon occasions to Communist causes. I have signed petitions for Communist causes. I attended caucuses at an FE convention at which Communist Party officials were present. Since I freely cooperated with the Communist Party I have no motive for making the distinction between cooperation and membership except the simple fact that it is the truth. I never carried a Communist Party card. I never accepted discipline and indeed on several occasions I opposed their position.

"In a special convention held in the summer of 1947 I led the fight for compliance with the Taft-Hartley Act by the FE-CIO International Union. This fight became so bitter that it ended any possibility of future cooperation."

He was asked: ". . . with whom did you participate in the Communist Party in [its] activities . . . ?" He named several people. Mr. Kunzig, Committee counsel, said: "Now, I have here a list of names of people, all of whom were identified as Communist Party members by Mr. Rumsey during his recent testimony in Chicago. I am asking you first whether you know these people." He did not know the first three. He knew the fourth, who was Spencer, and the fifth, one Harold Fisher. He was asked, "Do you know Harold Fisher to be a member of the Communist Party?" [1] He consulted his counsel and then read this statement to the Committee: "I would like to get one thing perfectly clear, Mr. Chairman. I am not going to plead the fifth amendment, but I refuse to answer certain questions that I believe are outside the proper scope of your committee's activities. I will answer any questions which this committee puts to me about myself. I will also answer questions about those persons whom I knew to be members of the Communist Party and who I believe still are. I will not, however, answer any questions with respect to others with whom I associated in the past. I do not believe that any law in this country requires me to testify about persons who may in the past have been Communist Party members or otherwise en-

[1] As to all except Fisher and one other, the Committee's questions were expressly about past Party membership. As to those two persons, the questions were phrased in the present tense. But in view of the earlier testimony of Rumsey and Spencer, who set the dates of appellant's Party affiliation from 1943–46, and appellant's uncontradicted statement that he had ceased co-operation with the Party in 1947, it is plain that the Committee was questioning appellant about the past. He did not refuse to testify about the present. His statement which we proceed to quote shows that when he replied to a question about present membership by standing on the statement, he was in effect denying that he knew the named individual to be a present member of the Party and refusing to answer about past membership.

gaged in Communist Party activity but who to my best knowledge and belief have long since removed themselves from the Communist movement.

"I do not believe that such questions are relevant to the work of this committee nor do I believe that this committee has the right to undertake the public exposure of persons because of their past activities. I may be wrong, and the committee may have this power, but until and unless a court of law so holds and directs me to answer, I most firmly refuse to discuss the political activities of my past associates."

After testifying that Joseph Stern, one of the men on the Committee's list, had carried on Party activities, he said: "In regard to the other names that you have read, I will not answer, based upon the statement that I read into the record. . . ." The Committee directed him to answer. He refused again. The Committee did not question him further.

He was indicted in November 1954 and tried in May 1955. He waived a jury. The government called only one witness, the Committee counsel, who put into the record the transcript of the Committee's examination of Watkins. The court found Watkins guilty, fined him $500, sentenced him to a year's imprisonment, suspended the sentence, and placed him on probation.

I

The Committee on Un-American Activities is a standing committee of the House of Representatives. The Committee and its subcommittees are authorized by a Joint Resolution "to make from time to time investigations of (i) the extent, character, and objects of un-American propaganda activities in the United States, (ii) the diffusion within the United States of subversive and un-American propaganda that is instigated from foreign countries or of a domestic origin and attacks the principle of the form of government as guaranteed by our Constitution, and

(iii) all other questions in relation thereto that would aid Congress in any necessary remedial legislation." 60 Stat. 812, 823, 828.

A witness before a congressional committee is guilty of a misdemeanor if he "refuses to answer any question pertinent to the question under inquiry. . . ." 2 U.S.C. § 192, R.S. § 102, 52 Stat. 942, as amended. Pertinence is part of the government's case. In order to convict, the government must plead and prove that the questions the witness would not answer were pertinent to an inquiry Congress had authorized. . . .

An important preliminary question is whether the Joint Resolution is to be construed broadly or narrowly for the purpose of deciding whether the questions Watkins would not answer were pertinent to the inquiry authorized by the Resolution. The Resolution must be construed narrowly if a narrow construction avoids a serious constitutional question. *United States* v. *Rumely*, 345 U.S. 41.

If the questions Watkins would not answer were pertinent to the inquiry authorized by the Resolution, we should have to decide whether they were within the constitutional power of Congress. Like the question in the *Rumely* case, this question is serious, as we shall presently show. It follows that, for the purposes of this case, the Joint Resolution must be construed narrowly if the questions Watkins refused to answer would otherwise appear pertinent. . . .

It is very questionable whether exposure of individuals to public contempt or hostility is a "valid legislative purpose." Since Congress has "no powers of law enforcement" it would have no power, in the absence of a valid legislative purpose, to expose former Communists, even if there were a law requiring that former Communists be exposed. If we were obliged to decide what the Committee's purpose was in asking the questions Watkins would not answer, we might be forced to conclude that the Committee asked them for the sole purpose of exposure.

By "exposure" we mean injurious publicity. The fact that Rumsey, at Chicago in March, publicly called Fisher a Communist, does not mean that if Watkins had done so at Washington in April, this new publicity and its repetition in and out of the press would not have been injurious. Obviously the new publicity would have been injurious. As the law of slander and libel recognizes, the fact that a derogatory statement has been made previously does not make it harmless. And the fact that Rumsey had called Fisher a Communist does not show that the Committee sought to serve some other purpose than injurious publicity when it asked Watkins "Do you know Harold Fisher to be a member of the Communist Party?"

II

The government argues that the Committee's purpose in asking the questions was to investigate Communist infiltration of labor unions, in order to determine the need for pending legislation to deprive Communist-infiltrated unions of the use of the National Labor Relations Board.[2] But several aspects of the Committee's

[2] In opening the hearing in Washington at which Watkins testified, on April 29, 1954, the chairman said nothing directly about purpose. He said: "The hearing this morning is a continuation of the hearings which were held in Chicago recently. . . ." In opening the Chicago hearings, in March 1954, the chairman said Congress had directed the Committee "to ascertain the extent and success of subversive activities directed against these United States," and mentioned bills of two sorts as pending before the Committee, one of which would make evidence "secured from confidential devices" admissible in "cases involving the national security." Another, he said, "would provide that the Subversive Activities Control Board should, after suitable hearings and procedures, be empowered to find if certain labor organizations are in fact Communist-controlled action groups. Following this action, such labor groups would not have available the use of the National Labor Relations Board as they now have under the provisions of the Labor-Management Relations Act of 1947."

examination of Watkins tend to show that the Committee did not ask these questions for that purpose, or for any purpose except exposure.

(1) The Committee made no attempt to learn from Watkins either the total number of Communists in his union, or what positions Communists held in the union, or whether or how, or how far, or in what direction, they influenced the union. The Committee showed no interest in anything but a list of names. Whether Communist infiltration of unions creates a need for legislation would seem to depend on the number, and the nature, extent, and effectiveness of the activities, of Communists in unions. Watkins named several people, who apparently had been fellow-members of his union, as having been Communists while he co-operated with the Party. If the Committee had been questioning him for a legislative purpose, it could hardly have failed to question him about what, if anything, these Communist members of the union did.

(2) It is not clear, and the government does not suggest, how the questions Watkins would not answer could have served the purpose the government now attributes to the Committee.

These questions concerned the presence of Communists in a union between 1942 and 1947. Their presence or absence in unions then had little or nothing to do with the question whether, at the time of the Committee hearing in 1954, Communists in unions were so numerous, so active, and so effective as to create problems that called for legislation. This is true partly because of the lapse of time, but chiefly because times had changed and legislation had changed.

Communist affiliation between 1942 and 1947 did not mean what Communist affiliation meant in 1954. In December 1941 the United States joined Russia in the war against Germany. President Roosevelt wrote to Admiral Land in January 1942: "I am still terribly disturbed about the fact that an adequate number of ships are not available for Russia. . . . This Government has made a firm pledge to Russia and we simply cannot go back on it." In February 1942 General MacArthur honored the 25th [*sic*] anniversary of the Red Army with a message in which he said: ". . . the hopes of civilization rest upon the worthy banners of the courageous Russian Army. . . ." (Quoted in Robert E. Sherwood, *Roosevelt and Hopkins* [1948], pp. 496, 497.) Friendly relations between the United States and Russia continued throughout the war and did not cease immediately at the end of the war.

The Labor Management Relations Act, which requires non-Communist affidavits from officers of unions that use the National Labor Relations Board, was not passed until 1947, close to the end of the period to which the Committee's questions relate. Whether the Act is adequate or requires strengthening would seem to depend upon what has happened since, not what had already happened. Likewise the Internal Security Act and the Immigration and Nationality Act, passed in 1950 and 1952, were in effect at the time of the Committee hearing but not at the time to which the Committee's questions relate.

(3) When Watkins refused to answer the Committee's questions, saying he thought their purpose was "public exposure of persons because of their past activities," the Committee was under no obligation to reply. However, the chairman chose to reply. His reply did not suggest that the questions had a legislative purpose related to unions. It did not mention unions. Instead, it claimed for the Committee unlimited authority to question Watkins concerning his knowledge of former Communists. The chairman said: "This committee is set up by the House of Representatives to investigate subversion and subversive propaganda and to report to the House of Representatives for the purpose of remedial legislation. The House of Representatives has by a very clear majority, a very large majority, directed us to engage in that type of work, and so we do, as a committee of the House of Representatives, have the authority,

the jurisdiction, to ask you concerning your activities in the Communist Party, concerning your knowledge of any other persons who are members of the Communist Party or who have been members of the Communist Party, and so, Mr. Watkins, you are directed to answer the question propounded to you by counsel."

(4) The Committee seems to have had in its possession, before it questioned Watkins, the information about other persons which it asked him to supply.

(5) The purpose the government attributes to the Committee, and practically any other purpose except exposure, might have been served by questioning Watkins in a closed session. But the Committee questioned him at a public hearing.

III

Words and conduct of the Committee on other occasions go far to confirm the inference that its purpose on this occasion was exposure.

"The Committee and its members have repeatedly said in terms or in effect that its main purpose is to do by exposure and publicity what it believes may not validly be done by legislation."

At the trial, the defense offered in evidence "excerpts from House committee reports, House committee hearings, Congressional Record statements and newspapers, going to the point that the House committee asserts an independent power all apart from legislation to expose persons to public knowledge." The court excluded these excerpts as evidence, but they are in the record as an offer of proof. They cover some 64 printed pages. They show beyond doubt, and it is not disputed, that the Committee on Un-American Activities claims an independent power of exposure and sometimes investigates for the purpose of exposure. We give a few illustrations.

Mr. Dies, the first chairman of the Committee, said during debate in the House on his resolution for the appointment of such a Committee, "I am not in a position to say whether we can legislate effectively in reference to this matter, but I do know that exposure in a democracy of subversive activities is the most effective weapon that we have in our possession." 83 *Congressional Record* 7570 (May 26, 1938).

The Committee said in 1951: "Exposure in a systematic way began with the formation of the House Committee on Un-American Activities, May 26, 1938. . . . The House Committee on Un-American Activities was started on its way May 20, 1938, with instructions from the United States House of Representatives to expose people and organizations attempting to destroy this country. That is still its job, and to that job it sticks." *100 Things You Should Know About Communism* (1951), 82d Cong., 1st Sess., House Document No. 136, pp. 19, 67.

Mr. Velde, the Chairman of the Committee in the 83d Congress, who presided at the Watkins hearing, said at another hearing: "we feel that we have a duty and that duty has been imposed upon us by Congress not only to report to Congress for the purpose of remedial legislation but to inform the people who elected us about subversive activities. . . ." Hearing Before the Committee on Un-American Activities, House of Representatives, 83d Cong., 1st Sess., p. 1106.

Chairman Walter said in 1955: "Unlike most congressional committees, in addition to the legislative function we are required to make the American people aware if possible of the extent of the infiltration of Communism in all phases of our society." U.S. News and World Report, August 26, 1955, p. 71.

The Committee has publicized the names of persons identified to it as Communists or former Communists. Its Report for 1952 devotes 54 out of a total of 89 pages to the names and addresses of such persons. Its Report for 1953 devotes 59 out of 193 pages to a similar list.

Though the Committee's Report for 1954, the year of the Watkins hearing, does not contain a list of names, it points to exposure as the Committee's function. It says, *e.g.*, that in 1952 the Committee "reported that during its investigation the identity of over 600 individuals as Communist Party members was obtained. . . . During the committee's investigation, it uncovered members of the Communist Party holding influential positions in the school systems of Detroit and other communities. . . . Most of the teachers called have been suspended or permanently removed from their positions. The Committee on Un-American Activities approves of this action . . ." Committee on Un-American Activities, Annual Report for the Year 1954, pp. 14–15, 17. In a separate pamphlet issued in 1954 the Committee said: "This committee and the special committee have over the past 16 years held hundreds of hearings and issued and distributed throughout the United States hundreds of thousands of reports exposing the operations of the Communist Party and its fronts." *This is YOUR House Committee on Un-American Activities*, p. 25.

The District Court ruled that express claims of an independent power of exposure, made without particular reference to the Watkins hearing, do not tend to prove that the Committee's purpose in the Watkins hearing was exposure. In our opinion this was error. Although general propositions do not decide concrete cases, they help to decide them. Intentions tend to result in acts. By claiming that it had the authority and duty to expose, the Committee implied that it intended to expose. And as the Fifth Circuit recently said, "of course it may be inferred from a person's statement that he intended to do something, that he later actually did it. Mutual Life Ins. Co. of New York v. Hillmon, 145 U.S. 285, 295, 12 S. Ct. 909, 36 L. Ed. 706." *Shurman* v. *United States*, 219 F. 2d 282, 290, fn. 9 (1955).

IV

In our opinion the questions Watkins refused to answer are not pertinent to the inquiry authorized by the Joint Resolution, even if the Resolution is not construed narrowly. If it is construed narrowly, the questions are clearly not pertinent.

The key words of the Resolution are (i) "extent, character and objects of un-American propaganda activities"; (ii) "diffusion . . . of subversive and un-American propaganda"; and (iii) "questions in relation thereto that would aid Congress in any necessary remedial legislation." The questions do not relate in any clear or direct way to the extent, the character, the objects, or the diffusion, of any propaganda, subversive and un-American or otherwise. The government has not shown that in asking these questions the Committee was seeking, even indirectly, information about the extent or character or objects or diffusion of propaganda. It has not shown that Watkins, or his union, or the persons about whom the Committee inquired, engaged in propaganda, or that the Committee sought to learn whether they did.

As to clause (iii) of the Resolution: possibly questions concerning Communist Party membership might be considered "questions in relation" to the "extent, character and objects" or the "diffusion" of propaganda, if the phrase "in relation" were construed very broadly, but these questions certainly cannot be so considered if the phrase is construed narrowly. Moreover, clause (iii) contains the further requirement that the questions "would aid Congress in any necessary remedial legislation." If a mere theoretical chance of very slight aid were to be considered sufficient, possibly it might be thought that the questions "would aid." But that would be a broad construction of those words. Construed narrowly, the words require more than a theoretical chance. The questions Watkins would not answer plainly do not meet this requirement.

"The United States suggests that the presumption of regularity is sufficient without proof. But, without determining whether that presumption is applicable to such a matter, it is enough to say that the stronger presumption of innocence attended the accused at the trial." *Sinclair* v. *United States*, 279 U.S. 263, 296. We conclude that the government failed to show, either beyond a reasonable doubt or even by a preponderance of the evidence, that the questions Watkins would not answer were pertinent to any investigation the Committee was authorized to make.

Barsky v. *United States*, 83 U.S. App. D.C. 127, 167 F. 2d 241, is not to the contrary. The court held that, in the circumstances of that case, Congress and the Committee on Un-American Activities had "power to make an inquiry of an individual which may elicit the answer that the witness is a believer in Communism or a member of the Communist Party." 83 U.S. App. D.C. at 136, 167 F. 2d at 250. But the circumstances of that case and of this are very different. (1) As the court pointed out, Barsky and his co-defendants "were not asked to state their political opinions. They were asked to account for funds." 83 U.S. App. D.C. at 130, 167 F. 2d at 244. (2) As the court pointed out, the Congressional Committee had been informed that Barsky's organization, the Joint Anti-Fascist Refugee Committee, was engaged in "political propaganda." 83 U.S. App. D.C. at 129, 167 F. 2d at 243. It has not been shown that the Congressional Committee had any comparable information in this case. (3) The question Barsky refused to answer related, though indirectly, to his *present* Communist membership. The questions Watkins refused to answer related to Communist membership of other persons at a time long past. To hold, as *Barsky* does, that the Committee may inquire whether members of an organization shown to engage in propaganda are now Communists, does not imply that it may inquire whether members of a union not shown to engage, or to be likely to engage, in propaganda were once Communists.

METHODIST FEDERATION FOR SOCIAL ACTION

v.

JAMES O. EASTLAND *et al.*

Decided May 25, 1956

Before EDGERTON and PRETTYMAN, *Circuit Judges,*
and WILKIN, *District Judge*

The Methodist Federation for Social Action is one of the un-happy organizations that has been grievously weakened by an in-ternal struggle against Communist sympathizers who gained positions of power within the group. It was founded in 1908, under the name Methodist Federation for Social Service, by leaders in the church who felt that Methodists should play their part in the struggle for social justice. The common goal of the founders is said to have been "economic justice, racial and religious goodwill, and world-wide peace." The Federation was not a branch of the church, and it was clearly understood within the church that the organization did not speak for it. The General Conference did approve it at its birth, reiterated that approval when it was first under attack, and until very recently housed it in the Methodist Building in New York City, but after 1936 required it to add the word "unofficial" on its stationery.

By 1924 the more conservative elements in the church began active opposition to the Federation, and by the middle of the 1930's it had become the subject of serious internal controversy and had also been subjected to public attack by the Hearst papers.

Beginning in the late forties the Federation was again subjected to bitter public attack. A series of articles appeared in the Scripps-Howard papers accusing it of consistently following the Communist line, the House Un-American Activities Committee described it as a "tool of the Communist Party," and in 1950 a sensational article in the *Reader's Digest* repeated the charges. The Federation itself had discovered that its executive secretary had been sympathetic to a number of Communist causes and that the Federation's *Social Questions Bulletin* often supported the Communist line. It took steps to correct this situation. In 1952 the General Conference formally voiced its disapproval of the policies of the Federation, requesting it to remove the word "Methodist" from its title and to leave its quarters in the Methodist Building. In 1953 the Federation was reorganized, the controversial executive secretary was transferred from his post to a less important one, and the move from the Methodist Building was accomplished. In the course of the struggle many of the leading Methodist liberals had resigned, and the membership had been cut nearly in half. Nevertheless, a substantial number of respectable liberals have remained in the organization. The Federation has never been placed upon the Attorney General's list of subversive organizations.

In 1956 the Senate Subcommittee on Internal Security planned to republish and circulate a pamphlet in which the Federation was named as a Communist front. The organization asked the District Court to enjoin the subcommittee members, the Public Printer, and the Superintendent of Documents from printing and distributing the pamphlet. Judge Wilkin, a visiting district judge, issued a temporary restraining order, and the case was then heard by a statutory three-judge court. Judge Edgerton spoke for the court, dismissing the complaint, and Judge Wilkin dissented vigorously.

In the earlier cases the court had, in effect, been asked to refuse to use its process in order to enforce a power of Congress. This time the plaintiff requested it to forbid a committee of the Senate to act, thus exercising direct control over the activities of Congress. Such an action would have involved a serious breach of the "separation of powers," instituted by the American Constitution as one guarantee of a free society.

EDGERTON, *Circuit Judge:* A 100-page pamphlet entitled *The Communist Party of the United States—What It Is—How It Works—A Handbook For Americans,* issued by the Subcommittee on Internal Security of the Senate Committee on the Judiciary, was printed December 21, 1955. A Concurrent Resolution, passed by the Senate January 16, 1956 and by the House of Representatives April 23, 1956, orders this pamphlet "printed as a Senate Document. . . . There shall be printed seventy-five thousand additional copies of such Senate Document for the use of the Subcommittee on Internal Security of the Senate Committee on the Judiciary." S. Con. Res. 62 [Report No. 2025], 84th Cong., 2d Sess., 102 Cong. Rec. 441, 6069.

The pamphlet contains these statements: "With an eye to religious groups, the Communists have formed religious fronts such as the Methodist Federation for Social Action. . . . Sometimes fronts will merge to avoid exposure or prosecution. At times they have been known to assume a name similar to some well-known and respectable organization. An example is the Methodist Federation for Social Action which has no official connection with the Methodist Church. . . ." Pp. 91, 95.

The Methodist Federation for Social Action filed a complaint in the District Court against the members of the Senate Subcommittee, the Public Printer, and the Superintendent of Documents. The complaint says the charge that the plaintiff is a Communist front is false as well as defamatory, was made without a hearing, and causes irreparable injury. It says the Concurrent Resolution abridges the plaintiff's rights of free speech, assembly, press and religion, deprives the plaintiff of liberty and property without due process of law, and is a bill of attainder. It asks a declaration that the Concurrent Resolution is unconstitutional, an order enjoining the defendants from printing and distributing the Senate Document, and a temporary restraining order.

On May 3, 1956 Judge Wilkin in the District Court issued a temporary restraining order against the Public Printer and the Superintendent of Documents. He also asked for the appointment of this three-judge District Court in accordance with 28

U.S.C. § 2282, 62 Stat. 968. In his view, which we have adopted, the restraining order expired when this court convened.

The Public Printer and the Superintendent of Documents have answered the complaint, and have also filed a motion to dismiss or in the alternative for summary judgment. No appearance has been entered on behalf of the members of the Senate Subcommittee. Whatever the facts may be, for the purpose of deciding whether the complaint should be dismissed we must assume that its factual assertions are true.

By express provision of the Constitution, members of Congress, "for any Speech or Debate in either House . . . shall not be questioned in any other Place." Art. I, Sec. 6. It would be paradoxical if members could be questioned in any other place for statements in a document which both houses have ordered published.

Nothing in the Constitution authorizes anyone to prevent the President of the United States from publishing any statement. This is equally true whether the statement is correct or not, whether it is defamatory or not, and whether it is or is not made after a fair hearing. Similarly, nothing in the Constitution authorizes anyone to prevent the Supreme Court from publishing any statement. We think it equally clear that nothing authorizes anyone to prevent Congress from publishing any statement.

No previous case has been called to our attention in which it has even been attempted to prevent publication of anything Congress has ordered published. In *Hearst* v. *Black*, 66 App. D.C. 313, 87 F. 2d 68, the plaintiff sought among other things to enjoin the members of a Senate Committee from publishing telegrams alleged to have been obtained in violation of his constitutional rights. The United States Court of Appeals for the District of Columbia said in denying relief: "If a court could say to the Congress that it could use or could not use information in its possession, the independence of the Legislature would be destroyed and the constitutional separation of the powers of government invaded." 87 F. 2d at 71–72. Since Congress has ordered publication of the Senate Document involved in this case, and had not ordered publication of the telegrams involved in the *Hearst* case, it is even plainer here than there that a judgment for the plaintiff would invade the constitutional separation of powers.

The premise that courts may refuse to enforce legislation they think unconstitutional does not support the conclusion that they may censor congressional language they think libelous. We have no more authority to prevent Congress, or a committee or public officer acting at the express direction of Congress, from publishing a document than to prevent them from publishing the Congressional Record. If it unfortunately happens that a document which Congress has ordered published contains statements that are erroneous and defamatory, and are made without allowing the persons affected an opportunity to be heard, this adds nothing to our authority. Only Congress can deal with such a problem.

The constitutional history called to our attention includes no instance in which an English court has attempted to restrain Parliament, or an American court to restrain Congress, from publishing any statement. This history therefore tends to confirm our view.

In *Joint Anti-Fascist Refugee Committee* v. *McGrath*, 341 U.S. 123, neither the President nor Congress had directed the Attorney General to take the particular action which the Court restrained him from taking; and the action restrained was an adverse ruling that had legal consequences, not a mere defamatory publication.

We need not consider whether an injunction would violate the First Amendment as well as the prerogative of Congress.

As to the members of the Senate Subcommittee, the complaint is dismissed for lack of jurisdiction. *Cf. Hearst* v. *Black, supra.* As to the Public Printer and the Superintendent of Documents, the complaint is dismissed for failure to state a claim on which relief can be granted.

Lloyd Barenblatt

v.

United States of America
Decided January 16, 1958
Heard in banc

On the same day that it decided the *Watkins* case the Supreme Court granted a petition by Lloyd Barenblatt asking for a writ of certiorari to review a judgment of the Court of Appeals affirming his conviction in the District Court for contempt of Congress. The Court thereupon remanded the case to the Court of Appeals for reconsideration in the light of the *Watkins* case.

The petitioner, Lloyd Barenblatt, was a former student at the University of Michigan who was called before a subcommittee of the Un-American Activities Committee in the course of an investigation by that body of communism in education. He did not challenge the pertinency of the questions put to him but simply refused to answer, attempting instead to read a statement attacking the jurisdiction of the Committee.

The Court of Appeals sat in banc to review the case and again sustained the conviction. In a 5 to 4 decision the court found that the *Watkins* case did not strike down the resolution that created the Un-American Activities Committee but permitted the necessary clarification to be made when hearings are held. It found further that this clarity had been achieved in Barenblatt's case by the opening statements of the chairman and the committee counsel as to the purpose and scope of the session in Michigan, by the consistency of the questions asked, all of which related to Communist activity at the University of Michigan, and by the pertinency of the questions put to Barenblatt to the stated purpose of the hearing.

Judges Fahy and Washington thought that under the *Rumely*,

Watkins, and *Sweezy* cases the Committee was barred from any inquiry in the field of education unless specifically authorized by Congress. Judge Edgerton, with whom Judge Bazelon agreed, took the position that the *Watkins* case did invalidate the Committee's authorizing resolution.

The Supreme Court agreed to review the case. In May, 1958, it ordered it to be reargued in the next term of court and on June 8, 1959, in a 5 to 4 decision, affirmed Barenblatt's conviction. The Court found that the mandate of the Committee to investigate communism in education was made sufficiently clear by a long legislative history, that the pertinency of the questions asked was manifest, that they were related to a legislative purpose, and that the First Amendment does not under all circumstances forbid an inquiry into "associational relationships." In view of this situation the Court was without authority to inquire into the motives of the legislative body.

Three Justices joined Justice Black in a vigorous dissent to all these points.

EDGERTON, *Chief Judge,* whom BAZELON, *Circuit Judge,* joins, *dissenting:* A unanimous panel of this court decided that "the opinion of the Supreme Court in *Watkins* v. *United States . . .* requires reversal" of the conviction of Singer. Barenblatt, like Singer, was convicted of refusing to answer questions of a subcommittee of the Un-American Activities Committee investigating Communists in the field of education. There is no difference pertinent to *Watkins* between Singer's case and Barenblatt's. I think this court errs in overruling our *Singer* decision.

I understand *Watkins* to hold that the Committee on Un-American Activities had no authority to compel testimony because it had no definite assignment from Congress. The Supreme Court said: "[W]hen First Amendment rights are threatened, the delegation of power to the Committee must be clearly revealed in its charter. [354 U.S. at p. 198] . . . An essential premise in this situation is that the House or Senate shall have instructed the Committee members on what they are to do with the power delegated to them. . . . [T]he responsibility of the Congress . . . to insure that compulsory process is used only in furtherance of a legislative purpose . . . requires that the instructions to an investigating committee spell out that group's jurisdiction and purpose with sufficient particularity. [p. 201] . . . It would be difficult to imagine a less explicit authorizing resolution. [p. 202] . . . Combining the language of the resolution with the construction it has been given, it is evident that the preliminary control of the Committee exercised by the House of Representatives is slight or non-existent. No one could reasonably deduce from the charter the kind of investigation that the Committee was directed to make. [pp. 203–4] . . . The Committee is allowed, in essence, to define its own authority . . . [This] can lead to ruthless exposure of private lives in order to gather data that is neither desired by the Congress nor useful to it. . . . Protected freedoms should not be placed in danger in the absence of a clear determination by the House or the Senate that a particular inquiry is justified by a specific legislative need. . . . An excessively broad charter, like that of the House Un-American Activities Committee, places the courts in an untenable position. . . . [p. 205] It is impossible in such a situation to ascertain whether any legislative purpose justifies the disclosures sought. . . . The reason no court can make this critical judgment is that the House of Representatives itself has never made it. . . . Plainly these committees are restricted to the missions delegated to them, *i.e.*, to acquire certain data to be used by the House or the Senate in coping with a problem that falls within its legislative sphere. No witness can be compelled to make disclosures on matters outside that area." [p. 206]

In summary: (1) The "instructions to an investigating committee [must] spell out that group's jurisdiction and purpose with sufficient particularity." (2) "It would be difficult to imagine a less explicit authorizing resolution. . . . No one could reasonably deduce from the charter the kind of investigation that the Committee was directed to make." (3) "No witness can be compelled to make disclosures on matters outside that area." Since Congress did not define that area, there can be no proof that the Committee's questions were within it. It follows that the defendant must be acquitted.

Even if, contrary to my clear understanding of *Watkins*, Congress did "with sufficient particularity" authorize the Committee to investigate something, it by no means follows that Congress authorized the Committee to investigate Communists in the field of education. Four Justices of the Supreme Court recently said: "It is particularly important that the exercise of the power of compulsory process be carefully circumscribed when the investigative process tends to impinge upon such highly sensitive areas as freedom of speech or press, freedom of political association, and freedom of communication of ideas, particularly in the academic community. . . . [T]he areas of academic freedom and political expression" are "areas in which government should be extremely reticent to tread." Two other Justices said in the same case: "These pages need not be burdened with proof, based on the testimony of a cloud of impressive witnesses, of the dependence of a free society on free universities. This means the exclusion of governmental intervention in the intellectual life of a university." *Sweezy* v. *New Hampshire*, 354 U.S. 234, 245, 250, 262. The Court there held that Sweezy, a university teacher, could not constitutionally be required to answer certain questions about his political activities and connections. Barenblatt was a university teacher. He was convicted because he would not answer certain questions about his political activities and connections. Though the two cases are not identical and *Sweezy* does not prove that Barenblatt's conviction violates his constitutional rights, it does show that this conviction raises serious constitutional questions. Delegation of power to a congressional committee must be construed narrowly when a narrow construction avoids serious constitutional questions. *United States* v. *Rumely,* 345 U.S. 41. The words of the Committee's charter, "investigations of . . . un-American propaganda activities," need not and therefore should not be interpreted to authorize the Committee to select for investigation political activities and connections of university teachers. We must suppose that if Congress had intended to authorize such an investigation it would have done so explicitly.

We need not consider whether the Committee's questions to Barenblatt were pertinent to an investigation of Communists in the field of education. The force of the Court's decision in *Watkins* that the Committee had no definite assignment, and therefore no authority to compel testimony, is not destroyed by the Court's decision that the questions Watkins refused to answer were not clearly pertinent to the investigation in which the Committee was then engaged. "[W]here there are two grounds, upon either of which an appellate court may rest its decision, and it adopts both, 'the ruling on neither is *obiter,* but each is the judgment of the court and of equal validity with the other.'" *United States* v. *Title Ins. & Tr. Co.,* 265 U.S. 472, 486. And even if the Supreme Court's demonstration that the Committee on Un-American Activities had no authority to compel testimony were *obiter,* this court should defer to it.

Although, on examination, the answer to a question is plain, higher courts commonly require lower courts to make the examination and decide the question in the first instance. The Supreme Court followed the usual practice in this case.

III

Loyalty and the Safety
of the Nation

On March 21, 1947, President Truman issued Executive Order 9835 establishing a federal employee loyalty program. The order was intended primarily to meet the danger of espionage or other improper activity within the government service in behalf of Russia by persons who were either Communists or too sympathetic to communism and to Russia. That such a danger existed had been made clear by documents taken from the Russian Embassy in Canada by Igor Gouzenko, a Russian code clerk who sought sanctuary with the Canadian government, and by the report of the Royal Commission that investigated his charges, as well as by the revelations of ex-Communists who had told a story of espionage within our Government to the FBI.

The order provided that every officer and employee of the Government must be investigated to determine his loyalty to the Government of the United States. It directed that a board should be established in each agency to review investigative reports turned in by the FBI. In appropriate cases these boards were to issue formal charges to the employee. He was permitted to answer them, to have a hearing if he desired it, and to appeal from an unfavorable decision, first to the head of the agency and then to a central Loyalty Review Board composed of distinguished citizens from outside the Government. This Review Board was also to exercise over-all supervision over the operations of the program. The standard of proof to be met to reach a decision unfavorable to the employee was that "on all the evidence reasonable grounds exist for belief that [the person involved] is disloyal to the Government of the United States." In 1951 the President amended the standard of proof to provide that an employee should be dismissed if it was found that "on all the evidence there is a reasonable doubt as to the loyalty of [the person involved] to the Government of the United States."

The order permitted concealment, in the interest of national security, of information and of the identity of informers.

Six criteria for judging disloyalty were listed. The sixth, which proved to be the most important, was "membership in, affiliation with, or sympathetic association with any foreign or domestic organization, association, movement, group or combination of persons, designated by the Attorney General as Totalitarian, Fascist, Communist or Subversive, etc." The order further provided that the Loyalty Review Board was to be given the names of all organizations "which the Attorney-General, *after appropriate investigation* and determination, designates as Totalitarian, Fascist, Communist, Subversive. . . ."

The screening of employees suspected of subversive activities was not new when the President's order was issued. Since 1939 the Hatch Act had forbidden the employment of anyone who belonged to an organization which advocated the overthrow of our constitutional form of government, and riders to the appropriation acts made it a crime for any such person to accept payment from the federal Treasury. During the war years the Civil Service Commission, with the approval of the President, had refused to appoint anyone if it entertained "a reasonable doubt as to his loyalty to the Government of the United States," and it interpreted the right to dismiss employees in the interest of the efficiency of the service to cover situations where it suspected employees to be either Communists or Nazis.

In 1942 the military agencies were authorized by Public Law 808 of the 77th Congress to dismiss summarily anyone "whose immediate removal is . . . warranted by the demands of national security." Later the State Department was given similar powers. The Atomic Energy Commission and the Central Intelligence Agency had from their inception their own screening programs. Special investigation of employees was provided for when various agencies were set up to operate in the international and foreign fields. In 1950 Public Law 808 was superseded by Public Law 733 of the 81st Congress. It gave eleven named agencies, including the military departments and the Department of State, the right to suspend employees summarily in the interests of national security. The law provided certain procedural safeguards for the employee, but gave no right of appeal from the head of the agency in the event of dismissal. It permitted the President to extend its provisions to other agencies "in the best interests of national security" and required him to report any such extension to the Committee on the Armed Services of the Congress.

The President's loyalty order and its amendment provoked bitter criticism. It was charged on the one hand that it violated constitutional guarantees of free speech and due process, on the other that it dealt far too leniently with suspected subversives in the government service. "Communists in Government" became a campaign issue in the 1952 election, and President Eisenhower, in his first inaugural address, promised a better program.

On April 23, 1953, President Eisenhower issued Executive Order 10450 in which he revoked E.O. 9835 and extended Public Law 733 to cover every agency and every position in the Government. The new order defined national security broadly, extending it to include "the economic and productive strength of the United States." To the six criteria listed in the old loyalty order it added others, broadly inclusive, some of which had been used hitherto only in security proceedings involving highly "sensitive" positions. It made certain procedural changes, the most important of which was the abolition of the central Loyalty Review Board and the right of appeal beyond the head of the agency. A more stringent standard of proof was established, namely, that the head of the agency must find that the employee's retention is "clearly consistent with the interests of national security."

On June 11, 1956, in the case of *Cole* v. *Young* (infra, p. 138) the Supreme Court ruled that Public Law 733 did not apply to nonsensitive positions in the Government. This meant that about 280 out of 342 security risk dismissals under E.O. 10450 were invalid and that the subjects thereof could ask to be restored to duty.

Official screening of individuals for loyalty and security has not been limited to government employees. Four additional programs are now in operation in the Federal Government. Two, the industrial security program and the military personnel program, are administered by the Department of Defense. The former affects all persons who work in industry, in laboratories, or in universities on government contracts that involve access to classified material; the latter applies to the selection, assignment, and discharge of military personnel in the active service and the reserves and to persons serving with the Armed Forces. On June 29, 1959, in the case of *Greene* v. *McElroy* the Supreme Court ruled that the Department had not been given authority either by Congress or the President to establish the industrial security program. A passport program has been established in the State Department. A port security program affecting all seamen and many dock workers is administered by the Coast Guard.

The sixth criterion of the Loyalty Order, which was broadened in scope in Personnel Security Order, E.O. 10450, has resulted in what is popularly called the Attorney General's list of subversive organizations. The first list issued was sent to the Loyalty Review Board in November, 1947, and made public on March 20, 1948. It contained the names of 82 organizations, 47 of which had previously been used in screening employees under the requirements of the Hatch Act and the Civil Service Commission's rule as to loyalty. Although a few organizations have been dropped from the list, it now includes more than 270 names.

In the first listing the organizations were not classified according to their character. In later editions, organizations were placed in the categories listed in the Loyalty Order. When this was done, only eight were labeled "subversive," although a large number were classified as Communist. When the list was reissued and enlarged under E.O. 10450, the Attorney General again dropped the classification system, and all are referred to simply as organizations designated under Executive Order 10450.

In preparing the lists the Attorney General interpreted "appropriate investigation" to mean careful study, within the Department, of its available investigative reports. For six years none of the organizations was given a hearing or even notified of the Attorney General's proposed action against them. Under the rules issued by the Loyalty Review Board, employees accused of some connection with these organizations were not permitted to question the Attorney General's findings as to their subversive character. In May, 1953, the Attorney General for the first time issued regulations providing for notice to be given to organizations that he intended to designate as subversive and for proceedings, including a hearing if desired, to contest the designation.

The Government has consistently taken the position that the list is nothing more than a piece of advice from the Attorney General to the heads of departments and the Loyalty Review Board. The current list as published in the Federal Register contains the note that it is prepared only for the information of federal civilian officers and employees and for the convenience of persons completing applications for federal employment. In fact, it has had far-reaching consequences, affecting many persons entirely outside the Government. The list has been used by the Federal Government to determine the eligibility of would-be immigrants, foreign visitors, passport applicants, tenants of publicly financed housing projects, voluntary organizations seeking tax exemption, and applicants for fellowship grants and by the Army in connection with assignments to duty and as a basis for a less than honorable discharge. It has been adopted by reference in state laws and municipal ordinances relating to the eligibility of state and municipal employees, including teachers, students in publicly supported institutions of learning, authors of textbooks to be used in public schools, public speakers, insurance agents, candidates for admission to the bar, would-be lobbyists, jurors, participants in boxing matches, and even persons entering or passing through a state.

It is acknowledged that in all these programs both the criteria and the procedures do in fact contravene or diminish individual rights guaranteed by the Constitution. When this result is weighed against the needs of national security in a period of serious international tension, it is said that the latter must prevail. This position has been or is being challenged in about 65 reported cases, six directly attacking the Attorney General's list, twenty the screening of government personnel, eleven the industrial security program, eleven the military personnel program, eleven the passport program, three the port security program, several the requirement of loyalty oaths from the tenants of government housing projects. Only seventeen of these cases have reached the Supreme Court. The major responsibility for the development of the law in this field has rested upon the Court of Appeals for the District of Columbia.

Loyal Servants of the Government

JOINT ANTI-FASCIST REFUGEE COMMITTEE

v.

TOM C. CLARK, ATTORNEY GENERAL OF THE
UNITED STATES

Decided August 11, 1949

Before EDGERTON, CLARK, and PROCTOR,
Circuit Judges

When the Attorney General published his list of subversive organizations, three of those on the list, the Joint Anti-Fascist Refugee Committee, the International Workers Order, and the National Council of American-Soviet Friendship, promptly brought suit, contending that the list violated constitutional guarantees of free speech and due process of law. They asked that the Attorney General be ordered to strike their names from the list and enjoined from further designating them as subversive.

The Joint Anti-Fascist Refugee Committee was an unincorporated organization, allegedly charitable in character and engaged in relief work under a license from the President's War Relief Control Board. The purpose of the National Council of American-Soviet Friendship was said to be the development of friendly relations between the United States and Russia by means of cultural exchange between the two nations. The International Workers Order was a fraternal benefit society incorporated under the insurance laws of New York State and in good standing there and in other states. One of the members of the International Workers Order, who had been dismissed from the government service, allegedly because of his membership, joined with this organization in bringing suit.

All three cases suffered the same fate in the District Court in the District of Columbia. In each one the Government moved for summary judgment on the ground that the organization had no cause of action, and the motion was granted. By this legal move, for the purpose of argument, all the allegations as to the benevolent and harmless purposes of each of these organizations were admitted.

All three organizations appealed. The first case to reach the Court of Appeals for the District of Columbia was that of the Joint Anti-Fascist Refugee Committee. Judge Proctor wrote the majority opinion in the case sustaining the action of the District Court, and Judge Edgerton dissented. The Court of Appeals agreed with the District Court that the organization had no cause of action, and it adopted the Government's position that the Attorney General, in listing organizations, did nothing more than give information and advice to the Loyalty Review Board and the heads of the agencies. It found that any injury suffered by the Committee was indirect and incidental since "the Executive Order imposes no obligation or restraint upon the Committee. It commands nothing of the Committee. It denies the Committee no authority, privilege, immunity or license. It subjects the Committee to no liability, civil or criminal." The constitutional objections were met by the statement:

> Contrary to the contentions of the Committee, nothing in the Hatch Act or the loyalty program deprives the Committee or its members of any property rights. Freedom of speech and assembly is denied no one. Freedom of thought and belief is not impaired. Anyone is free to join the Committee and give it his support and encouragement. Everyone has a constitutional right to do these things, but no one has a constitutional right to be a Government employee.

On appeal to the Supreme Court the cases of the three organizations were joined. On April 30, 1951, the Court, in a 5 to 3 decision, reversed the Court of Appeals and found that the organizations did have a cause of action, although the Justices disagreed as to its nature. Four of the Justices agreed with Judge Edgerton, that listing without notice or hearing violated the Due Process Clause of the Constitution. The fifth, Justice Burton, avoided the constitutional question by adopting Judge Edgerton's interpretation of the pleadings, concluding with him that, as a matter of law, by admitting the alleged innocent purposes of the organizations, the Attorney General convicted himself of arbitrary action that was not authorized by the Order.

The three cases were sent back to the District Court, and nine years of litigation followed, as they were tossed back and forth between the District Court and the Court of Appeals. Judgment was sometimes for the organizations, sometimes for the Government. During the nine years the President's Loyalty Order, E.O. 9835, was superseded by the President's Personnel Security Order, E.O. 10450. On May 6, 1953, while the case was still in the courts, the Attorney General issued regulations that gave a listed organization an opportunity to protest. The organizations refused to avail themselves of the administrative remedy thus offered. Finally, on February 28, 1957, in the case of *National Council of American-Soviet Friendship et al. v. Brownell*, 243 F. 2d 22, the Court of Appeals sustained an order of the District Court granting the Government's request for summary judgment against the organization.

Later another organization, the Independent Socialist League, sought a hearing under the regulations and after a ten-year fight won a favorable decision from the Attorney General. Its predecessor, the Workers Party, and its youth group, the Socialist League, were struck from the list at the same time. A Justice Department official explained that this did not mean that membership in these groups could not be considered in deciding security cases. The Association of Lithuanian Workers and a companion organization challenged the constitutionality of the regulations, but before their cases could be heard by the Supreme Court, the Attorney General removed them from the list.

EDGERTON, *J., dissenting:* The facts have not been tried and we know nothing about them. Appellant may be charitable as it says or subversive as appellees' ruling says. By moving to dismiss appellant's complaint on the ground it did not state a justiciable controversy or a claim on which relief could be granted, appellees elected to try only the sufficiency and not the truth of appellant's statements of fact. Since the District Court granted the motion to dismiss, appellant's statements must be assumed to be true for purposes of this appeal. No other facts are before us.

According to appellant's complaint: "Plaintiff, an unincorporated association located in the City and State of New York, is a charitable organization engaged in relief work. . . . The aims and purposes of the plaintiff organization are to raise, administer and distribute funds for the relief and rehabilitation of Spanish Republicans in exile and other anti-fascist refugees who fought in the war against Franco. Before the end of the war in Europe, this relief consisted of: (1) the release and assistance of those of the aforesaid refugees who were in concentration camps in Vichy France, North Africa and other countries; (2) transportation and asylum for those of the aforesaid refugees in flight; (3) direct relief and aid, to those of the aforesaid refugees requiring help, through the Red Cross and other international agencies. At the present time, the Joint Anti-Fascist Refugee Committee relief work is principally devoted to aiding those Spanish Republican refugees, and other anti-fascist refugees who fought against Franco, located in France and Mexico. Pursuant to its aims and purposes, the plaintiff organization has, from its inception in 1942 through the end of 1947, disbursed a total of $1,011,448.00 in cash and $217,903.00 in kind for the relief of anti-fascist refugees and their families. The relief included money, food, shelter, educational facilities, medical treatment and supplies, and clothing to recipients in France, North Africa, the Dominican Republic, Portugal, Switzerland, Cuba, Venezuela, Mexico, the Netherlands, Spain, and the United States.

"By means of voluntary and paid assistance, the plaintiff organization has raised funds from contributors at social affairs, rallies, meetings, dinners, theatre parties, etc. In order to carry on the aforesaid work, plaintiff has built up and is dependent upon the continued good will of the people of the United States and upon the continued maintenance of its reputation of engaging in relief work for the benefit of anti-fascist refugees."

According to the complaint: the appellees, purporting to act under an Executive Order, have issued for the guidance of government officials in employing and discharging employees a ruling that the appellant is "subversive." They issued this ruling without giving appellant any notice or hearing. They gave it wide publicity. It has caused appellant to lose reputation, members, supporters, contributions from government employees and others, valuable privileges, speakers, and meeting places. It has caused appellant's members to be subjected to ridicule, obloquy and economic loss.

However indefinite the word "subversive" may be, it is more or less synonymous with "disloyal." It is highly defamatory. No common meaning of the term fits the appellant if the appellant's "aims and purposes" are what it says they are. In other words, if the complaint is true the appellant is not subversive. Whatever the actual facts may ultimately prove to be, it must be assumed for purposes of this appeal that appellees' ruling is not only damaging but contrary to fact.[1]

I. *The Executive Order.* Executive Order No. 9835, on which appellees rely, provides in Part V that: "1. The standard for the

[1] It is immaterial that, as the opinion of the court points out, the complaint "contains no express denial that the Committee falls within the designation." If the complaint did not, as it does, contain a denial by necessary implication, that also would be immaterial. No complaint based on defamatory words need allege that the words are false; it is for the defendant to allege and prove, if he can, that they are true. And regardless of the nature of the suit, things not asserted or admitted in the complaint cannot be treated as true on the present appeal even if they are not denied in the complaint.

If appellees had described appellant as "totalitarian, fascist, communist, or subversive . . . ," and not specifically as "subversive," the difference would be immaterial, since either description is defamatory and, on this record, contrary to fact.

refusal of employment or the removal from employment in an executive department or agency on grounds relating to loyalty shall be that, on all the evidence, reasonable grounds exist for belief that the person involved is disloyal to the Government of the United States.

"2. Activities and associations of an applicant or employee which may be considered in connection with the determination or disloyalty may include one or more of the following: . . . f. Membership in, affiliation with or sympathetic association with any foreign or domestic organization, association, movement, group or combination of persons, designated by the Attorney General as totalitarian, fascist, communist, or subversive, or as having adopted a policy of advocating or approving the commission of acts of force or violence to deny other persons their rights under the Constitution of the United States, or as seeking to alter the form of government of the United States by unconstitutional means." 12 Fed. Reg. 1935, 1938.

An organization of the aims and purposes asserted in the complaint is not "subversive" within the meaning of that term in the Executive Order. Whatever it means in other connections, in this connection the term describes organizations "sympathetic association" with which may be evidence "that the person involved is disloyal to the Government of the United States." Advocacy of revolution is disloyal to the government. Greater or equal loyalty to a foreign government is disloyal to the government of the United States. Nothing less is. Helping former Spanish Republicans is not evidence of disloyalty to the government of the United States. A charitable organization such as the appellant must now be assumed to be is therefore not subversive in the sense in which the word is used in the Executive Order. Neither is it "totalitarian, fascist, communist, . . ." or otherwise within the Order. On the present record, the Order does not justify appellees' ruling.

The Order fails for another reason to justify the ruling. The Order provides (Part III, § 3) that "The Loyalty Review Board shall currently be furnished by the Department of Justice the name of each foreign or domestic organization, association, movement, group or combination of persons which the Attorney General, *after appropriate investigation* and determination designates as totalitarian, fascist, communist or subversive . . ." (Emphasis added.) An investigation that may result in the making and publication of a defamatory ruling which limits employment throughout the government service, limits the freedom of government employees, and harms not only the appellant but many persons outside as well as within the service, is not appropriate unless it conforms to basic standards of fairness. These include notice and a hearing. If the complaint is true, appellant was given none.

Appellees' ruling is not only outside the Executive Order but outside the authority on which the order is said to rest. Section 9A of the Hatch Act, 53 Stat. 1148, 18 U.S.C. 61 i, forbids employment of members of an organization that "advocates the overthrow of our constitutional form of government in the United States." If the facts alleged in the complaint are true the appellant is not such an organization. The Civil Service Act, R.S. § 1753, 5 U.S.C. 631, authorizes the President to "prescribe such regulations for the admission of persons into the civil service of the United States as may best promote the efficiency thereof . . ." On the present record, appellees' ruling against appellant has no more tendency to promote the efficiency of the civil service than a similar ruling against the Republican party or the Methodist Church would have.

Moreover, the ruling is invalid on constitutional grounds.

II. *Due process of law.* Arbitrary official action that inflicts damage takes liberty or property without due process of law. On this record, appellees' ruling is arbitrary because it is contrary to fact, because it is not authorized by law or Executive Order, because it has no tendency to benefit the public service, and because it was made without notice and hearing. . . .

What is practically necessary may be reasonably fair, and what is reasonably fair may be due process. It is not practical to require a public official to hold a hearing before he makes a casual damaging statement. But it is neither fair nor necessary to enact and publish a defamatory permanent regulation restricting eligibility for public employment, restricting the freedom of government employees, and inflicting damage on many persons, without giving the accused group an opportunity to be heard in its defense. The same circumstances that make the Attorney General's investigation less than appropriate make it less than due process of law.

III. *Freedom of speech and assembly.* Read literally, the First Amendment of the Constitution forbids only *Congress* to abridge these freedoms. But as the due process clause of the Fourteenth Amendment extends the prohibition to all state action, the due process clause of the Fifth must extend it to all federal action.

According to the complaint, appellant uses meetings and speakers in raising funds. Appellees' ruling, in its context, is a public warning that sympathetic association with appellant may cause government employees to be dismissed. It therefore puts government employees, present and prospective, under economic and social pressure not to support any of appellant's activities, verbally or otherwise, and in particular to stay away from appellant's meetings. In other words the ruling restricts the freedom of speech and assembly of government employees. According to the complaint, the ruling has deprived appellant of speakers and meeting places as well as supporters and funds. In other words it has restricted appellant's freedom of speech and assembly. To restrict appellant is to restrict the members who compose it.

The Supreme Court has repeatedly held that restrictions on

freedom of expression are not valid in the absence of a clear and present danger. There is no evidence of such a danger in this case. In the *Mitchell* case the Court held that "For regulation of employees it is not necessary that the act regulated be anything more than an act reasonably deemed by Congress to interfere with the efficiency of the public service." *United Public Workers* v. *Mitchell*, 330 U.S. 75, 101. But if appellant's purposes are truly stated in the complaint, sympathetic association with appellant cannot reasonably be deemed to interfere with the efficiency of the public service. It follows that if, as we must now assume, the complaint is true, the restraint imposed upon government employees, and not merely that imposed upon appellant and its members, is unconstitutional.

Executive power to control public employment stands on no higher constitutional ground than legislative power to tax. The taxing power does not extend to sales of propaganda not made for profit; license taxes, though imposed for the legitimate purpose of raising revenue, are unconstitutional in their application to such sales. Such taxes, even if they are too small to be a "substantial clog" on the circulation of propaganda, are "on their face . . . a restriction of the free exercise of those freedoms which are protected by the First Amendment." *Murdock* v. *Commonwealth of Pennsylvania*, 319 U.S. 105, 114. The threat to reputation and livelihood that appellees' ruling imposes is on its face a greater restriction of the free exercise of those freedoms than the small license taxes the Supreme Court held void. It is a substantial clog. It is therefore more clearly unconstitutional than the taxes.

IV. *Standing to sue.* Appellant, an unincorporated association, has standing to sue for the claimed injury to its reputation.

Appellant has standing to sue for the claimed impairment of its freedom of speech and assembly.

Appellant has standing to sue for its claimed loss of contributions. Even a charity, which appellant claims to be, cannot operate without funds. In *Pierce* v. *Society of Sisters* private schools, some of them charitable, got relief because a state law requiring children to attend public schools caused the plaintiffs to lose tuition fees. "Their interest is clear and immediate, within the rule approved in *Truax* v. *Raich* . . . and many other cases where injunctions have issued to protect business enterprises against interference with the freedom of patrons or customers." *Pierce* v. *Society of Sisters*, 268 U.S. 510, 536. In *Truax* v. *Raich*, 239 U.S. 33, enforcement of a state law restricting the right of employers to hire aliens but not the right of aliens to work for hire was enjoined at the suit of an alien. In *Buchanan* v. *Warley*, 245 U.S. 60, an ordinance forbidding Negroes to move into white neighborhoods was set aside at the suit of a white man who wished to complete a sale to a Negro. In each case an unconstitutional interference with persons other than the plaintiff was enjoined because it put pressure on them to sever, or not to create, relations of value to him. Similarly the unconstitutional pressure of appellees' ruling upon present and prospective government servants has injured appellant by depriving it of contributions. Its relations with its contributors were terminable at will, but so were the relations involved in the *Pierce* and *Truax* cases. . . .

Threatened publication by government officers of damaging information about a plaintiff, even when its truth is conceded, gives him standing to test the propriety of the publication. There would seem to be no less standing where, as here, truth is not conceded and continuance rather than the first occurrence of the publication is threatened.

V. *Liability to suit.* "Under our constitutional system, certain rights are protected against governmental action and, if such rights are infringed by the actions of officers of the Government, . . . courts have the power to grant relief against those actions." *Larson* v. *Domestic and Foreign Commerce Corporation*, 337 U.S. 682. Equitable jurisdiction extends to cabinet officers. The theory that an officer who is or claims to be executing an order of the President cannot be restrained would end due process of law and subject all life, liberty, and property to the will, or alleged will, of one man.

Cabinet officers are not liable in damages for statements made in connection with official duties, for they should be under no apprehension that personal harm might result from saying what they think they should say. But their liability in equity causes no such apprehension. No claim for injunctive or declaratory relief, or that a regulation was invalid, was involved in the *Spalding* and *Glass* cases on which appellees rely. No claim for damages is involved in this case.

The rule of *Standard Scale Co.* v. *Farrell*, 249 U.S. 571, that mere administrative advice cannot be reviewed by a court, is equally irrelevant here. Standard manufactured scales that did not agree with "specifications" published by a state Superintendent of Weights and Measures. Standard's bill to set aside the specifications was dismissed. No law or order required any inspector, purchasing officer, or other person to treat the specifications as correct; they were (p. 574) "at most, advisory." But Executive Order No. 9835 requires all loyalty boards to treat as correct appellees' ruling that appellant is subversive. On March 9, 1948, the appellee Chairman of the Loyalty Review Board called this fact to the attention of all executive departments and agencies. . . .

Appellees' ruling is said to be a mere matter of internal management. Even in such matters the Constitution governs. But there was nothing internal about the publication of the ruling. It was chiefly this publication that injured the appellant and its members and restricted the freedom of government employees. The right to hire and fire is not a right to broadcast statements that appellant, and so the members who compose it, are criminals or that they are subversive.

If the assertions of fact in the complaint are true the appellees' ruling is contrary to fact, unauthorized, and unconstitutional, and the appellant is entitled to relief against the appellees. The judgment dismissing the complaint should therefore be reversed.

Dorothy Bailey

v.

Seth W. Richardson

Decided March 22, 1950

Before Edgerton, Prettyman, and Proctor, *Circuit Judges*

Dorothy Bailey was the first employee to be dismissed from the government service on grounds of disloyalty after review of her case by a panel of the Loyalty Review Board. The case received a great deal of publicity, and the action of the Review Board was announced to the press and reported on the front page in Washington newspapers. The proceedings in the case were so contrary to accepted standards of fair play that the *Bailey* case became the subject of heated controversy.

Miss Bailey had been in the government service almost continuously since November, 1933, had reached a position of responsibility in the United States Employment Service, and had gained a national reputation as an expert in her field. She had been separated from the Government in the course of a reduction in staff but had been recalled a few months later. On March 28, 1948, she received an interrogatory from the Civil Service Commission that contained three unfavorable allegations as to her past activities. It was alleged (1) that she had been a member of the Communist Party and the Communist Political Association, had attended meetings of the Party, and had associated with Communists on numerous occasions, (2) that she had belonged to the American League for Peace and Democracy, and (3) that she had been a member of the Washington Committee for Democratic Action. The last two organizations had been listed by the Attorney General as "subversive" on the first list issued by him under E.O. 9835 and as "Communist" on the second. Miss Bailey replied to the interrogatory, flatly denying any Communist activity, admitting a brief membership in the American League for Peace and Democracy, and asserting her loyalty to the United States. She was given no further particulars as to the time and place of her alleged attendance at Communist meetings or the identity of the alleged Communist associates, until she came before the Board in a hearing. She then presented witnesses and affidavits in her own behalf from a number of highly respected members of the community. No one appeared to testify against her, but in the course of the hearing she was informed of a number of other unfavorable statements in the investigative file and was questioned as to her association with various named persons whom she refused to identify as Communists. Her request for further particulars as to her alleged Communist activities and as to the identity of her accusers continued to be denied. She had been active in a government employees' union, the leaders of which were said to be Communist. When her lawyer asked if this was the basis of the charges against her, he was told that union activities as such would not be held against her. At the hearings her activities within the union proved to be important.

The hearing board found against her, she appealed, and at her hearing before the Review Board it developed that the board members themselves did not know the particulars for which she had asked, had no information as to the identity of her accusers, did not think that their testimony had been given under oath, and were relying simply upon the FBI's assurance that their testimony was reliable. The Review Board sustained the finding of the hearing board and directed that Miss Bailey be removed from the government service. The Civil Service Commission graded her "ineligible," ordered her dismissal on November 1, 1948, and barred her from the Civil Service for a period of three years.

Miss Bailey took her case to court and asked that her reinstatement be ordered. She challenged the constitutionality of the Order itself and of her dismissal and also claimed that the procedures followed in her case were not in conformity with the provisions of the Order which required that an adverse finding must be based "on all the evidence." She said that no adverse "evidence" in the legal sense had been presented. The District Court summarily dismissed her complaint on the ground that the President's authority over government employees, except as checked by Congress, is absolute and that "the Court has no function to perform in connection with the hiring and firing of employees."

Miss Bailey appealed, and in a 2 to 1 decision, Judge Edgerton dissenting, the Court of Appeals sustained the District Court except in one particular. As in the *Barsky* case, Judges Prettyman and Edgerton each wrote a comprehensive opinion setting forth fully and carefully the opposing views on the issues presented in the case. Judge Prettyman, after reciting the facts of the case, introduced his opinion by saying: "The case presented for Miss Bailey is undoubtedly appealing. She was denied reinstatement in her former employment because Government officials found reasonable grounds to believe her disloyal. She was not given a trial in any sense of the word, and she does not know who informed upon her. Thus viewed, her situation appeals powerfully to our sense of the fair and the just."

The Court of Appeals found that the President's power to hire or fire executive personnel is not limited by the Due Process Clause of the Fifth Amendment and that, even if it were, Miss Bailey had received such due process as was required; that when the President used the word "evidence" in his Order he meant "information"; and that there was no disparity between the provisions of the Order and the practice of the Board. It accepted the Government's premise that government employment is a privilege, not a right, and that any injury suffered by the employee is incidental. The court also rejected Miss Bailey's contention that her dismissal was punishment in the constitutional sense entitling her to the procedural protections of the Sixth Amendment. It concluded that the order of the Loyalty Board was valid, but it found that the provisions barring her from Civil Service for three years went beyond the terms of the Order and did amount to unconstitutional punishment.

The Supreme Court agreed to review the case. Justice Clark, who had been Attorney General when the Loyalty Order was issued, did not participate. The Justices divided 4 to 4 on the issues and handed down a *per curiam* decision that left the decision of the Court of Appeals standing, but the constitutional issues unresolved.

EDGERTON, *Circuit Judge, dissenting:* Without trial by jury, without evidence, and without even being allowed to confront her accusers or to know their identity, a citizen of the United States has been found disloyal to the government of the United States.[1]

For her supposed disloyal thoughts she has been punished by dismissal from a wholly nonsensitive position in which her efficiency rating was high. The case received nation-wide publicity. Ostracism inevitably followed. A finding of disloyalty is closely akin to a finding of treason. The public hardly distinguishes between the two.

No charges were served on appellant. The chairman of the Regional Board said "Nobody has presented any charges." The Board told appellant it was inquiring whether there were reasonable grounds for believing she was disloyal to the government of the United States. The Federal Bureau of Investigation had reported that informants believed to be reliable had made general statements purporting to connect her with the Communist Party. These reports were not disclosed to the appellant and have not been disclosed in court. The informants were not identified to the appellant or even to the Board. Their statements were admittedly not made under oath. The appellant denied under oath any membership in and any relationship or sympathy with the Communist Party, any activities connected with it or with communism, and any affiliation with any organization that advocated overthrow of the government of the United States. She asserted her loyalty to the government of the United States. She admitted

---

[1] The form of the finding against the appellant is that "reasonable grounds exist for belief" that she is disloyal to the government of the United States. The only important difference between this finding and a direct adjudication of disloyalty is that the former finding is easier to make. Once made, there is no practical difference. Executive Order 9835 recognizes this. In Part I, 2a it describes the form of finding prescribed in the Order and made here as an "adjudication of disloyalty"; in Part V, 2 as a "determination of disloyalty."

attending one Communist meeting in 1932 in connection with a seminar study of the platforms of the various parties while she was a student at Bryn Mawr.

Appellant had no power to subpoena witnesses. Though it takes courage to appear as a voluntary defense witness in a loyalty case, four appeared. One was the pastor of the Methodist church of which appellant is an active member. He testified: "When this charge or information came to me I was not only surprised, I was dumfounded. . . . People in our community and in our church think of her and her family in the highest terms." Three officials of appellant's government agency, the United States Employment Service, who had known appellant professionally and socially for years, testified respectively that they were "extremely shocked" by the suggestion of her being disloyal, that it was "inconceivable" and "out of reason." Persons prominent in business, government and education who knew appellant but could not be present submitted affidavits.

No witness offered evidence, even hearsay evidence, against appellant. No affidavits were introduced against her. The record consists entirely of evidence in her favor. Yet the Board purported to find "on all the evidence" that there were reasonable grounds for believing she was disloyal to the government of the United States. Appellees admit the Board made this finding "after considering all the evidence, including the confidential reports of the Federal Bureau of Investigation." The Board directed the Federal Security Agency to suspend appellant pending her appeal to the Loyalty Review Board, and told her she was barred from civil service examinations for three years.

Appellant appeared and testified before a panel of the Loyalty Review Board. She submitted her own affidavit and the affidavits of some 70 persons who knew her, including bankers, corporate officials, federal and state officials, union members, and others. Again no one testified against her. She proved she had publicly and to the knowledge of a number of the affiants taken positions inconsistent with Communist sympathies. She showed not only by her own testimony but by that of other persons that she favored the Marshall Plan, which the Communist Party notoriously opposed, and that in 1940, during the Nazi-Soviet Pact, she favored Lend-Lease and was very critical of the Soviet position. In her union she urged its officers to execute non-communist affidavits, opposed a foreign policy resolution widely publicized as pro-Russian, and favored what was then the official CIO resolution on foreign policy.

Against all this, there were only the unsworn reports in the secret files to the effect that unsworn statements of a general sort, purporting to connect appellant with Communism, had been made by unnamed persons. Some if not all of these statements did not purport to be based on knowledge, but only on belief. Appellant sought to learn the names of the informants or, if their names were confidential, then at least whether they had been active in appellant's union, in which there were factional quarrels. The Board did not furnish or even have this information. Chairman Richardson said: "I haven't the slightest knowledge as to who they were or how active they have been in anything." All that the Board knew or we know about the informants is that unidentified members of the Federal Bureau of Investigation, who did not appear before the Board, believed them to be reliable. To quote again from the record: "Chairman Richardson: I can only say to you that five or six of the reports come from informants certified to us by the Federal Bureau of Investigation as experienced and entirely reliable." "Mr. Seasongood: Here is a statement that it was ascertained you were a member of the Communist Party in the District of Columbia as early as 1935, and that in the early days of her Party membership she attended Communist Party meetings. . . . Here is another that says you were a member of the Communist Party, and he bases his statement on his knowledge of your association with known Communists for the past seven or eight years. That is part of the evidence that was submitted to us." "Mr. Porter: Is it under oath? Chairman Richardson: I don't think so. Mr. Seasongood: It is a person of known responsibility who had proffered information concerning Communist activity in the District of Columbia. . . . Here is another one: 'considers appointee a member of the Communist Party, and if not an actual member, one who is entirely controlled by the wishes of the Communist Leaders in the District of Columbia.' "

On such material, the Review Board sustained the action of the Regional Board and directed the Federal Security Agency to dismiss the appellant. However respectable her anonymous accusers may have been, if her dismissal is sustained the livelihood and reputation of any civil servant today and perhaps of any American tomorrow are at the mercy not only of an innocently mistaken informer but also of a malicious or demented one unless his defect is apparent to the agent who interviews him.

Appellant's dismissal violates both the Constitution and the Executive Order.

I. *Executive Order 9835 requires evidence and an opportunity for cross-examination.* The Executive Order provides that "The standard for the refusal of employment or the removal from employment in an executive department or agency on grounds relating to loyalty shall be that, on all the evidence, reasonable grounds exist for belief that the person involved is disloyal to the Government of the United States." Despite the plain words "all the evidence," the court rules that the Order requires no evidence and authorizes findings based on unsworn confidential reports of unsworn statements of anonymous informants as to their beliefs concerning an employee's affiliations. I think the Order does no such thing.

The court derives its paradoxical conclusion from premises that do not support it. The court points out that the Order and a supplementary order require the names of confidential informants, and reports of the proceedings, to be kept confidential. But no order requires the Board to consider only confidential information. To say that confidential informants shall not be disclosed is not to say that willing government witnesses shall not be heard or that findings may be made without evidence. Neither is the prohibition against publication of reports a prohibition against hearing witnesses. On the contrary, Executive Order 9835 expressly authorizes testimony by witnesses for the accused employee. If anything so unprecedented as a prohibition of testimony by witnesses for the government had been intended it would have been plainly expressed. Unsworn anonymous statements may be used and useful as leads to evidence but not as substitutes for evidence.

The requirement of the Order that findings be based on evidence is not merely uncontradicted by the context. It is confirmed by the context. The preamble of the Order says that both the United States and the accused employee must be afforded "maximum protection." Such protection plainly includes an opportunity to introduce witnesses and to cross-examine opposing witnesses. Even the minimum standards of fairness that are known as due process of law include as much. Hardly any protection at all is possible against vague assertions of unseen and unknown persons. The accused employee can only deny such assertions and prove, as the appellant did, that they are inconsistent with her reputation and with some of her acts. She can prove no specific contradictions, no mistaken identities, and no alibis, for she cannot discover just when and where she is supposed to have done or said anything. However prejudiced, mistaken, untruthful, delinquent, or defective her accusers might prove to be if they could be cross-examined, an unidentified agent's recorded belief in the reliability of their reports and inferences must go unchallenged. "The many possible deficiencies, suppressions, sources of error and untrustworthiness, which lie underneath the bare untested assertion of a witness, may be best brought to light and exposed by the test of

Cross-examination. . . . It is beyond any doubt the greatest legal engine ever invented for the discovery of truth." Wigmore, *Evidence* (3rd edition, 1940), 1362, 1367.

Moreover the Order provides that "an officer or employee who is charged with being disloyal shall have a right to an administrative hearing . . ." Particularly in the light of the guarantee of maximum protection, this must mean a full administrative hearing. Even a normal administrative hearing, to say nothing of one that affords maximum protection, includes the right of confrontation and cross-examination and the requirement that findings be based on evidence. Evidence has been required in administrative hearings even where, as here, the substantive matter at stake may be considered a privilege rather than a right. Aliens are entitled to a fair hearing in deportation proceedings, and this despite the fact that "there is no express requirement for any hearing or adjudication in the statute authorizing deportation." *Wong Yang Sung* v. *Clark*, 339 U.S. 33. Even in deportation proceedings against aliens charged with advocating, or with membership in organizations advocating, overthrow of the government by force, evidence is required. The Supreme Court has said in such cases: "If the hearing was fair, if there was evidence to support the finding of the Secretary, and if no error of law was committed, the ruling of the Department must stand and cannot be corrected in judicial proceedings. If, on the other hand, one of the elements mentioned is lacking, the proceeding is void and must be set aside." *Kessler* v. *Strecker*, 307 U.S. 22, 34. . . . It follows that even if the Executive Order did not expressly require findings based on evidence, or promise maximum protection, the administrative hearing which the Order guarantees to the employee whose job and reputation are at stake would still require evidence and an opportunity for cross-examination. As the Supreme Court has said, "manifestly there is no hearing when the party does not know what evidence is offered or considered and is not given an opportunity to test, explain, or refute." *Interstate Commerce Commission* v. *Louisville and Nashville Railroad*, 227 U.S. 88, 93.

No doubt cases arise in which investigation of an employee produces only anonymous accusations. The Executive Order elects to preserve their anonymity. No one questions the validity of that election. But its effect is that the employee must be cleared or the proceedings dropped. The Executive Order does not, and could not constitutionally, provide that he may be found disloyal without evidence.

II. *Dismissal for disloyalty is punishment and requires all the safeguards of a judicial trial.* Most dismissals, including among others dismissals for colorless or undisclosed reasons and dismissals for incompetence, are plainly not punitive. They do not require a judicial trial or even a full administrative hearing. They are within the authority of the executive. Likewise most tax laws are within the authority of the legislature. It does not follow that all legislative taxation is constitutional or that all executive dismissals are constitutional.

Punishment is infliction of harm, usually for wrong conduct but in appellant's case for wrong views. Dismissals to provide jobs for persons of certain affiliations, whatever else may be said of such dismissals, are not punitive. But dismissals for disloyal views are punitive. This is what the Supreme Court squarely held in the *Lovett* case. *United States* v. *Lovett*, 328 U.S. 303. It overruled no cases in so holding. The earlier decisions of the Supreme Court on which this court relies are irrelevant because they involved dismissals for undisclosed reasons, not for disloyal views.

The question whether the rule of the *Lovett* case extends to dismissals of "disloyal" persons from sensitive positions in which their presence might threaten substantial harm to the government does not arise in the present case and I express no opinion on it. Appellant was dismissed from a nonsensitive position. She was a staff training officer in the United States Employment Service.

Congress attempted to dismiss Lovett and two others from their government positions as of November 15, 1943, because of their supposed disloyal views. Their agencies kept them at work on their jobs for varying periods after November 15 but discontinued their salaries after that date. They sued for and recovered salaries for their post-November 15 work. The Supreme Court held that their dismissals for supposed disloyalty, "which stigmatized their reputation and seriously impaired their chance to earn a living," were equivalent to punishment for crime and therefore could not be imposed by Congress or without judicial trial. The validity of an incidental attempt of Congress to make them ineligible for possible future appointments was not the question before the Court. They did not ask for, and it does not even appear that they would have been willing to accept, either reinstatement in their old positions or appointments to new positions. The Court *said* "This permanent proscription from any opportunity to serve the government is punishment . . ." But the question before the Court was whether the attempted dismissals were valid. This was the question the Court *decided*.

This court is deciding this case as if the Supreme Court had sustained the attempt of Congress to dismiss Lovett and the others, denied their claims to salaries, and awarded them nothing but an assurance that they would be eligible for possible future appointments if they were ever offered any that they cared to accept. This court interprets the *words* of the Supreme Court regarding "permanent proscription" as contradicting and overruling the *decision* of the Supreme Court regarding dismissals. If the Court's words had been inconsistent with its decision our duty would of course have been to follow the decision, not the words. But they were not inconsistent. The dismissals that the Court held invalid were the immediate phase of the permanent proscription that the Court said was invalid.

The distinction this court draws between dismissal as punishment and ineligibility as punishment not only contradicts the *Lovett* case but has no basis in reason. Dismissal is more certainly damaging than ineligibility, for the necessary combination of vacancies, qualifications, and desire for public appointment may never occur again. A person dismissed as disloyal can obtain no normal employment, public or private. The President's Committee on Civil Rights said in 1947: "It is a severe punishment to be discharged from the government for disloyalty, as the Supreme Court pointed out in 1946 in *United States* v. *Lovett.* . . . Loss of job and inability to obtain another one is a severe punishment to impose on any man." *To Secure These Rights*, Report of the President's Commission on Civil Liberties, p. 51. It makes no present or probable future difference to the appellant and it should make no difference to a court whether the appellant is told that she is separated from the civil service for life, for three years, or only for the moment. Whatever she is told, if her dismissal is sustained she will not be re-employed while the present climate of opinion continues.

Since dismissal from government service for disloyalty is punishment, due process of law requires that the accused employee be given all the safeguards of a judicial trial before it is imposed. The Supreme Court in the *Lovett* case did not stop with holding that *Congress* could not dismiss employees for disloyalty. It went on to say, with particular reference to this punishment: "Those who wrote our Constitution . . . intended to safeguard the people of this country from punishment without trial by duly constituted courts. . . . And even the courts to which this important function was entrusted were commanded to stay their hands until and unless certain tested safeguards were observed. An accused in court must be tried by an impartial jury, . . . he must be clearly informed of the charge against him, the law which he is charged with violating must have been passed before he committed the act charged, he must be confronted by the witnesses against him . . . and even after conviction no cruel and unusual punishment can be inflicted upon him." 328 U.S. at 317–318.

Not only the basic right to judicial trial but every one of these basic safeguards, unless it be the last, was violated here. (1) The appellant was not tried by a jury. (2) She was not clearly informed of the charge against her. This is true not only because there was no formal charge and, according to the Chairman of the Regional Board, no charge at all, but also because of the vagueness of the term "disloyal." It is so indefinite that neither the Executive Order nor, as far as appears, the Loyalty Review Board has attempted to define it. It means different and sometimes opposite things to different people. Since section 9A of the Hatch Act forbids employment of members of an organization that advocates (and, by necessary implication, of persons who advocate) "the overthrow of our constitutional form of government in the United States," the Executive Order is plainly meant to cover more ground, but how much more no one can say. As the Supreme Court has repeatedly held, very indefinite standards cannot be used as a basis for punishment. (3) The appellant violated no law. (4) Even the Executive Order was issued after the activities from which her disloyalty is inferred took place, if they took place at all. (5) She was not confronted with any witnesses against her. (6) Forced idleness may well be considered a cruel as well as unusual punishment. It has been considered more severe than forced labor.

Because certain officials should be free from apprehension that personal harm to them may result from their official acts they cannot, as the court points out, be required to pay damages for their official errors. But that is irrelevant here. The present appellant asks compliance with the Constitution, not damages for its violation. . . .

III. *Appellant's dismissal abridges freedom of speech and as-*

sembly. Mr. Justice Holmes' famous statement, made in 1892 when he was a member of the Supreme Judicial Court of Massachusetts, that "the petitioner may have a constitutional right to talk politics, but he has no constitutional right to be a policeman," *Mc Auliffe* v. *Mayor of New Bedford*, 155 Mass. 216, 220, is greatly oversimplified. "As pointed out in *Frost Trucking Co.* v. *Railroad Comm.*, 271 U.S. 583, 594, 46 S. Ct. 605, 607, 70 L. Ed. 1101, even in the granting of a privilege, the state 'may not impose conditions which require the relinquishment of constitutional rights . . .' " including the rights of free speech, press, and assembly. In the *Esquire* case the Supreme Court said: "We may assume that Congress . . . need not open second-class mail to publications of all types. . . . But grave constitutional questions are immediately raised once it is said that the use of the mails is a privilege which may be extended or withheld on any grounds whatsoever. See the dissents of Mr. Justice Brandeis and Mr. Justice Holmes in *Milwaukee Publishing Co.* v. *Burleson*, 255 U.S. 407, 421–423, 430–432, 437–438. Under that view the second-class rate could be granted on condition that certain economic or political ideas not be disseminated." *Hannegan* v. *Esquire, Inc.* 327 U.S. 146, 155, 156. Similarly, the premise that government employment is a privilege does not support the conclusion that it may be granted on condition that certain economic or political ideas not be entertained. Though members of minority parties have often been dismissed, in the past, to make room for members of a party in power, any comprehensive practice of that sort would today be unthinkable as well as illegal, and the Supreme Court has plainly indicated it would also be unconstitutional. The Court pointed out in the *Mitchell* case that Congress could not " 'enact a regulation providing that no Republican, Jew or Negro shall be appointed to federal office, or that no federal employee shall attend Mass or take any active part in missionary work.' " *United Public Workers* v. *Mitchell*, 330 U.S. 75, 100.

The dismissal which the Court upheld in the *Mitchell* case

was not based on views but on conduct. The Hatch Act sought
to restrain civil servants, regardless of their views, from devot-
ing more than a limited amount of energy to politics. The Court
held that "For regulation of employees it is not necessary that
the act regulated be anything more than an act reasonably
deemed by Congress to interfere with the efficiency of the public service." Since the present appellant was not a policy-making
officer, had no access to state secrets, and was not even in a sensitive agency, it is doubtful whether any political opinions of
hers, however obnoxious, could reasonably be deemed to interfere with the efficiency of the service. But the question is, I
think, immaterial here, for the "vague and indeterminate . . .
boundaries," *Herndon* v. *Lowry*, 301 U.S. 242, 264, of the term
"disloyal" have made the Executive Order as construed and applied a restraint on many opinions that certainly cannot be
deemed to interfere with the efficiency of the service. . . .

A record filed in this court shows that an accused employee
was taken to task for membership in Consumers Union and for
favoring legislation against racial discrimination. The record
in the present case contains the following colloquy between a
member of the Regional Board and the present appellant: "Mr.
Blair: Did you ever write a letter to the Red Cross about the
segregation of blood? Miss Bailey: I do not recall. Mr. Blair:
What was your personal position about that? Miss Bailey: Well,
the medical—. Mr. Blair: I am asking yours."

No doubt some boards are quite aware that unconventional
views and conduct have no tendency to indicate disloyalty. But
the fact remains that some boards imagine the contrary. This
fact is only too well known. It puts government employees
under economic and social pressure to protect their jobs and
reputations by expressing in words and conduct only the most
orthodox opinions on political, economic, and social questions.

A regulation that restrains constitutionally protected speech
along with other speech cannot be enforced against either. . . .

Freedoms that may not be abridged by law may not be abridged by executive order. Executive power to control public employment stands on no higher constitutional ground than legislative power to tax. The taxing power does not extend to sales of propaganda not made for profit; license taxes, though imposed for the legitimate purpose of raising revenue, are unconstitutional in their application to such sales. Such taxes, even if they are too small to be a "substantial clog" on the circulation of propaganda, are "on their face . . . a restriction of the free exercise of those freedoms which are protected by the First Amendment." *Murdock* v. *Commonwealth of Pennsylvania*, 319 U.S. 105, 114. The loss of employment, reputation, and earning power here involved is on its face a very substantial clog on the free exercise of those protected freedoms. It is therefore more clearly unconstitutional than the taxes.

Appellant's dismissal abridges not only freedom of speech but freedom of thought. Whatever loyalty means in the present connection, it is not speech but a state of mind. The appellant was dismissed for thinking prohibited thoughts. A constitution that forbids speech control does not permit thought control.

Appellant's dismissal attributes guilt by association, and thereby denies both the freedom of assembly guaranteed by the First Amendment and the due process of law guaranteed by the Fifth. The appellant was dismissed as disloyal because she was believed to be a member or associate of the Communist Party. Undoubtedly many such persons are disloyal in every sense to the government of the United States. But the Supreme Court has held that a particular member of the Communist Party may be "attached to the principles of the Constitution" within the meaning of those words in a naturalization act: . . .

The court thinks Miss Bailey's interest and the public interest conflict. I think they coincide. On this record we have no sufficient reason to doubt either Miss Bailey's patriotism or the value of her services to the government, or to suppose that an unpatriotic person could do substantial harm in her sort of job. Even if her services were on the whole undesirable, to oust her as disloyal on rumor and without trial is to pay too much for protection against such harm as she could do in such a job. The cost is too great in morale and efficiency of government workers, in appeal of government employment to independent and inquiring minds, and in public confidence in democracy. But even if such dismissals strengthened the government instead of weakening it, they would still cost too much in constitutional rights. We cannot preserve our liberties by sacrificing them.

KENNETH M. COLE

v.

PHILIP YOUNG

Decided June 28, 1955

Before EDGERTON, PRETTYMAN, and BASTIAN,
Circuit Judges

When Congress passed Public Law 733, permitting summary suspension of government employees in eleven agencies, it made "national security" the basis and justification for summary action that deprived employees who were veterans of the special procedural rights granted to them by the Veterans' Preference Act, but it did not define the phrase. In the summer of 1952 a committee of the National Security Council reported to President Truman that in its opinion Congress did not intend the term to apply to all positions in the Government, but only to those activities that directly affected national safety, such as military and foreign affairs. Advisers to President Eisenhower took the opposite position, and by Executive Order 10450 he extended the application of P.L. 733 to every agency and position. This interpretation was challenged in the courts by Kenneth M. Cole when he was dismissed by the head of the Department of Health, Education and Welfare.

Cole was a veteran who at the time of his dismissal was a Food and Drug inspector in the New York District. He was suspended summarily in November, 1953, and was charged with "close association with individuals reliably reported to be Communists" and with "sympathetic association with the Nature Friends of America, an organization on the Attorney-General's list." At first he refused to answer the charges or to ask for a hearing, and he was dismissed by the head of the agency on the ground that his employment was not clearly consistent with the interests of national security. He twice asked that his case be reopened and was twice refused. He then invoked his right, under the Veterans' Preference Act, to appeal to the Civil Service Commission. The Commission declined to accept his appeal, and he brought an action in the District Court of the District of Columbia asking for an order requiring that he be reinstated.

Mr. Cole's principal contention was that Public Law 733 did not authorize the President to extend its provisions to nonsensitive, non-policy-making positions in derogation of employee rights under the Veterans' Preference Act. He further contended that the requirement of the Order that the head of the agency must dismiss an employee unless he finds that his continued employment is "clearly consistent with the interests of national security" goes beyond the authority granted in Public Law 733 which permits dismissal when "necessary and advisable in the interest of national security."

The District Court dismissed Mr. Cole's complaint and he appealed. The appellate court found that the statute explicitly gave the President the right to extend its application to all agencies, that the President clearly acted within his broad constitutional powers as head of the Executive Branch in whom all executive power is vested, and that the standard adopted in the Executive Order was a proper exercise of his judgment as to the needs of national security. Judge Edgerton dissented.

The Supreme Court agreed to review the case and on June 11, 1956, handed down an opinion sustaining Judge Edgerton's contention that Public Law 733 was intended to be applied only to sensitive positions or agencies. The Supreme Court further found that if Public Law 733 is to be invoked an agency head must first make the determination that the position held by the employee is in fact related to the national security. The Court's opinion did not deal with the other points made in Judge Edgerton's dissenting opinion.

Following the decision of the Supreme Court, Mr. Cole was restored to duty.

EDGERTON, *Circuit Judge, dissenting:* As we held a year ago, enforcing the Lloyd-LaFollette Act's requirement that "No person in the classified civil service of the United States shall be removed" without notice and reasons in writing: "The power of Congress thus to limit the President's otherwise plenary control over appointments and removals is clear." *Roth* v. *Brownell,* 215 F. 2d 500, 502. It does not follow, of course, that Congress could impose absurd and crippling limits. But this is irrelevant here.

In the Lloyd-LaFollette Act and the Veterans' Preference Act, Congress limited the President's control over removals. No one claims that these limitations are unreasonable. By the Act of August 26, 1950, Congress authorized exceptions to these limitations. 64 Stat. 476, 5 U.S.C. §§ 22-1, 22-3. The question is whether this case is within the exceptions. I think it is not, for three reasons.

1. The exceptions do not cover the Food and Drug Administration, in which the appellant was employed.

The Act of 1950 provides in § 1: "Notwithstanding the provisions of section 652 of this title [Lloyd-LaFollette Act], or the provisions of any other law, the Secretary of State; Secretary of Commerce; Attorney General; the Secretary of Defense; the Secretary of the Army; the Secretary of the Navy; the Secretary of the Air Force; the Secretary of the Treasury; Atomic Energy Commission; the Chairman, National Security Resources Board; or the Director, National Advisory Committee for Aeronautics, may, in his absolute discretion and when deemed necessary in the interest of national security, suspend, without pay, any civilian officer or employee. . . ." Section 1 also provides that a suspended employee may be dismissed if the agency head thinks it "necessary or advisable in the interest of the national security." Section 3 provides that the Act "shall apply to such other departments and agencies of the Government as the President may, from time to time, deem necessary in the best interests of national security."

In Executive Order No. 10450 the President, ostensibly "deeming such action necessary in the best interests of the national security," undertook to extend the Act to "all other departments and agencies of the Government." I think this blanket extension unauthorized and invalid. Congress had specified some agencies that have something to do with national security. Committee reports describe them as "sensitive" or "concerned with vital matters" affecting national security. H.R.Rep. No. 2330, 81st Cong., 2d Sess. 4 (1950); S.Rep. No. 2158, 81st Cong., 2d Sess. 2 (1950); S.Rep. No. 2264, 80th Cong., 2d Sess. 2 (1948). Evidently Congress thought some other agencies might likewise be concerned with national security. Accordingly Congress authorized the President to extend the Act. There is, I think, not the slightest reason for supposing that Congress intended to authorize the blanketing in of all agencies. A committee report said: "the bill makes ample provision for the employment in nonsensitive agencies of certain of those employees who may be classified in sensitive departments and agencies as security risks." H.R.Rep. No. 2330, 81st Cong., 2d Sess. 4 (1950). Accordingly Section 1 of the Act provides "That the termination of employment herein provided shall not affect the right of such officer or employee to seek or accept employment in any other department or agency of the Government. . . ." Since many agencies, including the Food and Drug Administration in the Department of Health, Education and Welfare, in which the

appellant was employed, have nothing to do with national security, the Act of 1950 has nothing to do with them. The authorization to bring "other" departments and agencies within
the Act should be recognized, in accordance with the purpose
and intent of Congress, as limited to those that might reasonably be deemed "necessary in the best interests of national
security." It could not reasonably be deemed necessary in the
best interests of national security that employees in all agencies,
including not only the Food and Drug Administration but the
Fish and Wildlife Service, be subject to summary unappealable
dismissal. . . .

2. The Act of 1950 authorizes the head of an agency covered
by the Act to dismiss suspended employees "whenever he shall
determine such termination necessary or advisable in the interests of the national security." Appellant's agency head did not
make that determination concerning the appellant, but determined only that appellant's continued employment "is not
clearly consistent with the interests of national security." In
Executive Order 10450 the President purported to adopt the
"clearly consistent" test, but he had no authority to adopt it. It
differs vitally from the "necessary or advisable" test that Congress prescribed.

The difference is closely parallel to that between the test,
"reasonable grounds exist for belief that the person involved is
disloyal," used in Executive Order 9835, and the test, "There is
a reasonable doubt as to the loyalty of the person involved,"
used in the later Executive Order 10241. As this court has
held, that "amended standard applied a more rigid test of suitability for government employment. It contemplated the possible
existence of proof or information which, while not capable of
inducing a belief that the person 'is disloyal,' does cause a reasonable doubt as to whether he is in fact loyal." *Jason* v. *Summerfield*, 214 F. 2d 273, 276, *cert. denied*, 348 U.S. 840. Just so
here, the amended standard applied a more rigid test of suita-

bility for government employment. It contemplated the possible existence of information which, while not capable of inducing a belief that the person's dismissal is "necessary or advisable in the interests of national security," does cause a reasonable doubt as to whether his continued employment is consistent with the interests of national security. Under the new standard, but not under the old, no matter how important to the country a man's continued employment may be he must be dismissed if there is doubt about him from a security standpoint. The new standard gives employees less protection than Congress authorized, and thereby makes a deeper inroad on the safeguards of the Lloyd-LaFollette Act and the Veterans' Preference Act.

3. The procedure used in appellant's dismissal does not even comply with the Act of 1950. Even that Act requires "a written statement of the decision of the agency head." Frequently, in legal connections, "decision" means not only a result but the reasons for the result. The Administrative Procedure Act follows this usage. It requires that "All decisions (including initial, recommended, or tentative decisions) shall become a part of the record and include a statement of (1) findings and conclusions, as well as the reasons or basis therefor, upon all the material issues of fact, law, or discretion presented on the record; and (2) the appropriate rule, order, sanction, relief, or denial thereof." Sec. 8(b); 60 Stat. 242, 5 U.S.C. § 1007(b). The letter telling appellant he was dismissed, but not telling him why, was evidently not "a written statement of the decision" as Congress uses that term in connection with administrative procedure. The required statement is plainly intended to be a safeguard against arbitrary action. Unless reasons are given no safeguard is provided. *Cf. Mulligan* v. *Andrews,* 211 F. 2d 28.

JOHNNIE C. DUNCAN

v.

ARTHUR E. SUMMERFIELD

Decided December 31, 1957

Before EDGERTON, *Chief Judge,* and WILBUR K.
MILLER and BAZELON, *Circuit Judges*

Following the *Cole* case the Attorney General, on August 1, 1956,
sent a memorandum to all agency heads establishing the conditions
to be met by persons seeking reinstatement after being discharged
under E.O. 10450 from nonsensitive positions in the Government.
He set a time limit of eighteen months from the time of dismissal
for the filing of an application for reinstatement and advised that
employees should be warned that if they are restored to their jobs
they may be subject to the reissuance of the charges against them.
He suggested that they be permitted to resign.

Johnnie Duncan, a former letter carrier, was one of some 280
former employees who had been dismissed from nonsensitive positions and who sought reinstatement. His request was denied on
the ground that too much time had elapsed between his dismissal
and the filing of his application. Judge Edgerton spoke for the court,
overruling the Government. His opinion gives the relevant facts
of the case.

EDGERTON, *Chief Judge:* Plaintiff Duncan, a veteran's preference eligible with classified civil service status, was employed as
a letter carrier in the Washington Post Office. He was dismissed
for "security" reasons February 12, 1954 and filed this suit for
reinstatement October 24, 1956. The defendant pleaded laches.
The District Court granted his motion for summary judgment
and the plaintiff appeals.

We think the court erred. Normally a dismissed government

employee who waited two years and eight months before bringing suit would be guilty of laches, but in this case we think circumstances excuse the delay.

The plaintiff was dismissed "under the provisions of Executive Order 10450" which was based on the Act of August 26, 1950. But in *Cole* v. *Young*, 351 U.S. 536, 543, the Supreme Court determined that this Act "relates only to those activities which are directly concerned with the Nation's safety." That decision was rendered June 11, 1956. It reversed the District Court and this court. The District Court in October 1954, and this court in 1955, had held that the Act, supplemented by the Executive Order, applied to all government employees. Duncan had discussed with his counsel the advisability of suing, but had been advised in the summer or late spring of 1954 to await the result of Cole's suit, which would be controlling. We think he acted reasonably in following this advice.

In the summer of 1955 Duncan learned that this court had decided against Cole and that Cole was seeking review in the Supreme Court. In June and again in August, 1956, after the Supreme Court ruled in favor of Cole, Duncan applied for reinstatement. The Postmaster General and the Civil Service Commission denied relief, and on September 17, 1956 the Chairman of the Civil Service Commission wrote to Duncan's counsel: "You may consider this notice to exhaust Mr. Duncan's administrative remedies before the Commission." This suit was filed between five and six weeks later.

In suits for reinstatement in government employment, as in equitable actions generally, laches has two elements, (1) unreasonable delay in prosecuting a claim and (2) resulting prejudice. *Gurley* v. *Wilson*, 239 F. 2d 957. In the present case the second element is not clearly present, and the first element is absent.

(1) The Court of Claims and a number of other courts have held that a dismissed government employee acts reasonably,

and is not guilty of laches, if he awaits the result of a suit by another employee who was dismissed in similar circumstances. The Court of Claims said in *Kaufman* v. *United States:* "We do not see how any good purpose could have been served from the standpoint of either the Government or the three persons affected by instituting three different suits and having the Government defend all three and the plaintiffs put to the expense of employing attorneys and possibly paying court costs in all three cases. It was natural that only one should file suit since it was apparent that whatever decision was rendered in that suit would apply to all three cases. This it seems to us fully explains the delay of plaintiff in not filing suit until after the final decision in the Borak case. . . ." 93 F. Supp. 1019, 1021 (1950). In *State* v. *Kansas City,* 261 S.W. 112, 114 (Mo., 1924), the Supreme Court of Missouri said: "In the case before us the delay was 24 months in formally asking reinstatement and in bringing suit, but we think that the relator reasonably, under the circumstances, so refrained until the case of Rundberg, involving the same question, was finally decided. This suit was brought and demand for reinstatement made within about 4 or 5 months after we denied the writ of certiorari in the Rundberg Case." . . .

(2) If Duncan recovers back pay for work he did not perform and another man did, the government will be prejudiced by its wrongful discharge of Duncan, but not by his awaiting the result of another suit before filing his own. He gave no notice that he was doing so, but neither did the discharged employee in the Court of Claims case or in the Missouri case. We think this fact immaterial, not only on the question of reasonableness but also on the question of prejudice. The government says it was prejudiced because it "converted" a substitute carrier to regular carrier in place of Duncan. But it cannot reasonably be assumed that if a man dismissed for security reasons in 1954 had

immediately sued, or given notice that he might sue, his job
would have been kept open for him.

Workers in Industry

CAFETERIA AND RESTAURANT WORKERS UNION,
LOCAL 473, AFL-CIO

v.

NEIL H. McELROY

Decided August 21, 1959

Before EDGERTON, FAHY, and DANAHER,
Circuit Judges

The Supreme Court was not asked to pass upon the industrial
security program developed by the Department of Defense until the
October Term of 1958. On June 29, 1959, in the case of *William L.
Greene* v. *Neil H. McElroy et al.*, it handed down an opinion holding
that the Department had been given no authority either by Congress
or by the President for a program that deprived a worker in industry
of his job. In the case below the Department of the Navy sought to
achieve the same ends by barring a worker from access to the naval
installation where she was employed by a private contractor.

The District Court dismissed the Union's complaint and was overruled by a division of the Court of Appeals. On October 26, 1959,
that court ordered that the case be reheard in banc.

EDGERTON, *Circuit Judge:* A private corporation, M & M
Restaurants, Inc., under a contract with government officers,
operated a cafeteria in the Naval Gun Factory, property of the

United States. The corporation employed appellant Brawner, a civilian, as a cook. Without a hearing of any sort, the Superintendent and the Security Officer of the Naval Gun Factory excluded her from the premises and thereby deprived her of her job. They said she did not meet the "security requirements." No one told either her or the corporation which employed her what the security requirements were, or why she was believed not to meet them. The employer asked for "a hearing relative to the denial of admittance to the Naval Gun Factory of Rachel Brawner." The request was refused.

Brawner and her labor union sued the Secretary of Defense, the Secretary of the Navy, the Superintendent and the Security Officer of the Gun Factory, and also Brawner's employer, for the loss of her job, and have appealed from a summary judgment dismissing the complaint.

Except with respect to the employer, the District Court erred. This has now become clear. On June 29, 1959, the Supreme Court determined that the Secretary of Defense and his subordinates have not been empowered to deny a contractor's employee access to his work, and thereby deprive him of his job, on security grounds, "in a proceeding in which he was not afforded the safeguards of confrontation and cross-examination." *Greene* v. *McElroy*, 360 U.S. 474, —— (Slip op. pp. 33–34). What government officers are not empowered to do in such a proceeding, which includes a limited sort of hearing, they are not empowered to do in a proceeding that includes no hearing at all. As in the *Greene* case, if the action of the government officers was in accordance with Navy regulations, the regulations were unauthorized and invalid.

It is immaterial that Greene's working place does not appear to have been, as Brawner's was, on government property. From the premise that "the United States could validly exclude all persons from access to the Naval Gun Factory," appellees draw the conclusion that the Secretary of Defense could validly exclude Brawner from her work there, on "security" grounds, without giving her a hearing. If the conclusion followed from the premise, it would likewise follow that the Secretary could deprive government employees of their jobs on similar grounds, without giving them a hearing, by simply excluding them from the places where they work. But neither Congress nor the President has authorized any such thing. And it is clear that government officials may not deprive government employees of their jobs on security grounds except as authorized by Congress or the President. *Peters* v. *Hobby,* 349 U.S. 331; *Cole* v. *Young,* 351 U.S. 536.

The government challenges the standing of appellant labor union to sue. We think the union here had standing to protect the interests of its members. *Cf. Nat'l Ass'n for the Advancement of Colored People* v. *Alabama,* 357 U.S. 449, 459–460; *MacArthur Liquors, Inc.* v. *Palisades Citizens Ass'n,* 265 F. 2d 372.

Since Brawner's employer could not employ her within the Naval Gun Factory, the only place where it had contracted to employ her, when the government appellees would not let her enter the place, it is not responsible for ceasing to employ her. Appellants' claim against the employer is for alleged breach of contract, and impossibility of performance defeats the claim. The judgment in favor of M & M Restaurants, Inc., is therefore affirmed. The judgment in favor of the government appellees is reversed and the case is remanded to the District Court for proceedings consistent herewith.

Travelers Abroad

Although American citizens have been traveling abroad in great numbers for more than 150 years, the possible limits to their right to do so and the legal attributes of the passport they must now carry have never been clearly defined. In time of war the President has customarily restricted the right to travel, and the passport has been the tool by which the restriction was made effective. In 1856 Congress gave the Secretary of State the sole right to issue passports under rules prescribed by the President, and this authority has been confirmed by later Acts. In 1941 Congress amended the law to permit the President to restrict travel in times of national emergency as well as in war, and in 1952 it reaffirmed this power. Successive Presidents have exercised the right in a series of Proclamations, and the Secretary of State has been authorized by Executive Order to refuse, restrict, or withdraw a passport in his discretion. The Secretary has exercised this power freely and at times seemingly arbitrarily, sometimes adopting dilatory tactics that have made the passport useless in view of the purpose for which it was requested. In 1952 he established for the first time categories of persons to whom passports will not be issued: members of the Communist Party; persons who, because of their recent membership or their activities in support of the Communist movement, are believed to be under Communist discipline; and persons believed to be going abroad to further the Communist movement. Until very recently the Secretary has taken the position that since passports are "political documents" and instruments of foreign policy his discretion in regard to their issuance is absolute.

For many years this theory as to the Secretary's power was of little practical importance. An American citizen's passport was little more than a letter of introduction to officials abroad and a pleasant souvenir of foreign travel. Today the situation is very different. Continuously since 1941 it has been unlawful to leave the country without a passport, and the United States will not readmit anyone who has succeeded in doing so. Normally no foreign government will admit a traveler who is without a passport, and no international steamship or airline will accept him as a passenger.

A number of American citizens whose passports have been revoked or refused have turned to the courts for relief. All of their cases have been heard in the District of Columbia; nine of them have reached the Court of Appeals, which has heard three in banc. The result has been the development of a new body of law that has forced the Secretary of State to alter both his theory and his practice.

The Court of Appeals has ruled that an American citizen has a right—"a natural right"—to travel abroad, of which he may not be deprived arbitrarily, and that the granting of a passport does not necessarily involve "the conduct of foreign affairs on a political level." So far the majority of the court has refused to consider the constitutionality of the regulations issued by the Secretary, but it has asserted its right to review both the procedures and the findings of the Department and has in effect written a code of procedure for the passport office. The court has said that a passport may be denied only on grounds that would apply to all persons alike, not to a particular individual only, and that an applicant must be informed of the reasons for a proposed denial and given a quasi-judicial hearing if he so desires. In the event of a final adverse decision, specific findings must be made by the Secretary to show that the applicant falls within a general category of persons to whom passports will be denied. If the Secretary's decision is based on secret evidence, the court has requested him to explain whether secrecy has been adopted for reasons of internal security or of foreign policy, but it has refused to require him to disclose the information or names of confidential informants. In the case of *Dulles* v. *Nathan* (infra, p. 155) the court, by implication, rebuked the dilatory tactics of the Department, setting a definite time limit for each step of the procedure that it prescribed in detail for that case.

Until 1957 a decision by the Court of Appeals adverse to the acts of the Passport Division had usually been followed by the granting of the passport. In that year in the cases of Rockwell Kent and Walter Briehl (infra, p. 158) the Department, after complying with the procedural requirements laid down by the court, denied the passports. It was upheld by the Court of Appeals. The rejected applicants appealed to the Supreme Court, which heard their cases together. In June, 1958, that Court handed down a decision (357 U.S. 116) rejecting the theory of the inherent powers of the President and finding that Congress had never given the Secretary the authority he claimed.

MAX SHACHTMAN

v.

JOHN FOSTER DULLES

Decided June 23, 1955

Before EDGERTON, FAHY, and WASHINGTON,
Circuit Judges

Max Shachtman is the national chairman of the Independent Socialist League, a splinter of a splinter of the left-wing Socialists, the members of which are commonly referred to as the Shachtmanites. The number of adherents to the Independent Socialist League is negligible, although on a few campuses its youth organization has attracted students who believe in socialism and enjoy fighting the Communists. The organization uses the revolutionary language of Marxism, but it has no connection with the international Communist movement. Its members insist that when they use the term "revolution" they do not contemplate violence but the achievement of socialism through normal, political processes, especially by the formation of a Labor Party in the United States similar to that in Great Britain. Without a hearing the organization was put on the Attorney General's first list of subversive organizations and later classified as Communist. For six years it tried in vain to be heard. Its request was finally granted and ultimately it was taken off the list. Hearing procedures had not been completed when the *Shachtman* case came to the Court of Appeals.

The majority opinion in the case, written by Judge Fahy, found that the right to travel is a natural right that cannot be denied except in accordance with substantive as well as procedural due process. A unanimous court found that the State Department had accepted Shachtman's testimony that the Independent Socialist League was hostile to the Communist International and had refused the passport only because the organization was listed by the Attorney General as subversive. The major premise of the opinion was that an American citizen has a right to travel abroad of which he may not be arbitrarily deprived, and the court found that the action of the State Department in relying solely on the Attorney General's list was, in fact, arbitrary.

After the case was decided, the State Department issued a passport to Mr. Shachtman.

EDGERTON, *Circuit Judge:* I concur in the opinion of the court.

The Supreme Court has said: "Undoubtedly the right of locomotion, the right to remove from one place to another according to inclination, is an attribute of personal liberty, and the right, ordinarily, of free transit from or through the territory of any State is a right secured by the Fourteenth Amendment and by other provisions of the Constitution." *Williams* v. *Fears*, 179 U.S. 270, 274. Freedom to leave a country or a hemisphere is as much a part of liberty as freedom to leave a State.

Those who inflict a deprivation of liberty are not the final arbiters of its legality. Due process of law is a judicial question.

Arbitrary action is not due process of law. Taking the facts alleged in the complaint to be true, as we must on this record, denial of a passport to Shachtman because the Independent Socialist League was on the Attorney General's list was arbitrary for several reasons.

1. The League is "an anti-Communist educational organization." In this respect the case is similar to *Joint Anti-Fascist Refugee Committee* v. *McGrath*, 341 U.S. 123.

2. The Passport Division knew plaintiff had tried and failed to get the Attorney General to give the League a hearing.

3. The premise that a man is not fit to work for the government does not support the conclusion that he is not fit to go to Europe. The Attorney General's list was prepared for screening government employees, not passport applicants.

4. Even in connection with screening government employees, membership in a listed organization was intended to be only an inconclusive item of evidence.

5. In other connections, the list has not even any "competency to prove the subversive character of the listed associations. . . ." *United States* v. *Remington*, 191 F. 2d 246, 252.

The defendants cannot bring their denial of a passport into conformity with due process of law by merely ceasing to base the denial on the Attorney General's list. Due process requires more than that a deprivation of liberty be not based on facts that are insufficient. It requires that a deprivation be based on facts that are sufficient and are found after a hearing. In *Bauer* v. *Acheson*, 106 F. Supp. 445, a three-judge District Court interpreted the Passport Act as requiring a hearing when a passport is revoked or its renewal is refused. The District Court for the District of Columbia has recently held that a hearing is necessary before a passport is denied. *Nathan* v. *Dulles*, 129 F. Supp. 951.

The government urges that a passport involves foreign relations and that the issuance of a passport is therefore in the exclusive control of the State Department. But the State Department's control of activities that involve both foreign relations and domestic liberties is not exclusive. If it were exclusive, the State Department could put an American citizen in jail and keep him there permanently on the mere request of a foreign government. "[T]he very delicate, plenary and exclusive power of the President as the sole organ of the federal government in the field of international relations . . . like every other governmental power, must be exercised in subordination to the applicable provisions of the Constitution." *United States* v. *Curtiss-Wright*

Export Corp., 299 U.S. 304, 320. "Since denial of an American passport has a very direct bearing on the applicant's personal liberty to travel outside the United States, the executive department's discretion, although in a political matter, must be exercised with regard to the constitutional rights of the citizens. . . ." *Bauer* v. *Acheson*, 106 F. Supp. 445, 451.

To speak of "the Secretary's discretion with respect to the issue of a passport," *Perkins* v. *Elg*, 307 U.S. 325, 350, is not to say that the Secretary may in his discretion deprive a citizen of liberty without due process of law. Moreover, in 1939, when *Perkins* v. *Elg* was decided, Americans could, as now they cannot, leave the country for any destination without a passport. Yet even then, the Supreme Court overruled the Secretary's action in denying a passport.

Neither the Passport Act nor any Executive Order should be interpreted as intended to authorize the Secretary of State to deny a passport arbitrarily or without a hearing. "We must, of course, defer to the strong presumption . . . that Congress legislated in accordance with the Constitution. Legislation must, if possible, be given a meaning that will enable it to survive." *Association of Westinghouse Salaried Employees* v. *Westinghouse Electric Corp.*, 348 U.S. 437, 452–453, *rehearing denied*, 348 U.S. 925.

John Foster Dulles

v.

Otto Nathan

Decided June 23, 1955

Before Edgerton, *Chief Judge*, Bazelon and
Washington, *Circuit Judges*

Edgerton, *Chief Judge:* On December 24, 1952, Dr. Otto Nathan, now the executor of Albert Einstein's will, applied to the Department of State for a passport. When the application had been pending nearly 20 months, on August 17, 1954, he filed a complaint for a declaratory judgment and for an injunction to direct the Secretary of State to issue a passport. On March 15, 1955, when the application had been pending over two years, Judge Schweinhaut directed the Secretary of State to "promptly afford plaintiff an appropriate hearing on his application for a passport." On June 1, 1955, finding that the Secretary of State had not complied with that order, Judge Schweinhaut directed him to "forthwith issue to the plaintiff a passport in the standard form and of the standard duration."

The Secretary of State appealed from the order of June 1 and moved for a stay. We granted a stay pending hearing and disposition of the motion. On June 2 we held a hearing and orally asked the United States Attorney to tell us why a passport was denied. On June 2 he filed a memorandum in reply, accompanied by an affidavit of the Assistant Director of the Passport Division of the Department of State. The affidavit, executed June 2, says among other things: "The Department of State on the basis of the present file, including the classified investigative record, of Dr. Otto Nathan and after full and careful consideration has concluded that it would be contrary to the best interests of the United States to provide him with a passport . . ."

On June 2 we entered an order in which we said:

". . . whereas it appears that the appellee applied for a passport some two and a half years ago and was never accorded an evidentiary hearing or confronted with the evidence, if any, which led to the denial of a passport;

"It is ORDERED by the Court that the said order of the District Court entered June 1, 1955, be, and it hereby is, stayed until further order of this court, PROVIDED, HOWEVER,

"(1) That the Department of State accord a quasi judicial hearing on the appellee's application for a passport, with opportunity provided to the government and to the appellee to offer evidence, such hearing to be commenced on or before Tuesday, June 7, and to be concluded within three days unless this Court upon application extends the time;

"(2) That the hearing officer or officers render a report and recommendation, based on the record of such hearing, within five days after the conclusion of the hearing;

"(3) That the appellee be immediately furnished with a copy of such report and recommendation, and be allowed three days within which to file objections thereto with the Department of State;

"(4) That within ten days after the rendition of such report and recommendation, action be taken by the Department of State, either granting or denying a passport, and a statement of such action be immediately furnished to appellee and to this Court;

"(5) That if a passport is denied, the State Department immediately either (a) inform this Court and the appellee with particularity of the reasons for such denial or (b) show cause to this Court with particularity for any failure to supply such reasons.

"After final action by the Department of State this Court will consider what further action on its part, if any, is necessary."

On Monday, June 6, the United States Attorney informed us in a memorandum that "The Acting Secretary of State having referred the passport application of Otto Nathan to the Board of Passport Appeals for review and recommendation and having received the report and recommendation of that Board, advises the Court that the application of Otto Nathan for a passport has been approved and the passport has been issued. . . ." The memorandum does not say what the Board reported or recommended, or why. It does not suggest that the Board had new information. It does not say what the Board thought about information referred to in the affidavit of the Assistant Director of the Passport Division. However, since the Department of State has issued the passport, it must be assumed that its issuance was not contrary to the best interests of the United States.

The memorandum of June 6 suggests that the Secretary's appeal and his motion for a stay are now moot. Since they clearly are, they "will be dismissed as moot and the case remanded to the District Court with directions to vacate its judgment." *Acheson* v. *Droesse*, 90 U.S. App. D.C. 143, 147, 197 F. 2d 574, 578.

WALTER BRIEHL

v.

JOHN FOSTER DULLES
Decided June 27, 1957

Before EDGERTON, *Chief Judge*, and PRETTYMAN,
WILBUR K. MILLER, BAZELON, FAHY, WASHINGTON,
DANAHER, and BASTIAN, *Circuit Judges*,
sitting in banc

In April, 1955, Dr. Walter Briehl, a practicing psychiatrist, applied for the renewal of his passport so that he might attend an international psychoanalytical congress in Geneva and a World Health Organization congress in Istanbul. The Director of the Passport Office requested him to submit an affidavit stating whether he was at the time or ever had been a Communist and explaining his connection with certain organizations. Through his attorneys he flatly refused to comply with this request, contending that it violated his constitutional rights under the First and Fifth Amendments. The Passport Office then informed him that it was tentatively denying his application because he was alleged to be a Communist. After several demands by his attorney for an "evidentiary hearing" he was given an "informal hearing" before two State Department representatives at which he continued to refuse to deny or explain

the allegations as to his communism. Later he again refused to submit
an affidavit as to past or present Party membership. The Board of
Passport Appeals then refused to act upon his case on the ground
that he had not complied with the departmental regulations.

Dr. Briehl brought suit in the District Court, asking among other
things that the passport regulations be declared invalid and the refusal to renew his passport a violation of his rights under the Passport Act of 1926, the Constitution of the United States, and the
Declaration of Human Rights of the United Nations. The District
Court ruled against him and Dr. Briehl appealed, contending that
the right to travel could not be made dependent upon the "political"
test of Communist membership and that the State Department's
regulations deprived him of procedural due process, did not provide
for a quasi-judicial hearing, and were unauthorized.

The Court of Appeals, sitting in banc, sustained the judgment of
the District Court in a 5 to 3 decision. Judge Prettyman wrote an
opinion in which three other judges concurred. He found that since
the days when the English kings could forbid their subjects to leave
the realm the Executive has had an inherent right to restrict travel
abroad. He also found that the Secretary of State did not exceed
the broad powers he possessed both by statutes and by delegation
from the President in time of a national emergency when he ruled
that passports will not be issued to Communists. Judge Prettyman
thought that the ban is justified by the character of the Communist
movement and by the duty of the Secretary to prevent international
incidents. He ruled that the regulations conform to the requirements
of procedural due process and that an applicant can properly be
required to submit pertinent data required by them before his application will be considered.

Judge Washington agreed with the judgment of the court, but
felt that it should confine itself to consideration of the last point
since it was unnecessary to go farther to sustain the judgment of the
court below. He thought that the questions put to Dr. Briehl were
pertinent and that the Secretary might properly require them to be
answered before he made a decision.

Judge Fahy dissented. He thought that the facts of the case showed that the passport had been denied simply because the applicant had refused to file the affidavit. This amounted to an arbitrary denial of the right to travel. He said that the Secretary's control over passports could be exercised only "to prevent the reasonable likelihood of harm to our national defense or the conduct of our foreign affairs" and could not be used to prevent travel that would not have that effect. The existing emergency was not sufficiently acute to justify an automatic denial of a right on the ground that the regulations had not been complied with. The Secretary must make an independent judgment. For these reasons he thought that the judgment of the court below should be reversed and the case remanded to the Secretary for further action.

Judge Bazelon wrote a long dissenting opinion in which Judge Edgerton concurred. He read history differently from Judge Prettyman and rejected the conclusion that the President has an inherent right to restrict foreign travel. This right, he found, lies with Congress, and Congress has delegated to the President and the Secretary of State only the right to make procedural regulations for the issuance of passports and to designate geographical areas in which American citizens may not travel. It has never authorized the creation of categories of ineligibility for passports. The regulations, therefore, are invalid.

Judge Edgerton concurred in Judge Bazelon's dissent and wrote a brief dissent of his own.

The Supreme Court agreed to review the case and heard it together with that of Rockwell Kent, in which the same questions were raised. In a 5 to 4 decision it overruled the Court of Appeals.

EDGERTON, *Chief Judge, dissenting:* We have temporized too long with the passport practices of the State Department. Iron curtains have no place in a free world. I think the Secretary should be directed to issue a passport.

"Undoubtedly the right of locomotion, the right to remove from one place to another according to inclination, is an attribute of personal liberty, and the right, ordinarily, of free transit

from or through the territory of any State is a right secured by
. . . the Constitution." *Williams* v. *Fears*, 179 U.S. 270, 274. We
have held that the right to leave the country is an attribute of
personal liberty and that restrictions on it "must conform with
the provision of the Fifth Amendment that 'No person shall be
. . . deprived of . . . liberty . . . without due process of
law.'" *Shachtman* v. *Dulles*, 225 F. 2d 938, 941.

But we need not and therefore should not decide any constitutional question. As Judge Bazelon's opinion shows, the President and Congress have not undertaken to delegate to the Secretary the authority he claims. This is very clear when the
statutes and executive orders on which he relies are construed
narrowly. Delegations of authority must be construed narrowly
when a narrow construction avoids serious constitutional questions. *United States* v. *Rumely*, 345 U.S. 41.

The Secretary proposes to continue restricting the personal
liberty of a citizen because statements by informants whom the
Secretary does not identify have led him to think that if the
citizen goes abroad he will do something, the nature of which
the Secretary does not suggest, which the Secretary thinks, for
reasons known only to him, will be contrary to what, for reasons
known only to him, he conceives to be "the national interest." If
Congress or the President had undertaken to authorize this,
serious constitutional questions would arise. May the government deprive a citizen of his constitutional liberty to go abroad
(1) without a jury trial, (2) without a definite standard of guilt,
(3) without sworn testimony, and (4) without an opportunity
to confront his accusers or know their identity? May it deprive
him of this liberty because of the way he has exercised his First
Amendment rights of free speech, press, and assembly? Since
neither Congress nor the President has undertaken to give the
Secretary the authority he claims, we need not consider these
constitutional questions.

Dangerous Tenants

JOHN RUDDER and DORIS RUDDER

v.

UNITED STATES OF AMERICA

Decided July 21, 1955

Before EDGERTON, BAZELON, and WASHINGTON,
Circuit Judges

On July 5, 1952, the Gwinn Amendment to the Housing Act of
1937 was passed providing that no one "who is a member of an
organization designated as subversive by the Attorney General"
shall be permitted to occupy any housing units built under the Act.
Thereafter the local housing authorities required all tenants to
certify that they did not belong to any of the organizations named
in a consolidated list issued by the Attorney General on November
10, 1952, under Executive Order 9835, in which he did not divide
the organizations into the categories named in the President's Loyalty
Order. Tenants who refused to sign the certificate were ordered to
vacate. Proceedings against recalcitrant tenants were brought in the
State courts in New York, Los Angeles, Chicago, and Milwaukee,
as well as in the District of Columbia. In all five jurisdictions the
courts ruled against the Government. On June 1, 1955, the Supreme
Court of Wisconsin found the amendment unconstitutional, and
the United States Supreme Court refused to review the case. In the
District of Columbia, Judge Edgerton spoke for a unanimous court.

EDGERTON, *Circuit Judge:* In 1952 the Rudders became tenants
from month to month of an apartment in Lincoln Heights
Dwellings, a low-cost housing development in the District of

Columbia constructed under the United States Housing Act of 1937. The United States owns the property and the National Capital Housing Authority manages it.

In 1953, in supposed compliance with the Gwinn Amendment, the Housing Authority asked the Rudders and other tenants to sign a so-called "Certification of Nonmembership in Subversive Organizations," which contains the words: "I hereby certify that I am not a member of any of the organizations listed in the document entitled 'Consolidated List, Dated November 10, 1952, of Organizations Designated by the Attorney General of the United States As Within Executive Order No. 9835'. . . ." A list, under that title, accompanied the Certification which the Rudders were asked to sign.

Executive Order 9835 authorized consideration, "in connection with the determination of disloyalty" of government employees, of various matters including "Membership in, affiliation with or sympathetic association with any foreign or domestic organization, association, movement, group or combination of persons, designated by the Attorney General as [1] totalitarian, [2] fascist, [3] communist, or [4] subversive, or [5] as having adopted a policy of advocating or approving the commission of acts of force or violence to deny other persons their rights under the Constitution of the United States, or [6] as seeking to alter the form of government of the United States by unconstitutional means." (Numbers added.) 3 C.F.R. 132, 1947 Supp., E.O. 9835.

The Consolidated List that accompanied the Certification named nearly 200 organizations. It did not indicate that the Attorney General had designated any as "subversive." It indicated nothing more than that all had been "designated by the Attorney General of the United States as within Executive Order No. 9835." The Attorney General had, in fact, designated very few organizations as subversive. In 1948 he designated many as "Totalitarian," many as "Fascist," more as "Communist," a few as advocating violent denial of the rights of others, and a few as seeking to alter the form of government by unconstitutional means. At that time he designated only six as "Subversive." 13 Fed. Reg. 6137–6138. A "List of Organizations Designated by the Attorney General Pursuant to Executive Order No. 9835 [Revised]," in the 1952 Cumulative Pocket Supplement to the 1949 edition of the CODE OF FEDERAL REGULATIONS, Title 5 (pp. 123, 126) designates only 13 organizations as "Subversive."

The Rudders refused to sign the Certification. For that reason the United States served them with notice to quit and afterwards brought this suit for possession. The Municipal Court of Appeals affirmed a judgment for the plaintiff, and we allowed this appeal.

The District of Columbia Code provides that a tenancy from month to month may be terminated on 30 days' notice, and that a landlord may recover possession in the Municipal Court. The Code does not require that a reason for termination be given. But those propositions do not decide this case. The government as landlord is still the government. It must not act arbitrarily, for, unlike private landlords, it is subject to the requirements of due process of law. Arbitrary action is not due process.

In our opinion the United States acted arbitrarily in undertaking to evict the Rudders. Their refusal to deny that they were members of any organizations on the Consolidated List was not proof that they were members. Even proof that they were members of, *e.g.*, a "totalitarian" organization, knowing nothing of its character, would be an arbitrary ground for an administrative decision to evict them from public housing. . . .

The Attorney General gave the organizations and their members no hearing before he designated the organizations as within Executive Order 9835. The Housing Authority gave the Rudders no hearing before it undertook to evict them. If it had used supposed membership only as "prima facie evidence of disqualification," a different question would have been presented. *Adler* v. *Board of Education*, 342 U.S. 485, 495. Moreover, the Attorney

General's list was intended for use in screening employees, not tenants. Yet even as an employee, a member of a listed organization is not automatically disqualified. "Neither Congress nor the President has seen fit to make membership in any organization designated by the Attorney General cause for removal from Government employment." *Kutcher* v. *Gray*, 199 F. 2d 783, 787. Even as against the organization itself, the designation is not conclusive. *Joint Anti-Fascist Refugee Committee* v. *McGrath*, 341 U.S. 123. As against a member of the organization, whatever validity the designation may have in connection with the purpose for which it was intended, in connection with other purposes it may not even be evidence. *United States* v. *Remington*, 191 F. 2d 246, 252. . . .

Accordingly this case does not present the question whether it would be arbitrary to evict persons proved to be, *e.g.*, "subversive." It does not present the question whether it would be arbitrary to evict the Rudders if it were proved that an organization was "subversive," that they were members of it, and that they knew its character. . . .

The government contends that the Gwinn Amendment required it to evict the Rudders. But construing the language of the Amendment strictly, as we must in order to avoid a serious question as to the constitutionality of this Act of Congress, we conclude that it does not touch this case. We have pointed out that most of the organizations on the Consolidated List were not designated as subversive by the Attorney General, and that the Rudders were not shown to be members of any organization.

IV

"Civilized Standards of Procedure"

With the exception of the Due Process Clause and the provisions for the protection of private property the three great procedural amendments to the Constitution, the Fourth, Fifth, and Sixth Clauses of the Bill of Rights, deal expressly with the rights of persons suspected or accused of crime. These rights were developed in the course of the long struggle for political and personal freedom in England and in this country, but the continuing effort to prevent their erosion must be carried on mainly in connection with trials for common crimes in which the defendants excite little public sympathy. The relation of the amendments to political liberty tends to be obscured. The burden of the fight so far as the federal courts are concerned falls largely upon the courts of the District of Columbia, for they alone have jurisdiction over the whole range of common crimes.

Since 1943 the Supreme Court has recognized a duty in connection with the administration of criminal justice that goes beyond the maintenance of what Justice Frankfurter has called "the Plimsoll line of due process" delimited by these amendments. In that year, in the case of *McNabb v. United States*, 318 U.S. 332, the Court declared that when the federal judiciary are the instruments of federal criminal administration they should "establish and maintain civilized standards of procedure." In accordance with this principle progressively stricter standards for the observance of the rights of persons accused of crime have been developed case by case.

In 1945 the Supreme Court formulated and Congress adopted a new code of federal criminal procedure that incorporates into statute law many of the requirements previously established by the cases and that goes well beyond the minimum requirements of the Constitution. Today in this field of law the Constitution establishes the underlying principles that guide the courts, but the federal cases are usually decided in terms of statutory interpretation.

The rules of federal criminal procedure and many of the cases deal with the activities of the police. In this area the Supreme Court has established the principle that the magistrate must be interposed between the individual and the police as promptly as possible, a rule aimed, among other things, at the elimination of the practice known as "the third degree." Since the courts cannot exercise direct control over any agency of the Executive Branch of the Government, they have devised a method of indirect enforcement of this and other rules relating to police activity. Evidence obtained in violation of them will be rejected by the courts. This sometimes means that on appeal a conviction for serious crime may be reversed on what appear to be technical grounds, with resulting popular indignation. Recent decisions restricting the police have been bitterly attacked. In June, 1958, in *Miller v. United States*, 357 U.S. 301, 313, the Supreme Court explained its position as follows:

> We are duly mindful of the reliance that society must place for achieving law and order upon the enforcing agencies of the criminal law. But insistence on observance by law officers of

traditional fair procedural requirements is, from the long point of view, best calculated to contribute to that end. However much in a particular case insistence upon such rules may appear as a technicality that inures to the benefit of a guilty person the history of the criminal law proves that tolerance of shortcut methods in law enforcement impairs its enduring effectiveness.

The result of the position taken by the Court has been a rapid and important development in the last two decades of the law of the procedural amendments.

"The Right of the People to Be Secure in Their Persons, Houses, Papers and Effects"

The Federal Rules of Criminal Procedure repeat the specific command of the Fourth Amendment that "no warrants shall issue, but upon probable cause supported upon oath or affirmation and particularly describing the place to be searched and the persons or things to be seized." The constitutional mandate establishes what is called in law the right of privacy. In spite of the Englishman's boast that "every man's home is his castle" the right was not fully respected in eighteenth-century England. The general warrant, which gave the right of indiscriminate search and arrest for the purpose of discovering whether some evidence of illegal acts could be turned up, was used in England to silence criticism of the Government by the press and was one of the weapons employed by the British to try to suppress the growing rebellion of the American colonists. The amendment, therefore, had a lively political significance for our forefathers that is now largely forgotten. Today it usually is invoked in cases in which there has been careless or overzealous police action in connection with ordinary crimes.

EARL H. McDONALD

v.

UNITED STATES OF AMERICA

Decided February 16, 1948

Before EDGERTON, CLARK, and WILBUR K. MILLER,
Associate Justices

One of the difficult problems of the police in the District of
Columbia is the enforcement of the laws relating to the various forms
of gambling—lotteries, betting on horses, playing the numbers, and
so on—that flourish there with the support of a very large segment
of the population. For the police, faced with an unco-operative
public, the temptation to cut corners is very great.

Numbers operators work in teams of three and live by rather an
exact schedule. Early in the afternoon the principal goes to headquarters to receive the "pickup man." This individual has a route
that he travels each day to pick up bets from "the writer," who
in turn has received them from the members of the public who place
them. At the headquarters the operator sorts and tallies until late
afternoon, when he leaves.

Earl H. McDonald had long been suspected of illegal gambling
activities. The police had kept him under surveillance, had noted
that he kept the regular hours of the numbers operator, and had
placed a watch on a house in which he rented a back room. On the
afternoon of June 22, 1946, they heard a sound in the house that
they thought was an adding machine. They had no warrant for
search or arrest, and the house was locked. One officer broke into
the landlady's apartment through a window and let the others in.
They then searched the house. The door of McDonald's room, when
they reached it, was locked, but they looked over the transom and
saw two men with an adding machine, numbers slips, and money.
They called to McDonald to open the door and when he did so arrested him and confiscated the adding machine, a suitcase full of

papers, and some money. Washington, who was with McDonald at the time, was also arrested. The defendants were tried and found guilty of promoting a lottery. They appealed on the ground that the evidence had been illegally obtained in violation of their constitutional rights and therefore should have been suppressed. The majority of the court found that the defendants could not complain of unlawful entry because the house and the room searched did not belong to them and that it is not a search to observe what is open to view. The court said that the only question in the case was whether it was unlawful to look through the transom, and this question was resolved in the negative. Judge Edgerton dissented.

The defendants appealed to the Supreme Court which reversed the majority decision, agreeing with Judge Edgerton's view of the right of privacy and calling it "one of the unique values of our civilization."

EDGERTON, *Associate Justice (dissenting)*: By guaranteeing freedom from "unreasonable searches and seizures," the Fourth Amendment "forbids every search that is unreasonable; it protects all, those suspected or known to be offenders as well as the innocent. . . ." *Go-Bart Importing Co. v. United States*, 282 U.S. 344, 357.

The search of the house was unreasonable and therefore illegal. The house was a dwelling. Search of a dwelling without a warrant is never reasonable except when incidental to a lawful arrest. Search of this house was not incidental to any arrest either lawful or unlawful. The officers had no right to, and did not, break into the house in order to arrest McDonald. It does not even appear that they knew he was present. They broke and entered the house in order to make the illegal search they made. Instead of being incidental to the arrests the search led to the arrests.

The officers searched McDonald's room before they entered it. Though it is "not a search to observe what is open to view" it is a search to open things to view and then observe them. The room and its contents were opened to view by forcible invasion of the house and corridor, and then observed from the corridor. This search of McDonald's room was illegal, like the previous search of the other rooms and for the same reasons. If this had been otherwise what the officers saw might perhaps have justified them in entering the room, making the arrests, and seizing the property. But that is quite immaterial. Since the search was illegal it justified nothing. The arrests and seizures were as illegal as the search itself. "A search prosecuted in violation of the Constitution is not made lawful by what it brings to light," *Byars* v. *United States*, 273 U.S. 28, 29, and evidence obtained by unlawful search is not made admissible by arresting its owner. The government cannot "justify the arrest by the search and at the same time . . . justify the search by the arrest." *Johnson* v. *United States*, 333 U.S. 10.

It is true that in order to complain of an unlawful search and seizure one must have an interest in the place searched or the property seized. Appellant Washington had neither, for he was only a guest of appellant McDonald. But McDonald had both. He rented the room searched and he owned the property seized. He was of course entitled to use the corridor. In my opinion illegal search of the room by illegal invasion of the corridor was a plain violation of his constitutional right.

The question is not whether officers may look in an unconventional way into another place, from a place in which they have a right to be and in which the person who complains has no interest. The question is whether officers may look into a room from a place in which they have no right to be and in which the person who complains does have an interest; the corridor that is the only means of access to his room. A roomer's constitutional right of privacy is a fiction that keeps the word of promise to the ear and breaks it to the hope unless it includes a right not to be spied upon by trespassers who force their way into his corridor. Yet the government contends that search by such trespassers is reasonable and the court decides that it is not a search. Neither of these propositions is comprehensible to me. No doubt a roomer's interest in a corridor is different from a householder's. Probably the one may be called an easement and the other an estate, as the government suggests. But I know of no reason why this difference should be critical here. To hold that McDonald cannot complain because he is only a roomer perverts the letter as well as the spirit of the constitutional guaranty against unreasonable searches and creates a discrimination in civil rights that is out of place in a democratic society.

UNITED STATES OF AMERICA

v.

PEGGY JEAN BLOK

Decided April 12, 1951

Before EDGERTON, BAZELON, and WASHINGTON, *Circuit Judges*

EDGERTON, *Circuit Judge:* District of Columbia police arrested appellee without a warrant on suspicion of petty larceny. They proceeded to search, without a warrant, a desk assigned to her exclusive use in the government office where she was employed. They searched it first in her absence and afterwards in her presence. She did not voluntarily consent to the search although her official superior did. The police found and seized alleged evidence in the desk. Appellee disclaims ownership of this evidence.

Petty larceny is not a felony and the alleged offense was not committed in the officers' presence. The arrest was illegal and did not justify the search. Appellee's counsel moved the Municipal Court, before trial, to rule that the arrest was illegal. The government does not dispute the ruling of the Municipal Court of Appeals that this motion was in purpose and effect a motion to suppress the evidence produced by the search. But the Municipal Court overruled the motion and admitted the evidence. Appellee was convicted of petty larceny.

The Municipal Court of Appeals reversed the conviction. It held that the appellee had a "possessory interest" in the desk assigned to her and that the search of the desk by the police "was such an invasion upon her privacy as to constitute a violation of the Fourth Amendment providing that 'The right of the people to be secure in their persons, houses, papers, and effects, against unreasonable searches and seizures, shall not be violated . . .'" The government appeals. It contends that in order to invoke the Fourth Amendment one who claims no interest in the property seized must have either a "proprietary" or a "possessory" interest in the place searched; that appellee had no such interest; and that her official superior's consent justified the police in searching the desk and its contents. . . .

Yet no clear rule has emerged as to what is necessary, over and above the introduction in evidence of that which was seized, to make one the victim of an unconstitutional search and seizure. . . .

The Fourth Amendment promises security against unreasonable searches. We think a person who has enough interest in a place to make a search unreasonable has enough to object to the search. Possession is a complicated and artificial concept. It is often hard to say whether or not a particular interest amounts to possession. We know of no reason why standing to object to a search should turn upon that question. We think appellee's exclusive right to use the desk assigned to her made the search of it unreasonable. No doubt a search of it without her consent would have been reasonable if made by some people in some circumstances. Her official superiors might reasonably have searched the desk for official property needed for official use. But as the Municipal Court of Appeals said, the search that was made was not "an inspection or search by her superiors. It was precisely the kind of search by policemen for evidence of crime against which the constitutional prohibition was directed." In the absence of a valid regulation to the contrary appellee was entitled to, and did, keep private property of a personal sort in her desk. Her superiors could not reasonably search the desk for her purse, her personal letters, or anything else that did not belong to the government and had no connection with the work of the office. Their consent did not make such a search by the police reasonable. Operation of a government agency and enforcement of criminal law do not amalgamate to give a right of search beyond the scope of either. Thus the government cannot, to find evidence of crime, search sealed mail in the possession of the Post Office Department. *Ex parte Jackson*, 96 U.S. 727, 733. In our opinion the search of appellee's desk by the police violated her right of privacy under the Fourth Amendment and the seized evidence should have been suppressed.

THOMAS HIGGINS

v.

UNITED STATES OF AMERICA

Decided January 28, 1954

Before EDGERTON, WILBUR K. MILLER, and WASHINGTON, *Circuit Judges*

EDGERTON, *Circuit Judge:* Appellant was convicted of unlawfully possessing marihuana. 26 U.S.C. § 2593(a), 53 Stat. 281. The drug was seized during a search of his room without a warrant. Seeds were found in a paper bag in a chest of drawers, and cigarettes in the pocket of a coat hanging in a closet. The seeds and cigarettes were introduced in evidence. The present question is whether appellant's motion to suppress the evidence, on the ground that the search was unlawful, should have been granted.

The trial court, sitting without a jury, found that appellant consented to the search.

At the hearing on the motion to suppress, a police sergeant testified: ". . . I identified myself to him as a police officer and asked him if I couldn't talk to him in his room. . . . He stated that that was all right and asked me to accompany him to his room. . . . I told him then about the information that I had, that I had received from the various sources, and he denied this information, denied that he was engaged in any narcotic drug traffic. I asked him then if I could look around. He stated that I could, was perfectly welcome to look anywhere in his room that I wanted to." Another policeman gave similar testimony. All this was repeated in substance at the trial. Appellant testified at the trial that the officers arrested him in the street, took him to his room, and searched it without asking or receiving permission.

We assume for present purposes that the officers' testimony was true and the appellant's false. Even so, we think the record does not support the finding that appellant consented to the search. We think the motion to suppress should have been granted.

Words or acts that would show consent in some circumstances do not show it in others. "Non-resistance to the orders or suggestions of the police is not infrequent . . . ; true consent, free of fear or pressure, is not so readily to be found." *Judd* v. *United States*, 190 F. 2d 649, 651. If a valid confession precedes a search by police, permission may show true consent to the search. That was the situation in *United States* v. *Mitchell*, 322 U.S. 65, on which appellee relies. But no sane man who denies his guilt would actually be willing that policemen search his room for contraband which is certain to be discovered. It follows that when police identify themselves as such, search a room, and find contraband in it, the occupant's words or signs of acquiescence in the search, accompanied by denial of guilt, do not show consent; at least in

the absence of some extraordinary circumstance, such as ignorance that contraband is present. No such circumstance is shown
here.

Johnson v. *United States*, 333 U.S. 10, illustrates the principle.
There policemen knocked on a door and "a voice inside asked
who was there. 'Lieutenant Belland,' was the reply. There was
a slight delay, some 'shuffling or noise' in the room and then the
defendant opened the door. The officer said, 'I want to talk to
you a little bit.' She then, as he describes it, 'stepped back acquies-
cently and admitted us.'" 333 U.S. at 12. The Supreme Court
held that the search which followed was unlawful and the evidence seized should have been suppressed. The Court said:
"Entry to defendant's living quarters, which was the beginning
of the search, was demanded under color of office. It was granted
in submission to authority rather than as an understanding and
intentional waiver of a constitutional right." 333 U.S. at 13. . . .

WILLIAM MILLER

v.

UNITED STATES OF AMERICA

Decided October 18, 1956

Before EDGERTON, *Chief Judge,* and
WILBUR K. MILLER and DANAHER, *Circuit Judges*

William Miller and three others were convicted of conspiracy to
violate the narcotics laws. At their trial they objected to the introduction in evidence of marked bills that had been seized after the
police, acting without a warrant, had forced their way into Miller's
apartment. Upon appeal the majority of a division of three judges
found that the seizure was legal and that the requirement that police
who have no warrant must identify themselves and state their purpose before entering a private dwelling to make an arrest had been

met. They based this conclusion on the assumption that the defendant recognized the officers, who said they were police, and must have known their purpose. Judge Edgerton dissented. The essential facts are stated in his opinion.

The Supreme Court granted certiorari. In a 7 to 2 opinion it found that there had been no express announcement of the purpose of the police as required by law and agreed with Judge Edgerton that the defendant's knowledge of their purpose could not be inferred from the surrounding circumstances.

EDGERTON, *Chief Judge, dissenting:* Officers arrested Clifford Reed, for whom they had a warrant, about 1:35 A.M. March 26, 1955. He told them he had been buying narcotics from appellant Shepherd who got them from appellants Miller and Byrd. The police arranged with Reed that he would make a purchase from Shepherd. About 3 A.M. Reed, in the presence of a narcotics agent, handed Shepherd marked money which the agent supplied. Under police surveillance, Shepherd then went to 1337 Columbia Road N.W. and entered the basement. After he came out and got into a cab, the police stopped it and saw him put something under its front seat. They found narcotics there, and also found that Shepherd no longer had the marked money.

The officers then went to the basement apartment at 1337 Columbia Road, which was occupied by appellants Miller and Byrd. One of the officers testified: "Officer Wurms knocked on the door and a voice from inside asked 'Who is there?' Officer Wurms repeated the name 'Blue,' called 'Blue' [a name by which Miller was known]. Then he said in a very low voice, 'Police.' The door was opened slightly, and it had a chain lock on it, and as the door was opened the man looked around the door, he tried to close the door. . . . he didn't want to let us in. . . . We forced the door open and forced our way into the room. . . . I believe the chain latch on the door was broken." The officers immediately arrested Miller and Byrd in the apartment. They took some of the marked money from Byrd, searched the apartment, and found the rest of the money.

Miller and Byrd moved to suppress the money as evidence. The motion was overruled. Shepherd, Miller, and Byrd were all tried together and convicted.

In my opinion the search of the apartment was illegal and the motion to suppress should have been granted. The officers had no warrant of any sort. In my opinion they had no sufficient reason to suppose the evidence, which was money, would be destroyed if they waited till morning and got a warrant. "Where, as here, officers are not responding to an emergency, there must be compelling reasons to justify the absence of a search warrant." *McDonald* v. *United States,* 335 U.S. 451, 454.

The arrests of Miller and Byrd do not excuse the search. "Of course, a search without warrant incident to an arrest is dependent initially on a valid arrest." *United States* v. *Rabinowitz,* 339 U.S. 56, 60. The arrests of Miller and Byrd were illegal for two reasons, even if the officers had probable cause to believe them guilty. (1) "Unless the necessities of the moment require that the officer break down a door, he cannot do so without a warrant; and if in reasonable contemplation there is opportunity to get a warrant, or the arrest could as well be made by some other method, the outer door to a dwelling cannot be broken to make an arrest without a warrant. The right to break open a door to make an arrest requires something more than the mere right to arrest. If nothing additional were required, a man's right of privacy in his home would be no more than his rights on the street; and the right to arrest without a warrant would be precisely the same as the right to arrest with a warrant. The law is otherwise." *Accarino* v. *United States,* 179 F. 2d 456, 464. *McKnight* v. *United States,* 183 F. 2d 977, 978. (2) Just as in *Accarino,* the officers did not make known their reason for demanding entry but merely identified themselves as police. One of the officers testified that Miller "wanted to know what we were doing there," but it does not appear that they answered the question. I find no evidence, and the court cites no evidence, that supports an inference that Miller even recognized the officers as the narcotics squad.[1] As we held in *Accarino*, "Before an officer can break a door to a home, he must make known the cause of his demand for entry. There is no claim . . . that the officers advised the suspect of the cause of their demand before they broke down the door. Upon that clear ground alone, the breaking of the door was unlawful, the presence of the officers in the apartment was unlawful, and so the arrest was unlawful." 179 F. 2d at 465. *Gatewood v. United States*, 209 F. 2d 789.

The denial of the motion of Miller and Byrd to suppress the illegally seized evidence was error that was prejudicial to Shepherd as well. His conviction as well as theirs should therefore be reversed. . . .

"No Person Shall Be Compelled in Any Criminal Case to Be a Witness against Himself"

Some well-publicized abuse before congressional committees of the right to refrain from self-incrimination and the clever phrase of a demagogue, "Fifth Amendment Communists," have served to bring the exercise of that right into current disrepute. Recent court interpretation of the federal law that protects the right when persons suspected of crime are questioned by police has provoked hot controversy and has been attacked as a roadblock in the way of law enforcement.

The Court of Appeals for the District of Columbia has had

[1] I do not suggest that if he had recognized them they would have been relieved of the obligation to make known the cause of their demand for entry.

to deal with a number of cases involving the use of the privilege during congressional hearings. Throughout the years, however, the issue of self-incrimination has usually come before it in connection with confessions offered as evidence in a criminal trial. Until the decision in the case of *McNabb* v. *United States*, 318 U.S. 332, the question was dealt with in constitutional terms only. The test developed was whether the confession was voluntary or involuntary, the result of a threat or a promise. In deciding this issue the courts at times appeared to make a very high estimate of human powers of resistance to pressures, both physical and psychological. In 1924, for example, in the case of *Wan* v. *United States*, 289 Fed. 908, the Court of Appeals, believing it was following the precedents set by the Supreme Court, admitted in evidence as voluntary the confession of a man who had been held incommunicado for eleven days, denied medical care and sleep, and subjected to relentless questioning. The Supreme Court overruled this decision. 266 U.S. 1. Eighteen years later, in the case of *McNabb* v. *United States*, it abandoned the test of "voluntary or involuntary" when dealing with the activities of federal officers and formulated the test of a "civilized standard of procedure." The next year the Federal Rules of Criminal Procedure provided that "an officer making an arrest . . . shall take the arrested person without unnecessary delay before the nearest available magistrate." When a confession has been obtained by police questioning, the issue of its admissibility has turned on the interpretation of the phrase "without unnecessary delay." In a series of cases the courts have narrowed the area of permissible questioning by police after arrest and before arraignment.

In June, 1957, the Supreme Court reversed the conviction for rape of Andrew R. Mallory, a nineteen-year-old Negro of limited intelligence. It sent the case back for retrial in the District Court because a confession had been introduced in evidence that had been obtained after he had been held too long in police custody before he was brought to a magistrate. Mallory was arrested about 2 P.M. and questioned intermittently by the police until he had signed the confession about 12:30 A.M. During that time he was not warned or informed of his rights, and he was not taken before a magistrate until the following morning. The Court stated that under the federal rules the police may not delay arraignment for the purpose of first establishing probable cause for arrest or of extracting a confession. *United States* v. *Mallory,* 354 U.S. 449. The case aroused a storm of protest from prosecutors, police, and some members of the legal profession. Congress set about devising a new law that would limit the scope of the decision, but the legislators found that they were unable to agree upon the proper limits of police activity, and no statute has yet been passed.

WILLIAM McAFFEE

v.

UNITED STATES OF AMERICA

Decided March 28, 1939

Before GRONER, *Chief Justice,* and STEVENS,
MILLER, EDGERTON, and VINSON,
Associate Justices

The *McAffee* case arose after the Court of Appeals had been overruled in the *Wan* case, but before the decision of the Supreme Court in the *McNabb* case.

William McAffee was convicted of the brutal murder of one of the tenants of an apartment building of which he was the janitor. The body of the murdered woman was discovered about six o'clock on a Sunday afternoon, and at about the same time McAffee was found in a drunken sleep in the basement of the apartment house. The police were called. They arrested McAffee and questioned him at the station house. Early the next morning they accused him of being the murderer. He then told them that he had gone upstairs and struck the woman with the furnace shaker after they had had a quarrel during which she had chased him with an ice pick. The police then took him to the apartment house, where he told the officers how he had cleaned the shaker and where his clothing was found. He was still in a drunken condition, craving sleep. The police took him back to the police station. There he was awakened and questioned at frequent intervals, and his clothes were taken from him; he was also taken back to the scene of the killing more than once. About thirteen hours after the arrest he signed a written confession. All this time he was in a nervous and highstrung condition, due to a bad "hangover." His confession was admitted in evidence at the trial. He was convicted and appealed on the ground that the confession was not voluntary and should have been excluded. The case was heard by the Court of Appeals sitting in banc. The judges all agreed that the case should be reversed, but on grounds other than those relating to the confession. On this point four of the five judges took the position that if the trial judge found that there was any evidence that the confession was in fact voluntary the issue must be submitted to the jury. Judge Edgerton agreed with the judgment of the court, disagreed as to the admissibility in evidence of the written confession, and wrote an opinion dealing with that issue.

EDGERTON, *J.*: I infer from *Wan* v. *United States*, 266 U.S. 1, that the defendant's confession should have been excluded. It is true that Wan was sicker than McAffee, but McAffee was 70 years old, and obviously suffering toxic effects of alcohol. He had drunk a quart of liquor, more or less, during the day, and a good deal on the two previous days. It is not disputed that during most of the night he was drunk. At 6 P.M. he was so thoroughly unconscious that a witness had to shake him very hard to wake him. He was taken to the station house and put in a cell, and lost consciousness so promptly that there was difficulty in waking him again at 7 P.M. At some time in the middle of the night the assistant coroner, a physician, gave him an ounce and a half or two ounces of whiskey. It seems clear that the whiskey was by way of treatment for the defendant's "highstrung condition" to which the doctor testified. When defendant signed the confession at about 7 the next morning he was in "a very nervous state"; "a nervous and highstrung condition"; "a little shaky"; he looked "like a man who had just come out of a hangover." He was cold and wet, and told the doctor that he was not feeling well. Again at about 10 A.M., several hours after the confession, defendant was given whiskey to drink upon the advice of the doctor. Clearly he was not a well man at any time during the night.

It is true that the police increased the discomfort of McAffee far less than that of Wan: but they increased it a good deal. McAffee obviously wanted sleep, and he was not permitted to get it except during short intervals. At about 6:30 P.M. officers took him to the police station. They waked him at 7 and took him to the Captain's office for questioning. About 8:30 they questioned him for an hour or more. They questioned him about half an hour at 10 o'clock. Then they took him to the house where the crime was committed, and where the body still was, and questioned him there for half an hour. They questioned him about midnight. By 12:30 he had fallen asleep; they aroused him and brought him out of his cell for questioning. They questioned him in the Captain's office at some time between 1 and 2, and kept him there until 2 or 3. At 3 o'clock he was "talking in a rambling manner." From 3 until about 5 A.M. he seems to have been allowed to sleep. At about 5 he was questioned at the station, taken again to the scene of the crime for "quite some time," and then taken to headquarters, where he signed the confession a few minutes before 8 o'clock. The estimate of a police sergeant, not continuously present, that defendant had "possibly 5 hours of sleep" cannot be correct. Being repeatedly waked up, kept awake, moved about, and questioned, when he must have been in great need of sleep, necessarily inflicted great misery on the defendant and made further inroads on what power of resistance he had in his besotted condition. He got wet and cold from being taken about in the rain. Moreover, his shoes and trousers were taken from him about 8:30 P.M.; he was taken through the streets at least once in pajamas, and was in "underdrawers or pajamas, or something" a large part of the night. This, whatever its purpose, probably tended to weaken his resistance. In *Bram* v. *United States*, 168 U.S. 532, 561, 563, in which a confession was held inadmissible, the Supreme Court emphasized among other things the fact that the prisoner had been stripped of his clothing.

Blows, promises, or threats are not necessary to vitiate a confession. *Wan* v. *United States*, 266 U.S. 1; *Perrygo* v. *United States*, 2 F. (2d) 181. The confession in the *Wan* case was held not "voluntary" because the prisoner, who was ill and in pain, was kept awake, moved about, confronted with evidence, and questioned for many days. In the present case there was far less abuse, but I think there was enough to vitiate the confession. I do not suggest that no questions may be asked of a sick or drunken prisoner, or that he may complain of trifling interferences with his sleep. The misery inflicted upon McAffee was serious. It may have worn down his resistance until the need for peace drove him to say, regardless of the truth, what seemed necessary in order to get it.

From the point of view of one who is not sleepy and can go to bed when he likes, a prisoner makes a bad bargain if he risks his neck for a little rest; but it is human to discount the future when one is suffering from an immediate physical need. We are told that Esau, being hungry, sold his birthright for a mess of pottage. The craving for sleep which follows an overdose of alcohol is urgent. And powers of resistance vary. . . . Mental and physical condition at the time of the confession affect the question. . . .

I take the principle of the *Wan* case to be that, if serious and protracted discomfort is inflicted in the effort to get information about a crime, a confession which follows should be excluded as involuntary, at least when the prisoner's character is not shown to be peculiarly rugged and his condition is such as to make him specially susceptible to pressure. I think this case is within that principle. . . .

The government's brief points out that defendant was not "accused to his face" until 5 in the morning; but it is not denied that he was suspected earlier, and the taking of his clothing in the evening, to examine it for bloodstains, shows that he was. Moreover, it is not clear that the officers' motive for the treatment which they inflict is important. If a prisoner were brutally beaten, and then confessed, the confession would not be made admissible by proof that the officers told him, and told him truthfully, that they would be satisfied if he incriminated a third person. The questioning which was held to invalidate the confession in *State* v. *Powell* [258 Mo. 239] was devoted largely to efforts to implicate others. The probable ineffectiveness of protest from a colored janitor to police officers, and McAffee's besotted condition, are sufficient explanations of his failure to complain at the time; and his condition explains also his purported failure to remember the proceedings later. . . .

Other examples of murder confessions which proved false are given in the *Report on Lawlessness in Law Enforcement* of the National Commission on Law Observance and Enforcement (Wickersham Commission), p. 182 ff. *Cf.* Borchard, *Convicting the Innocent*, pp. 20, 110 ff.; Wigmore, *Evidence*, § 867, note 1. Those who studied the third degree for the Commission found that it not only involves danger of false confession, but actually impairs the efficiency of the police by making them lazy and unenterprising; impairs the administration of criminal law in the courts by making jurors suspicious of police testimony, diverting attention from the main issue, and requiring reversals of some convictions which could have been properly obtained; brutalizes the police, hardens the prisoner, and lowers public esteem for the administration of justice. (pp. 181-190) The Commission itself, which included among others Roscoe Pound, George W.

Wickersham, and Newton D. Baker, unanimously reached similar conclusions.

As the Virginia court said in the *Enoch* case: "The police detectives have testified with apparently great candor and fairness . . . They verily thought they were doing their duty, and the state a service, in their efforts to secure a confession. But in this they were in error." *Enoch* v. *Commonwealth*, 141 Va. 411, 126 S.E. 222, 226. The common-law rule excludes extorted confessions because they may be untrue. The Fifth Amendment excludes them because they are extorted. . . .

ANDREW UPSHAW

v.

UNITED STATES OF AMERICA

Decided April 19, 1948

Before EDGERTON, CLARK, and WILBUR K. MILLER,
Associate Justices

Andrew Upshaw was arrested at two o'clock on a Friday morning and accused of theft. He was questioned intermittently from the time of his arrest until shortly after nine o'clock Saturday morning, when he confessed. He was not arraigned before a committing magistrate until Monday morning. At his trial his confession was admitted in evidence, and he was convicted. After the conviction the Government "confessed error"; that is, the prosecutor concluded that the confession should not have been admitted because Upshaw was not brought before the committing magistrate with the promptness required by the Federal Rules of Criminal Procedure. The Government asked the Court of Appeals to send the case back to the District Court for retrial. The majority of the division hearing the case disagreed with the Government's position and confirmed the conviction. Judge Edgerton dissented.

On appeal the Supreme Court, in a 5 to 4 decision, reversed the Court of Appeals, rejecting, as did Judge Edgerton, the contention that only the usual police procedure had been followed. The Court said, "However usual this practice, it is a violation of law and confessions thus obtained are inadmissible."

EDGERTON, *J., dissenting:* I think the United States Attorney and his Assistants were eminently fair and right in confessing error.

Appellant was questioned by policemen for about thirty minutes soon after his arrest at 2 A.M. on Friday, June 6, 1947. He was questioned again at 9 or 10 A.M., at 11 A.M., at 5:30 P.M., and between 7:30 and 8 P.M.; in all, five times on Friday. Each time he denied guilt. On Saturday, June 7, about 9 A.M., he was questioned a sixth time and admitted guilt. Half an hour later he signed a confession which he repeated and acknowledged during the day. When he first confessed, he had been under arrest for more than 30 consecutive hours. That period included the whole of one regular working day (Friday). He was not taken before a committing magistrate until Monday, June 9. At the trial a police detective frankly explained why that was not done on Friday morning: "We didn't have anything to take him to the Police Court with. . . . I didn't feel that we had a sufficient case against him to have the Police Court hold him, and if the Police Court did not hold him we would lose custody of him and I no longer would be able to question him."

The law requires an arresting officer to "take the arrested person without unnecessary delay before the nearest available commissioner or before any other nearby officer empowered to commit persons charged with offenses against the laws of the United States." Rule 5, Federal Rules of Criminal Procedure. Arrested persons without money or influence are not excepted. An arrested person with a criminal record is not excepted. "It is furthermore both by law and practice true that application for hearing might have been made to . . . committing magistrates at any hour. It follows that the detention was inexcusable and illegal at the outset." *Akowskey* v. *United States,* 158 F. 2d 649, 650.

During the trial, the prosecutor described appellant's detention and questioning as "usual police procedure." The detective's explanation, and a number of cases that have reached this court, suggest that this procedure is not unusual in the District of Columbia. It is procedure in defiance of Congress and the courts. Unnecessary delay in producing a prisoner before a committing magistrate is false imprisonment. As this court says in its opinion, police executives should discipline officers who are guilty of this practice. It deprives the citizen of his liberty without due process of law. It is a violation of civil rights that cannot be tolerated in a democratic society.

Until appellant's confessions were obtained, there was "inexcusable detention for the purpose of illegally extracting evidence." *United States* v. *Mitchell,* 322 U.S. 65, 67. It extracted the evidence. An event is presumably a result, not a coincidence, when it follows an act intended and likely to produce it. The presumption may be rebuttable in some cases, but in this case there is nothing to rebut it. Nothing suggests that confession would have been obtained if the illegal detention had not occurred. The *Boone* case, *Boone* v. *United States,* 164 F. 2d 102, in which this court found no causal connection between illegal detention plus questioning and a confession that followed, is distinguishable from the present case on three grounds. (1) The illegal detention of Boone was not expressly shown to have been for the *purpose* of questioning him and extracting a confession from him. (2) The questioning of Boone was less exhausting than that of appellant. Boone was questioned twice, appellant six times. (3) Boone did not confess until long after the police stopped questioning him. Appellant confessed while he was being questioned.

I think the *Boone* case is not only distinguishable but wrong. "Causal connection between some kinds of pressure and subsequent confessions is obviously probable and should be assumed." *Hawkins* v. *United States*, 158 F. 2d 652, 654. Illegal detention plus questioning, and particularly illegal detention plus extensive questioning, is an example of such pressure. When, as in this case, detention leads to extensive questioning that leads to a confession, it seems to me obvious that the detention leads to the confession. The *Mitchell* case, from which this court inferred that the Boone confession was admissible, held only that subsequent illegal detention does not rule out a confession previously and legally obtained. I find nothing in the *Mitchell* case to suggest what this court held in the *Boone* case, *viz.* that a prisoner who has been illegally held and extensively questioned before he confesses, and is still illegally held when he confesses, must offer additional proof that the detention and questioning caused the confession. In the present case there is the very substantial additional proof mentioned in the preceding paragraph. But I think the court errs in holding that any additional proof is necessary. The *Mitchell* case does not support that view and I think the *McNabb* case refutes it.

It is unimportant, if true, that a confession may be "voluntary" although extracted by illegal detention and questioning. Voluntary or not, a confession so extracted is not acceptable evidence in a federal court. That is what the Supreme Court held in the *McNabb* case. If a confession is found to be involuntary it is necessarily excluded on constitutional grounds. But the Supreme Court did not exclude the *McNabb* confessions as involuntary, or on constitutional grounds, but on other grounds that are present here. . . .

We are concerned here, as the Supreme Court was in the *McNabb* case, with "the duty of establishing and maintaining civilized standards of procedure and evidence" in a federal court. Appellant's conviction should therefore be reversed. "Plainly, a conviction resting on evidence secured through such a flagrant disregard of the procedure which Congress has commanded cannot be allowed to stand without making the courts themselves accomplices in willful disobedience of law." *McNabb* v. *United States,* at 345.

MARCUS SINGER

v.

UNITED STATES OF AMERICA

Decided April 18, 1957

Before EDGERTON, *Chief Judge,* and PRETTYMAN and WILBUR K. MILLER, *Circuit Judges*

Marcus Singer was called before the Un-American Activities Committee to testify in the course of an investigation of communism in education. At the time he was teaching at Cornell University. He was questioned as to his activities when he was at Harvard University in the early 1940's. He answered freely all questions as to his own membership and activities in a Marxist study group, and he admitted his Communist sympathies at that time. He denied that he had ever been a member of the Party and insisted that the study group had no subversive purposes. When questioned as to whether certain persons, some of whom were believed to have been "hard core" Communists, attended the meetings of his group, he refused to answer on grounds of "honor and conscience," and at the same time he invoked the privilege against self-incrimination. He was cited for contempt, indicted in the District of Columbia on eleven counts, waived a jury trial, was convicted on one count only, and appealed.

One month before the *Watkins* and *Sweezy* cases were decided by the Supreme Court the Court of Appeals affirmed Singer's conviction in a 2 to 1 decision. The court dealt only with the Fifth Amendment issue. The majority took the position that by his previous testimony as to the study group and his membership in it Singer had been foreclosed from resort to the Amendment. If the group was innocent of any subversive purpose, he could not be incriminated by answering the question. If the group was in fact subversive, he had already incriminated himself by admitting membership. Judge Edgerton dissented.

Singer petitioned for a rehearing in banc. Before the Court of Appeals had announced its decision, the Supreme Court handed down its decisions in the *Watkins* and *Sweezy* cases. The Court of Appeals then dismissed the *Singer* case.

EDGERTON, *Chief Judge, dissenting:* Appellant, having waived a jury, was convicted by a District Judge of refusing to answer a question asked by a subcommittee of the House of Representatives Committee on Un-American Activities. 52 Stat. 942, 2 U.S.C. § 192. At a Committee hearing in 1956, appellant testified he was not then a Communist but that when he was at Harvard in 1940 or 1941, and until perhaps 1944 or 1945, he had considered himself a Communist and had "supported the Communist program" because he "was interested in it" and "believed in it." He said he had "met with a Communist Party group" which was engaged in study and discussion of Marxism and which "did nothing subversive." He denied having supported any program that involved violence. He said: "we were not subversive. . . . We didn't follow any slavish policy. We were intellectuals. We were scholars. . . . We were autonomous."

He refused, on grounds both of "honor and conscience" and of the Fifth Amendment, to answer several of the Committee's questions regarding other persons. He was indicted on several counts. He was convicted only on Count 11, which charged him with refusing to say whether nine named persons, all but one of whom he acknowledged that he knew, attended the meetings he attended. The court ruled that his refusal to answer that question was not privileged, because, in the court's opinion, an answer would not have subjected him to "any real danger of further incrimination."

I think the court erred. The privilege against self-incrimination protects a refusal to answer unless it is " '*perfectly clear*, from a careful consideration of all the circumstances in the case, that the witness is mistaken, and that the answer . . . *cannot possibly* have such tendency' to incriminate." *Hoffman* v. *United States*, 341 U.S. 479, 488 (Italics in original). For two distinct reasons, it is by no means "perfectly clear" that an answer to the question could not "possibly" have a "tendency to incriminate."

1. If appellant had answered in the affirmative, he would thereby have contributed directly to a "link in the chain of evidence needed in a prosecution . . . for violation of . . . the Smith Act." *Blau* v. *United States*, 340 U.S. 159, 161. The Smith Act makes it unlawful to be a member of a "society, group, or assembly of persons" who advocate overthrow of the government of the United States, or the government of any State, by force or violence, "knowing the purposes thereof." 54 Stat. 671, 62 Stat. 808, 18 U.S.C. § 2385. To convict a man under this section of the Act, the government would have to convince a jury (1) that there had been such a society, group, or assembly of persons, (2) that the defendant had been a member of it, and (3) that he had known its illegal purposes.

Testimony before the Committee had some tendency to show that the nine persons named in Count 11 had the purposes the Smith Act condemns. Five of the nine had testified that they had been Communist Party members. All nine had been publicly identified before the Committee as Communist Party members. One of the nine, Davis, had testified in effect that the members of the group to which Davis belonged were under strict Party control and were not mere rank-and-file Party members: "All the members used aliases on their cards, and the party membership of his group was kept secret from the rank-and-file members of the Communist Party . . . under instructions from the Communist Party." There was testimony that one of the nine persons named in Count 11 had been treasurer of the Harvard branch of the Party. One of the nine was actually under indictment for conspiring to advocate overthrow of the government of Massachusetts by force.

The fact that all this testimony was insufficient to convict anyone of anything is immaterial. Although Communist Party members, even if they are under strict Party control, and even if they are more than rank-and-file members, and even if they are under indictment, may have no purpose of overthrowing the government by force, the existence of a popular belief that they are much more likely than most people to have such a purpose is too notorious to be questioned or ignored. The premise that they may be innocent, and may never be prosecuted, is sound. But it does not support the conclusion that they are no more likely than ordinary people, or even ordinary "students of Marxism," to be prosecuted under the Smith Act.

The Smith Act term "society, group, or assembly of persons" is broad. It is not a term of art. It implies no more about the "persons" than that they repeatedly meet. If the nine persons named in Count 11 repeatedly met, they were members of a "society, group, or assembly of persons," and their membership had some tendency to show that the group had the purposes the Smith Act condemns. If appellant attended the meetings of such a "society, group, or assembly of persons," he also was a member of it. An affirmative answer to the question in Count 11 would therefore have tended to show both (1) that there had been the sort of group the Smith Act condemns and (2) that the appellant had been a member of it.

At the trial, the prosecutor said: "of course, it is going to incriminate Mr. Singer to admit that Struick, Amdur, and the rest were in his party. We don't say that is not incriminatory.

We say that he cannot avail himself of the silence with respect to it. Of course, he is going to be worse off. He is going to be far worse off. I concede that." This concession was fair and appropriate. No testimony the appellant had given was so incriminating as an affirmative answer to the question in Count 11 would have been. The Internal Security Act of 1950 provides that "Neither the holding of office nor membership in any Communist organization by any person shall constitute per se a violation . . . of this section or of any other criminal statute." 64 Stat. 992, 50 U.S.C. § 783(f). The appellant had not said, but an affirmative answer to the question in Count 11 would have said, that he had belonged to a group containing numerous Communists who were under strict Party control and were more than mere rank-and-file Party members, a group that contained an officer of a Communist organization, a group that even contained a person who was afterwards indicted for attempting to overthrow a government by force. The appellant testified that his group was autonomous. He testified he did not know Davis. He testified in effect that his group was simply one of the "Marxist study groups" which, according to Davis, were conducted by Communist Party "instructors." On this appeal the parties have stipulated that at appellant's trial, "Davis said one of the functions of his group was to conduct Marxist study groups. He said 'It was fairly easy to form them because at this time . . . there was lively interest in Marxism; and though I think persons joining these groups had some idea that the instructors were close to the Communist Party they, nevertheless, were ready to discuss Marxism with them, and in some cases actually the persons whom the party secured were not actually party members but were intellectual social scientists who knew a good deal about Marxism and were willing to discuss it before a group.'"

It does not matter whether the testimony the appellant had given is or is not regarded as having some incriminating tendency. Giving testimony that has some incriminating tendency does not obligate a witness to give other testimony that will subject him to a " 'real danger' of further crimination." . . .

2. The privilege against self-incrimination is not confined to testimony which tends directly to establish a fact the government would have to prove in a possible criminal prosecution of the witness. The privilege extends to testimony that might be used "to search out other testimony to be used in evidence against him . . . in a criminal proceeding. . . ." It extends to testimony that might lead to "the obtaining and the use of witnesses and evidence . . . on which he might be convicted. . . ." This is what the Supreme Court expressly held in *Counselman* v. *Hitchcock*, 142 U.S. 547, 564. It seems to me clear that *Counselman* v. *Hitchcock* covers this case and requires us to reverse the present conviction. I know of no argument to the contrary.

If the appellant had told the Committee that the persons named in Count 11 attended the meetings he attended, it might have enabled the government to "search out" from them, and also concerning them, evidence that could be used against him. It might have led to "the obtaining and the use of witnesses and evidence . . . on which he might be convicted . . ." either (1) of violating the Smith Act, or (2) of perjury in the testimony he had previously given the Committee. It would certainly have tended to validate any testimony against him which any of the persons named in Count 11 might give. Though the appellant had attributed an innocent character to his group, it did not follow that the government would not be able, in a prosecution under the Smith Act, to convince a jury that his group was not what he said it was but actually advocated overthrow of the government by force. It did not follow that the government would not be able, in a prosecution for perjury, to convince a jury that he had given the Committee testimony which was false and which he knew to be false.

The prosecutor recognized the fact that if the appellant had said the persons named in Count 11 attended the meetings he attended, it might have enabled the government to get from them evidence that would incriminate him. The prosecutor recognized the importance of this fact. In arguing a motion preliminary to appellant's trial, he said: "the committee surely had the right to inquire into whether or not he was telling the committee the truth when he made [his] denial of subversion, and in doing so to find who was there who would either refute it or affirm it."

I do not imply that I think appellant's other contentions unsound.

"The Right to Be Informed of the Nature and Causes of the Accusations; to Be Confronted with the Witnesses against Him"

The right to know all the charges against one and to confront and cross-examine adverse witnesses has long been fully established and protected so far as criminal trials are concerned. The Federal Rules of Criminal Procedure have extended this right to preliminary proceedings before a Commissioner, and they also permit examination before trial of much of the adverse documentary evidence. Recently the courts have ruled that a defendant must be permitted to see the statements made to the FBI by witnesses who appear against him, and Congress has passed a law confirming this right but restricting it to statements that bear on the testimony given in open court. Administrative tribunals, on the other hand, have asserted the right to refuse to produce confidential informants or to disclose confidential information that is the basis of adverse decisions as to fitness for various licensed businesses and professions, as well as for government employment and work on government contracts.

Since 1947 when President Truman issued the first order requiring all government employees to be investigated to determine their loyalty to the United States Government, the use of loyalty tests has spread until now about one-fifth of the total working force of the United States is subject to such tests. Disqualification for one job may mean that none in the same field of work will be open even though no government contracts are involved. The question whether the Due Process Clause of the Constitution is violated when so great an injury is inflicted on an individual on the basis of undisclosed information is being widely debated. The Supreme Court has had the issue before it. In several cases it has reversed the decision of an administrative body on the ground that procedures followed by it were irregular or unauthorized. So far, however, it has not dealt with the constitutional question.

IN THE MATTER OF JOHN W. CARTER

Decided January 18, 1951

Before EDGERTON, CLARK, and PRETTYMAN,
Circuit Judges

On November 18, 1947, a judge of the District Court for the District of Columbia granted John W. Carter a license to engage for two years in the bonding business in the District. This action involved a finding that Carter was morally and financially qualified to act as a bondsman. About a month later the same judge revoked Carter's license in order to investigate further the question of Carter's moral fitness.

A report was turned in to the judge by the FBI. It was kept secret, but on the basis of it four judges of the District Court, on

June 8, 1948, denied Carter's application. The Court of Appeals reversed their decision on the ground that, in revoking a license already granted without disclosing the contents of the FBI report which was the basis of their adverse judgment, the judges had deprived Carter of property without due process of law. On December 12, 1949, the Supreme Court refused to review the decision of the Court of Appeals.

The next day the judges of the District Court, without a hearing and still without disclosure of the contents of the FBI report, denied Carter's application for a *renewal* of his license. Carter again appealed. The case was heard by a division of three judges of the Court of Appeals. In a 2 to 1 decision the Court of Appeals again reversed the District Court.

Six months later a petition for a rehearing in banc was granted. This time the Solicitor General as *amicus curiae* argued on behalf of the judges of the District Court. Seven judges of the Court of Appeals sat in the case and by a 4 to 3 decision affirmed the judgment of the division.

EDGERTON, *Circuit Judge:* An Act of Congress declares that "The business of becoming surety for compensation upon bonds in criminal cases in the District of Columbia is impressed with a public interest." D.C. Code (1940) § 23-602. It requires the District Court and other trial courts "to provide, under reasonable rules and regulations, the qualifications of persons and corporations applying for authority to engage" in this business, and provides that no one shall engage in it "in any such court until he shall by order of the court be authorized to do so. Such courts, in making such rules and regulations, and in granting authority to persons to engage in the bonding business, shall take into consideration both the financial responsibility and the moral qualities of the person so applying, and no person shall be permitted to engage, either as principal or agent, in the business of becoming surety upon bonds for compensation in criminal cases, who has ever been convicted of any offense involving moral turpitude, or who is not known to be a person of good moral character . . ." D.C. Code (1940) § 23-608.

In 1947 the District Court licensed appellant Carter to engage in the bonding business for two years. It revoked his license in 1948, after learning that in applying for it he had sworn that he had "never been charged and/or convicted of any offense involving moral turpitude" whereas actually, many years before, he had been charged once with receiving stolen property and three times with violations of the gambling laws. He had never been convicted, or even brought to trial, and under the court's rules about license applications the fact that he had been charged was immaterial. Applicants were required to state whether they had been convicted, but not whether they had been charged. Appellant did not misrepresent any fact about which he was asked. Moreover, he did not intentionally misrepresent any fact whatever. As the District Court found, such misrepresentation as he made "was not made willfully or with a purpose to deceive the Court, but was made on the advice of counsel who informed the petitioner that the language used would not constitute a misrepresentation." The court revoked appellant's license despite these favorable findings, and regarded his application as pending. It obtained a report from the F.B.I. which is not before us. The court did not put the report in the record or even disclose its contents to counsel but "placed it in a sealed envelope, not to be opened." Six months later the court denied appellant's application. On appeal we held the revocation invalid for lack of "a hearing and revelation of all data upon which a decision is to be based." We held that whatever might be true of the grant of the right to engage in the bonding business, "the deprivation of that right, once granted, is a judicial act, requiring due process of law." *In re Carter*, 177 F. 2d 75.

When appellant's license expired he applied for its renewal. His application was verified and was supported by affidavits of good moral character. It conformed to all the rules and regulations of the District Court. The record before that court showed without dispute that the appellant has the qualifications for a bondsman. Yet the District Court denied his application "on the ground that in the opinion of the Court he lacks the qualifications for a bondsman." The present appeal is from that order.

The District Court did not disclose what qualification it believed appellant lacked. Against the background of the sealed envelope its present action seems, as its former action seemed, to imply a belief that appellant's character is not good. It did not disclose the source of its belief. It said appellant's application was "in the administrative discretion of the Court." From that premise it seems to have drawn the conclusion that it could deny the application without a hearing, without evidence, and without possibility of review to determine whether its discretion was abused. On this appeal the Solicitor General as *amicus curiae* takes substantially the same position. Though some of the language in our opinion on the former appeal may seem to support this position, we think it erroneous.

In re Summers, 325 U.S. 561, involved an order of the Supreme Court of Illinois which had denied the application of Summers for admission to the practice of law. The Illinois court regarded its order as "ministerial," like the appointment of a clerk or bailiff, but the Supreme Court of the United States held it "a judgment in a judicial proceeding" (p. 566) and subject to review on certiorari. The Supreme Court said: "A claim of a present right to admission to the bar of a state and a denial of that right is a controversy. When . . . denial of the right is made by judicial order, it is a case which may be reviewed . . ." 325 U.S. at 568–569.

In *Carver* v. *Clephane* we affirmed an order of the District Court dismissing a complaint for admission to the bar. We pointed out that the order was entered "after a hearing." *Carver* v. *Clephane*, 137 F. 2d 685. It was based on a finding against the applicant's character. The record supported the finding.

Despite the differences between a lawyer's profession and a bondsman's business, they are alike in all the respects that seem even remotely or possibly pertinent to the question whether a court's order denying a license is judicial. Both differ from some occupations in that they plainly require good moral character, and from most occupations in that they are carried on in connection with courts and require licenses from courts. But both lawyers and bondsmen are on quite a different footing from a court's clerk or bailiff. They are not completely under a court's control, or obligated to deal with the public impartially; within wide limits they may choose how, when, where and whom they will serve. They are not commonly paid from public funds, their callings are not necessarily limited to a single person or to a few persons, and they cannot be deprived of their functions in a court's discretion. Since a court's order denying an application to practice law is a judicial act, as the Supreme Court determined in the *Summers* case, so is a court's order denying an application to do business as a bondsman. Since the District Court's order is judicial it is (1) appealable and (2) erroneous because not based "upon a proceeding which contains the elements of due process of law, i.e., a hearing and revelation of all data upon which a decision is to be based." *In re Carter*, 177 F. 2d 75. Old charges never brought to trial, and appellant's innocent mistake of fact on an immaterial matter, do not support the order. Neither do any secret charges that may have been made by anonymous informants whom the appellant has had no opportunity to confront and cross-examine.

The idea that this decision means courts must grade examination papers is erroneous. Expert opinion properly before a court on a technical question, such as the extent of an applicant's professional ability as shown by an examination, is of course a proper basis for either judicial or administrative action. A court is under no more obligation to form a judgment independently of expert opinion about an applicant's knowledge of law than about his knowledge of medicine or pharmacy. But no qualification of a bondsman appears to turn on technical questions requiring expert opinion. Certainly character does not. And the record contains no opinion unfavorable to the appellant except the District Court's own.

We do not imply that in our opinion the appealed order would be valid if it were administrative. Like the order involved in Carter's previous appeal, if it were upheld it would destroy an established business. We do not imply that in our opinion a purely administrative refusal to renew, or to grant, a license to do a lawful business could be supported if based on arbitrary ground or made without such a "hearing and opportunity to answer . . . as would constitute due process." *Goldsmith* v. *Board of Tax Appeals*, 270 U.S. 117, 123.

HOMER BROOKS

v.

BOLITHO LAWS

Decided June 26, 1953

Before STEPHENS, *Chief Judge,* and EDGERTON
and PRETTYMAN, *Circuit Judges*

The Committee on Admissions for the District Court of the District of Columbia rejected the application of Homer Brooks for admission to the bar of that court and after reconsideration affirmed its original action. About a year later Brooks filed a motion in the District Court asking for further reconsideration by the court and an order admitting him to the bar. He received a letter telling him that the judges had considered his application in executive session and sustained the action of the Committee. The court then denied him the right to file a motion of appeal, on the ground that the action taken by the judges was purely ministerial, not judicial. Brooks then asked the Court of Appeals for leave to file a complaint asking that court to order the District Court to hear his appeal. His motion was denied, on the ground that rejection of an application for admission to the bar is not appealable because it is not a judicial decision and involves no case or controversy. The court supported this position in part by citing the practice of basing decisions as to an applicant's suitability on materials gathered in a confidential inquiry rather than on evidence placed on the record.

EDGERTON, *Circuit Judge, concurring in the result:* As the court points out near the end of its opinion, Brooks made no attempt to appeal within the time fixed by the Federal Rules of Civil Procedure. We should therefore deny his present motion. Moreover it is, as the court says, "obvious that Brooks failed, in the papers he filed with the District Court, to show that he was entitled to admission to the bar of that court . . ." He showed he was not entitled. Therefore an appeal, even if promptly filed, would have been dismissed on motion. This is a second reason why we should deny Brooks's present motion. Accordingly we have no occasion to consider the question the court discusses and answers in the negative, "whether rejection by the District Court of an application for admission to its bar is a decision within the meaning of Section 1291 of Title 28 of the United States Code" and is therefore appealable. What the court says on this subject appears to me to be dictum rather than decision. But lest it be followed in future cases I think it should not go unanswered.

The Supreme Court has held recently, expressly, and without qualification that "A claim of a present right to admission to the bar of a state and a denial of that right is a controversy." *In re Summers*, 325 U.S. 561, 568 (1945). No one suggests that there is a difference in this respect between the bar of a state and the bar of the District Court. Yet this court says it is "holding

. . . that an application for admission to the bar is not a case, cause or controversy, that the rejection of an applicant . . . is not a decision . . ."

The Supreme Court reviewed, as the decision of a controversy, the Illinois court's refusal to admit Summers to the Illinois bar. The Supreme Court was indeed concerned with "the circumstances of the refusal" but only for a reason that has nothing to do with the present case. Whether a final decision of a state court may or may not be reviewed in the Supreme Court depends upon circumstances. Accordingly the Court said: "For the purpose of determining whether the action of the Supreme Court of Illinois in denying Summers' petition for an order for admission to practice law in Illinois is a judgment in a judicial proceeding which involves a case or controversy *reviewable in this Court* under Article III, § 2, Cl. 1, of the Constitution of the United States, we must for ourselves appraise *the circumstances of the refusal.*" 325 U.S. at 566. (Emphasis supplied.) To like effect, immediately after the Court's unqualified statement that "A claim of a present right to admission to the bar of a state and a denial of that right is a controversy" the Court said: "When the claim is made in a state court and a denial of the right is made by judicial order, it is a case which *may be reviewed* under Article III of the Constitution *when federal questions are raised* and proper steps taken to that end, *in this Court.*" 325 U.S. at 568–569. (Emphasis supplied.)

This court treats the proposition (1) that circumstances determine whether a controversy over a claimed present right to admission to a state bar is reviewable by the Supreme Court, as if it meant (2) that circumstances determine whether denial of a claimed right to admission to a bar creates a controversy. But these two propositions are distinct, and the second does not follow from the first. This court suggests no technical, practical, or other reason for the second proposition. Moreover the Supreme Court, so far from announcing or suggesting the second proposition, contradicted it in the *Summers* case by stating categorically that a denial of a claimed present right to admission "is a controversy."

This court emphasizes the fact that the District Court's refusal to admit Brooks was not by formal order but by letter. It overlooks the fact that the Illinois court's refusal to admit Summers was not by formal order but by letter. 325 U.S. at 564. This court takes precisely the view the Illinois court took of the question whether such a refusal is an administrative matter or a judicial decision of a controversy. The Supreme Court took the opposite view of that question. This court quotes as if it were a statement of the Supreme Court's own view what I understand to be merely the Supreme Court's statement of the Illinois view, *i.e.* that the matter is administrative. The Supreme Court recognized that the Illinois decision would have ended the controversy but for the fact that the particular "circumstances of the refusal" to admit Summers made the decision reviewable in the Supreme Court. But that is irrelevant here, since all final decisions of the District Court are reviewable in this court or the Supreme Court and all decisions of this court are reviewable in the Supreme Court.

The *Summers* doctrine is not new. As long ago as 1866 the Supreme Court said, in discussing the admission of attorneys, "Their admission or their exclusion is not the exercise of a mere ministerial power. It is the exercise of judicial power, and has been so held in numerous cases." *Ex parte Garland,* 71 U.S. 333, 378–379. The Court cited with approval *Matter of Cooper,* 22 N.Y. 81 (1860), in which the New York Court of Appeals held that a trial court's order denying an application for admission to the bar was appealable, found error, and reversed.

In *Carver* v. *Clephane,* 137 F. 2d 685 (1943), the District Court, after a hearing, had dismissed a complaint that sought to require its Committee on Admissions and Grievances to certify Carver for admission to the District Court's bar. Carver ap-

pealed to this court. We considered and affirmed the validity of
the District Court's order denying Carver's claimed right to admission to the bar. We thereby gave an affirmative answer to the
question whether such an order is appealable.

The court says "the whole purport of admission to the bar in
this country, and in this jurisdiction, and in our own court, is
that the Committee and the court can inquire into the applicant's
character by confidential inquiry . . ." This seems to imply
that applicants may be finally rejected on the basis of secret attacks on their character by secret informants. I think the law is
otherwise. A report on Admission of Attorneys from Other
Jurisdictions, prepared by Goscoe O. Farley, Secretary of the
Committee of Bar Examiners of the State Bar of California, for
the Survey of the Legal Profession and published in BAR EX-
AMINATIONS AND REQUIREMENTS FOR ADMISSION TO THE BAR
(1952), seems to show that the prevailing practice in this country is not what this court supposes. The report says (pp. 161–
162): "the applicant who has never been convicted of a crime
or disciplined by a grievance committee, but nevertheless is
known to be an unethical practitioner by his fellow lawyers,
often is able to get his application accepted by the examining
board. There are several reasons for this. In the first place, the
information obtained by The National Conference of Bar Examiners is confidential (it needs to be so, else many sources of
information would be closed to it) and hence occasionally an
examining board will have derogatory information about an
applicant, and not be able to use it. This insufficiency can sometimes be overcome by skillful interrogation of the applicant so
as to get him to admit the wrongdoing, or by proving it through
another (not confidential) source." The Supreme Court said in
1866: "Attorneys . . . are officers of the court, admitted as
such by its order, upon evidence of their possessing sufficient
legal learning and fair private character. It has been the general

practice in this country to obtain this evidence by an examination of the parties." *Ex parte Garland*, 71 U.S. 333, 378.

I agree with this court that if, as I think, the District Court's rejection of petitioner's application was a judicial decision it should have been made upon a record of evidence presented in open court. But I disagree with the court's statement that if the rejection is appealable this court must assume the burden of evaluating qualifications for admission to the bar of the District Court. This seems to me as erroneous as it would be to say that if the District Court's denial of a claim in contract or tort is appealable this court must assume the burden of evaluating the evidence in such cases. Our function is not to retry cases but to determine whether in our opinion the trial court followed the law.

When secret informants have made secret charges against an applicant possibly a Committee on Admissions may decline to recommend his admission, for its action is not final if he chooses to take his application to court. But for a court finally to reject an applicant because of secret charges by secret informants would be as shocking as to disbar a lawyer, or convict a man of crime, on such charges. By innocent mistake or incompetence or carelessness or malice a confidential informant may make false charges. Elementary fairness and therefore due process of law forbid finally rejecting, on grounds of character, an otherwise qualified applicant without allowing him a public opportunity to confront his accusers and refute their charges. The right to a public hearing is also a necessary safeguard against rejection because of charges which are true but irrelevant, e.g. that an applicant has unconventional social, political, or economic views.

"*The Assistance of Counsel for His Defense*"

Before 1938 the judicial attitude toward the right to counsel in criminal cases was at times somewhat perfunctory. A mumbled question by the judge as to the accused's wishes in the matter might be treated as sufficient notice of the right, and a failure to request counsel as a waiver. In that year, in *Johnson v. Zerbst*, 304 U.S. 458, the Supreme Court ruled that the right is a substantive one and that it is the duty of the judge to determine whether a waiver is made with full understanding and by a person competent to deal with the question. Since then the right has been steadily expanded. The Federal Rules of Criminal Procedure now provide that an accused person is entitled to counsel at a preliminary hearing and at arraignment. The Court of Appeals for the District of Columbia had taken this position even before the rules were adopted, and in the case of *Johnson v. United States* it was the first federal court in the country to find that the right has not been accorded when assigned counsel proves to be grossly incompetent.

WILLIAM F. JOHNSON

v.

UNITED STATES OF AMERICA

Decided February 28, 1940

Before GRONER, *Chief Judge*, and EDGERTON
and RUTLEDGE, *JJ.*

EDGERTON, *J.:* Appellant Johnson shot and killed George Scandalis on December 18, 1938. He was convicted of first degree murder and sentenced to death. He moved for a new trial on the ground, among others, of newly discovered evidence. The District Court overruled the motion.

Johnson, a colored laborer 22 years old, worked in a bakery. George Scandalis was his foreman. On December 17, 1938, Scandalis discharged Johnson. On December 18 Johnson returned to the plant, ostensibly to learn why he had been discharged. Scandalis, a strong man heavier than Johnson, seized him and put him out. Some 30 or 45 minutes later Johnson returned to the bakery and shot Scandalis. Eye-witnesses testified variously that Scandalis was retreating, standing still, and coming forward; but no one who testified at the trial, except appellant himself, saw anything menacing in the conduct or appearance of Scandalis. Johnson and Scandalis were said to be five or six, or eight, feet apart when Scandalis was shot. Appellant alone testified that "He was coming toward me to jump on me again." The court was scrupulously fair to appellant, and charged the jury on self-defense and on manslaughter, but the total lack of corroboration of appellant made his story hopeless. At the trial it appeared to be, as the court later said that it was, "evident that Scandalis' movement from the oven room had nothing to do with defendant."

Robert Thomas was an eye-witness of the shooting. He testified at the coroner's inquest, and was on the list of witnesses which the government furnished to appellant's counsel, but he was not called at the trial. The government tried without success to locate him. Presumably appellant's counsel assumed he would be produced. After conviction they got from Thomas an affidavit which stated that at the time of the shooting George Scandalis "was advancing toward Johnson in a menacing manner. . . . When George came to a point about three or four feet from Johnson he made a lunge for Johnson and a shot was fired." The court thereupon held a hearing and examined Thomas. It appeared at this hearing that appellant's counsel, who drew the affadavit, and Thomas had misunderstood each other; for Thomas testified that Scandalis made his lunge after Johnson's first shot, though before his second. But Thomas insisted that Scandalis, before the shooting began, advanced toward Johnson "in a menacing manner." He testified that "Scandalis came from the oven room and started toward this boy Johnson, and I could see he was pretty mad." He testified that Johnson had stopped, Scandalis was going toward him, and the men were only two or three feet apart, when the first shot was fired. The court asked Thomas what he meant by "a menacing manner," and he replied: "Well, the look on his face. I think he was still mad at the first encounter he had with Johnson." Thomas also testified that "he was putting him out, there's no doubt about it. . . . George started toward Johnson and I knew there was going to be trouble." At the end of the hearing the court said: "Whether it was a menacing manner depends on whether or not he was walking toward him in such a manner. He has described that George's actions did indicate that. . . . He went forward toward Johnson and walked up close to him and went right toward him, when the shot was fired." Thomas confirmed this paraphrase of his testimony.

The court found that this testimony, "instead of helping defendant, tends strongly to corroborate in a general way the testimony presented by the government at the trial." The court's action in overruling the motion for a new trial was plainly based, in part, on this finding. We think the finding and the consequent ruling were erroneous. If Thomas's testimony had been given at the trial it would have furnished substantial support, which without it was wholly lacking, for appellant's claim that he shot Scandalis because of fear induced by a fresh assault. It therefore called for a new trial. The testimony, if believed, was calculated to raise in the minds of the jury a reasonable doubt whether appellant was guilty of murder in the first degree.

The government says that, even if this be conceded, Thomas's testimony was, in the exercise of due diligence, available to the defense at the trial and therefore ought not to be considered after conviction. We think this does not follow. The experienced counselor who represents appellant here did not represent him at the trial. Accused was a colored boy without funds or other means to employ counsel of his own selection, and the court appointed two attorneys to defend him. The defense was conducted by one of them and another member of the bar. These attorneys did not examine the transcript of the testimony taken at the inquest. After the trial, they filed no brief in this court within the time allowed by the rules. The trial court finally asked present counsel to represent the defendant on this appeal. In the circumstances the failure of counsel to produce all available evidence, in a case involving the life of the accused, should not be held against him. It would be a strange system of law which first assigned inexperienced or negligent counsel in a capital case and then made counsel's neglect a ground for refusing a new trial. The right to counsel is not formal, but substantial. It is hard to ask experienced counsel, of proved ability, to serve in cases of this sort without compensation; but the rights of poor persons can be protected in no other way until systematic provision is made for their defense.

RICHARD B. McJORDAN

v.

RAY L. HUFF

Decided February 1, 1943

Before GRONER, *Chief Judge,* and VINSON and
EDGERTON, *Associate Justices*

Richard B. McJordan was indicted for housebreaking and pleaded guilty on November 24, 1941. He was sentenced on December 5.

The following July he filed a petition for a writ of habeas corpus on the ground that he had not had counsel at the time of his arraignment and plea of guilty. The writ was denied, and he appealed.

The opinion of the Court of Appeals sums up the facts of the case as follows:

> The evidence taken below shows that when appellant was arrested he made a written confession to the police; that upon his subsequent arraignment in the District Court upon the indictment, he pleaded guilty; that he was reasonably familiar with court procedure and knew of his right to demand the assignment of counsel to defend him, but asked for no such assignment; that the Judge thereupon, on the same day, referred his case to one of the Probation Commissioners for investigation and report and appointed attorney Guervitz to represent him. The latter immediately obtained a copy of the indictment and interviewed appellant while he was still in the court building, advising him that he had been appointed by the court as his attorney; that he knew of his plea of guilty and the reference of his case to the probation department, but that he would like to talk to him to be sure that he was pleading exactly as he should; and that if the facts in his case did not justify his pleading guilty, he would at once ask to have the plea changed. Appellant replied that he was guilty, and described his part in the housebreaking and larceny which the indictment charged. As a result counsel concluded that it was inadvisable to apply to the court to have the plea of guilty set aside. Some ten days later appellant was brought into court and sentenced, at which proceeding his attorney was present.

The District Court concluded, in view of these facts, that McJordan had had the advice of counsel guaranteed to him by the Constitution. The Court of Appeals sustained the lower court in a 2 to 1 decision.

EDGERTON, *J., dissenting:* Appellant was entitled to counsel at his preliminary hearing, and again when he was arraigned on his indictment. He had none. It is undisputed that he had no counsel until after he had pleaded guilty. The question is whether he waived his right. He did not waive it unless he knew of it and intelligently chose not to enforce it. " 'Courts indulge every reasonable presumption against waiver.' " *Johnson* v. *Zerbst*, 304 U.S. 458, 464. It has been strongly intimated that the court must inform the accused of his right and ascertain his attitude.

There is no finding or evidence that appellant chose, intelligently or otherwise, not to enforce his right to counsel. There is no finding that he knew he had such a right. He knew that, despite his plea of guilty, he could have counsel before conviction and sentence, but there is no clear evidence that he knew he could have counsel before plea. If he knew it, he knew what was widely unknown in this jurisdiction until later, when the *Evans* and *Wood* cases were decided.

Counsel appointed after arraignment may have been less inclined to substitute a not guilty plea for a guilty plea already entered than he would have been to plead not guilty had he been in the case from the start; especially since appellant had pleaded guilty on preliminary hearing as well as on arraignment, and it was widely thought that a plea of guilty on preliminary hearing was competent evidence against the accused on his trial. But we cannot know and need not guess whether appellant was injured by having no counsel in the early stages of his prosecution. "The right to have the assistance of counsel is too fundamental and absolute to allow courts to indulge in nice calculations as to the amount of prejudice arising from its denial." "Compliance with this constitutional mandate is an essential jurisdictional prerequisite to a federal court's authority to deprive an accused of his life or liberty." *Johnson* v. *Zerbst*, 304 U.S. 458, 467.

WILLIAM M. WILLIAMS

v.

RAY L. HUFF

Decided April 7, 1944

Before GRONER, *Chief Judge,* and EDGERTON and
ARNOLD, *JJ.*

EDGERTON, *J.:* This appeal is from an order discharging a writ
of habeas corpus upon consideration of the petition and the answer. In 1941 petitioner pleaded guilty to an indictment which
charged assault with a dangerous weapon. According to the record of the trial court he was advised of his constitutional right
to counsel, was asked whether he desired counsel, and replied
that he did not. He was sentenced to imprisonment for two to
six years. He says that he was then seventeen years old.

Appellant's petition for habeas corpus, prepared without the
aid of counsel, states: "I am filing petition for Writ of Habeas
Corpus on the grounds that I was not represented by counsel
during my trial; no one asked me if I wished counsel to represent
me; taking advise from layman that: if I pleaded guilty I would
receive probation, and being ignorant of law I pleaded guilty,
without the assistance of counsel and received my present
term . . ."

Facts of record with regard to what occurred at a trial cannot
be attacked on habeas corpus. The record shows that appellant
was informed of his right to counsel and undertook to waive the
right. But the record does not show that the waiver was competent and intelligent. Appellant says in effect that it was not. This
issue must be decided, for if a person charged with crime "is not
represented by counsel and has not competently and intelligently
waived his constitutional right, the Sixth Amendment stands as a

jurisdictional bar to a valid conviction and sentence depriving him of his life or his liberty. . . ." A plea of guilty creates no exception to this rule. *Johnson* v. *Zerbst*, 304 U.S. 458, 468.

"In deference to common experience, there is general recognition of the fact that many persons by reason of their youth are incapable of intelligent decision, as the result of which public policy demands legal protection of their personal as well as their property rights. The universal law, therefore, is that a minor cannot be held liable on his personal contracts or contracts for the disposition of his property." *Bonner* v. *Moran*, 126 F. 2d 121. In the case just quoted we held that a boy of fifteen cannot give valid consent to a surgical operation. The marriage of a boy of seventeen may be annulled. A boy under twenty-one cannot make a valid will. When a minor is a defendant in a mere civil suit, the court must appoint a guardian *ad litem* for him and also, if in the court's opinion his interests require that he have counsel, must assign him counsel regardless of his own opinion on that point. Because the interests of society must be protected boys of seventeen are held competent, with certain limitations, to commit crimes and torts. But they are held incompetent, with few or no limitations, to protect their own interests in assuming legal obligations or defending legal rights.

It seems to me to follow as a matter of law that a boy of seventeen cannot competently waive his right to counsel in a criminal case. In saying this I do not speak for the court.

In the view of the majority of the court appellant's competence was a question of fact, in the determination of which his youth was entitled to serious consideration but was not necessarily conclusive. It follows that the District Court should take evidence and determine whether, in the light of his age, education, and information, and all other pertinent facts, he has sustained the burden of proving that his waiver was not competent and intelligent.

"An Impartial Jury"

HERBERT V. HALL

v.

UNITED STATES OF AMERICA

Decided April 5, 1948

Before EDGERTON, CLARK, and WILBUR K. MILLER,
Associate Justices

The constitutional requirement of an impartial jury in criminal trials—extended to the states through the Equal Protection Clause of the Fourteenth Amendment—has proved to be an important weapon in the Negro's long struggle for emancipation from the discrimination that has followed his emancipation from slavery. In 1875 Congress made it illegal to bar Negroes on grounds of race from jury service in any federal court. In 1880, in the case of *Strauder* v. *West Virginia*, 100 U.S. 303, the Supreme Court ruled that to do so in the trial of a Negro violated the constitutional right to an impartial jury. At the same time, in the case of *Virginia* v. *Rives*, 100 U.S. 313, the Court declared that a Negro is not entitled to have a member of his race sit on the particular jury that is trying him. Ingenious subterfuges have been devised to avoid compliance with the requirement but, at least since the decision of the Court in *Norris* v. *Alabama*, 294 U.S. 587, the courts have looked beyond the form to the reality to see whether the right has been denied "in substance and effect."

Three Negroes, Herbert Hall, Shirley Harris, and John M. Gray, decided to commit a holdup in the District of Columbia. They got possession of a revolver and the necessary bullets and found their victim waiting at a car stop. One of them fired the fatal shot. At the moment Herbert Hall had lagged behind a short distance. All three were convicted of murder in the first degree and sentenced to death. At the trial the prosecution eliminated all Negroes from the jury by the exercise of nineteen of its twenty peremptory challenges. Similarly, Hall's counsel used his peremptory challenges only against white members on the panel, but the result was an all-white jury. Hall claimed that his right under the Fifth Amendment had been violated by exclusion of Negroes from the jury and appealed his conviction on this ground. The Court of Appeals rejected this contention, taking the position that the requirements of due process were met when there was no discrimination in the selection of the whole panel from which the particular jury was chosen.

Judge Edgerton dissented. He began his opinion with a series of quotations from cases dealing with the requirement of an impartial jury. The rest of the opinion follows.

EDGERTON, J., *dissenting:* . . . The quoted cases involved systematic exclusion of Negroes or other groups from jury lists or panels. But the spirit and purpose as well as the letter of those cases forbid systematic exclusion of Negroes from a jury that tries Negroes. The rule against excluding Negroes from the panel has no value if all who get on the panel may be systematically kept off the jury. The government impliedly admits that all Negroes were systematically excluded from the jury that tried the Negro appellants. Nineteen Negroes and no other persons were challenged peremptorily by the government. Whether this discrimination against Negroes did or did not violate the Act of Congress I think it violated the plainly expressed policy of Congress, the plainly expressed policy of the Supreme Court, the prosecutor's obligation of fairness, and the due process clause of the Fifth Amendment. These principles, which the court overlooks, collide with the principle on which the court relies. The question is whether they limit it or it limits them.

In other respects I concur in the opinion of the court. The trial was otherwise fair and a properly chosen jury would doubtless have convicted the appellants. But "reversible error does not depend on a showing of prejudice in an individual case. The evil lies in the admitted exclusion of an eligible class or group in the community in disregard of the prescribed standards of jury selection. . . . The injury is not limited to the defendant—there is injury to the jury system, to the law as an institution, to the community at large, and to the democratic ideal reflected in the processes of our courts." *Ballard* v. *United States*, 329 U.S. 187, 195. I believe the prosecutor's unfortunate error makes a new trial necessary.

GERHARD EISLER

v.

UNITED STATES OF AMERICA

Decided April 18, 1949

Before EDGERTON, CLARK, and WILBUR K. MILLER,
Circuit Judges

Under the common law an employee could be challenged for cause if he was called as a juror in a case in which his master was a party. For many years this rule was applied in the District of Columbia to bar government employees from serving as jurors in cases in which the United States Government was a party. As the proportion of inhabitants working for the Federal Government increased in the District, the work of the courts piled up, and the rule made it difficult to get enough qualified jurors. In 1935 Congress passed a law to permit government employees to serve even when the Government is a party to the suit. The first case involving this issue to reach the Supreme Court was that of Robert Frazier, who was convicted under the Harrison Narcotics Act by a jury composed entirely of government employees, two of whom served in the Treasury Department that administered the Act. Frazier moved for a new trial on the ground of presumed rather than actual bias on the part of the jurors. The Court, in a 5 to 4 decision, rejected his contention. Special circumstances as to the manner of the selection of the jurors in his case apparently weighed heavily in the Court's decision so that the case was not considered conclusive as to the propriety of using government employees as jurors under all circumstances.

The question was again raised by Eugene Dennis in appealing from his conviction for contempt of Congress in defying the Un-American Activities Committee. He was overruled by the Court of Appeals on the authority of the *Frazier* case. *Frazier* v. *United States*, 335 U.S. 497.

Shortly after the *Dennis* case, the court had to deal with the same issue in connection with the appeal of Gerhard Eisler. Eisler was indicted in the District of Columbia in 1947 for making false statements in an application to the Secretary of State for permission to leave the United States, a necessary step under wartime regulations for the control of aliens. By the time his case came to trial, Mr. Eisler had become notorious as a result of the investigations of the Un-American Activities Committee. He was quite generally believed to be a high-ranking agent of the Comintern, sent to the United States for the purpose of furthering the Communist activities here. The indictment itself and the bill of particulars which followed it were specific as to his alleged long record of Communist activities in several countries in Europe. His sister, Ruth Fisher, had given damaging testimony against him before the Committee. At his trial he moved to exclude all government employees from the jury. The motion was denied. He appealed, and his conviction was affirmed by a 2 to 1 decision, Judge Edgerton dissenting.

Shortly after the case was decided in the Court of Appeals, Eisler fled from the country on the Polish steamer *Batory*, found asylum in the Russian Zone of Germany, and for a while held an important post under the Communist government there. His case, therefore, was never acted upon by the Supreme Court.

When the *Dennis* case reached the Supreme Court, it was decided,

in a 5 to 1 opinion, that government employees could be excluded
in Communist cases, but only for actual bias discovered by appropriate questioning and not for presumed bias. *Dennis* v. *United
States,* 339 U.S. 162.

Judge Edgerton began his opinion with a brief statement that the
case should have been tried in New York, where the statements in
question were mailed.

EDGERTON, *J., dissenting:* . . .

In my opinion an added reason for reversal is that the court
permitted three employees of the United States to serve as jurors.

The indictment shows that its paragraph (A) deals with question 23 of the application, (B) with 18, and (C) with 7. This
transposition makes it the head and front of the indictment that
the appellant's answer "None" to question 23 was fraudulent in
that he "had been and was then a member of and was affiliated
with the Communist Party." The indictment does not allege that
he was a most important and disruptive Communist, but this was
urged throughout the trial. The prosecutor in his opening statement told the jury that the appellant "was a representative of the
Comintern" and "that his real purpose for coming to this country . . . was the purpose of disrupting the economy of the
United States, to further the ends of Moscow." There was testimony that he had been "the head of the Comintern" and was to
direct the Communist Party in this country. He was represented
as having taken a leading part in Communist activities here and
abroad. The prosecutor in his closing argument told the jury that
the appellant was "anti Government."

Government employment alone does not disqualify a juror in
a prosecution for larceny, *United States* v. *Wood,* 299 U.S. 123,
or violation of the narcotics laws. *Frazier* v. *United States,* 335
U.S. 497. But government employment is not commonly known
to be endangered by sympathetic association with thieves or drug

peddlers. It is commonly known to be endangered by sympathetic association with Communists. Government employees are therefore anxious, in various degrees according to their temper and circumstances, to avoid seeming to sympathize with Communists. Acquittal sometimes indicates, and is often thought to indicate, that the jury sympathized with the accused. It is therefore prudent for government employees to convict an alleged Communist and imprudent to acquit him. For government employees to acquit this alleged Communist leader would have been particularly imprudent. Trial by jurors whose personal security will either actually or apparently be promoted by conviction and endangered by acquittal is not "trial by an impartial jury" and is not due process of law.

Even in the narcotics case four members of the Supreme Court dissented. They said concerning government employees: "Of late years, the Government is using its power as never before to pry into their lives and thoughts upon the slightest suspicion of less than complete trustworthiness. It demands not only probity but unquestioning ideological loyalty. A government employee cannot today be disinterested or unconcerned about his appearance of faithful and enthusiastic support . . . Even if we have no reason to believe that an acquitting juror would be subjected to embarrassments or reprisals, we cannot expect every clerk and messenger in the great bureaucracy to feel so secure as to put his dependence on the Government wholly out of mind. I do not doubt that the government employees as a class possess a normal independence and fortitude. But we have grounds to assume also that the normal proportion of them are subject to that very human weakness . . . which leads men to '. . . crook the pregnant hinges of the knee where thrift may follow fawning.' " *Frazier* v. *United States*, 335 U.S. 497, 515.

Although the Court did not think such considerations controlling in the narcotics case, nothing in the opinion of the Court suggests that they are not controlling here. I think the opinion of the Court affirmatively shows that they are controlling. It quotes these words among others from the larceny case: " 'We think that the imputation of bias simply by virtue of governmental employment, without regard to any actual partiality growing out of the nature and circumstances of particular cases, rests on an assumption without any rational foundation. . . . In dealing with an employee of the Government, the court would properly be solicitous to discover whether, in view of the nature or circumstances of his employment, or of the relation of the particular governmental activity to the matters involved in the prosecution, or otherwise, he had actual bias, and, if he had, to disqualify him.' " *Frazier* v. *United States*, 335 U.S. 497, 509–10, 512–13. "Actual bias" includes "not only prejudice in the subjective sense but also such as might be thought implicitly to arise" from the circumstances of a particular case. *Ibid.*, p. 511, note 19. It is an understatement to say that prejudice might be thought implicitly to arise from the circumstances of this case.

GEORGE A. ANDERSEN

v.

UNITED STATES OF AMERICA

Order filed February 21, 1958

Statement of *Chief Judge* EDGERTON and *Circuit Judge* BAZELON in support of their vote to grant the petition for a rehearing in banc

George Andersen was convicted of assault upon a policeman. He claimed that he had only made a protest against an arrest of a third person. The court refused to submit to the jury the question of whether he had interfered with the police in a disorderly fashion and itself ruled upon the point. Andersen's appeal was denied by a division of three judges. He petitioned for a rehearing in banc. This petition was heard in banc and denied. One judge thought that the case should be reheard by the division that heard it originally.

Chief Judge EDGERTON and *Circuit Judge* BAZELON: Appellant was convicted of an alleged assault upon a policeman who was trying to arrest him. "One has an undoubted right to resist an unlawful arrest, and courts will uphold the right of resistance in proper cases." *United States* v. *Di Re,* 332 U.S. 581, 594 (1948). Only "reasonable force" is permissible in resisting an unlawful arrest. *Abrams* v. *United States,* 237 F. 2d 42 (1956); *United States* v. *Angelet,* 231 F. 2d 190, 193. It is not contended that the force appellant used was unreasonable if the arrest he was resisting was unlawful. He was guilty of assault only if he was resisting a *lawful* arrest.

The policeman sought to arrest appellant for either "disorderly" or "interference." The circumstances leading to the arrest were that appellant was challenging the policeman's legal right to give a third party a parking ticket. The policeman testified at the trial that appellant's challenge was made in disorderly fashion. Appellant's testimony was that he was completely orderly. If the jury believed the policeman, appellant's arrest was lawful and his resistance was unjustified. If the jury believed the appellant, his arrest was unlawful and his resistance justified. *The trial court did not allow the jury to consider the critical and disputed factual question of orderliness.* As the Municipal Court of Appeals stated in its opinion: "The trial judge ruled that the arrest of appellant was legal as a matter of law and in substance so instructed the jury, leaving for their consideration only the question of whether the alleged assault took place." 132 A. 2d 155, 156 (1957).

The Municipal Court of Appeals affirmed the conviction. The court said: "It is true that ordinarily when the evidence on such a question [orderliness] is conflicting it would have to be resolved by the jury, and appellant's testimony tended to prove that he was not disorderly. His own admission, however, that he interjected himself into an affair between an officer and a third person and engaged the officer in a jurisdictional dispute which was not his concern, clearly shows that he was interfering, and thus that his own arrest was justified." *Id.* at 157.

The Supreme Court said in *District of Columbia* v. *Little*, 339 U.S. 1, 6 (1950): "Although force or threatened force is not always an indispensable ingredient of the offense of interfering with an officer in the discharge of his duties, mere remonstrances or even criticisms of an officer are not usually held to be the equivalent of unlawful interference." The Court cited an annotation in 48 A.L.R. 746, 749, 755, which discusses statutes similar to D.C. Code § 22-505 (1951 ed., Supp. V), the "interference" statute which appellant is alleged to have violated.

Since the jury was not permitted to consider whether appellant's remonstrances with the policeman were other than orderly, the only theory of law upon which the conviction can rest is that it is a crime, punishable by a fine of up to $5,000 or imprisonment of up to five years or both, to argue peaceably with a policeman about his right to give a third person a parking ticket. This gives a policeman on his beat the same privilege not to be questioned by a bystander that a judge has in his courtroom. The decision seems to create a new crime, contempt of police. We think the error is so serious that the petition for rehearing in banc should be granted.

A Fair Trial

Like other legal concepts, that of a fair trial has continued to develop since the adoption of the Bill of Rights. Today some additional requirements not specifically included in the procedural amendments have gained constitutional protection by incorporation into the concept of due process. Others have not achieved that status or are even so controversial that they are not yet a matter of statute law. The appeal in criminal cases, for example, was unknown in England until the middle of the nineteenth century. Today it is quite generally regarded as an essential element of a fair trial, is provided for by statute, but is not treated as a matter of due process. The obverse of the requirement that a defendant must be informed of the evidence against him is that he should also be told of any evidence in his favor that comes to the attention of the prosecutor. There still is no general agreement as to whether and under what circumstances such disclosure should be required.

These problems are dealt with in the cases that follow.

BAXTER GRIFFIN

v.

UNITED STATES OF AMERICA

Decided July 10, 1950

Before EDGERTON, CLARK, and PROCTOR,
Circuit Judges

Baxter Griffin was convicted of first-degree murder and sentenced to death. The Court of Appeals affirmed the conviction, and on March 15, 1948, the Supreme Court denied certiorari. A motion for a new trial was made on the ground of newly discovered evidence in the nature of an uncommunicated threat. The defense had learned after the trial that the dead man had an open knife in the pocket into which he had thrust his hand. His hand was not on the knife but held some playing cards. The prosecutor knew of the evidence but thought it inadmissible and did not report it to the defendant.

The Court of Appeals denied the motion for a new trial, and the Supreme Court granted certiorari. It sent the case back to the Court of Appeals with instructions to determine the law in the District of Columbia as to the admissibility of evidence concerning an uncommunicated threat. Judge Edgerton spoke for the court, which granted a new trial.

EDGERTON, *Circuit Judge:* We affirmed appellant's conviction of murder in the first degree. 164 F. 2d 903. The Supreme Court denied certiorari. 333 U.S. 857. The District Court afterward declined to grant a new trial on the ground of newly discovered evidence and we affirmed without opinion. The Supreme Court granted certiorari and remanded the case to us "with instructions to decide, in the first instance, what rule should prevail in the District of Columbia" with respect to the admissibility of "uncommunicated threats" of the deceased against the accused. *Griffin* v. *United States,* 336 U.S. 704, 709–711, 715, 718. The ultimate question is whether the District Court erred in refusing to grant a new trial when it appeared that after the homicide an open penknife was found in the same trousers pocket of the deceased in which his hand was, and that the prosecution knew at the time of the trial that such testimony was available but neither produced it in court nor disclosed it to the defense.

The appellant shot and killed one Hunter as the outcome of a quarrel. Whether the shooting immediately followed the quarrel was in dispute. The accused claimed self-defense. He said Hunter "jumped up and started around the table, with his hand in his pocket, and told me he would kick my teeth out of my head." 336 U.S. at 706. But the accused was the only witness who testified to any aggressive word or act of Hunter at the time of the shooting. Several eye-witnesses testified that the accused was the aggressor and Hunter made no move. The prosecution knew, but the defense did not, that a morgue attendant had said he found an open penknife in Hunter's pocket although playing cards were in his hand. The facts are more fully stated in the opinions of the Supreme Court and of this court.

The majority of the Supreme Court expressed no "preference among the competing rules about the admissibility of uncommunicated threats" and left us free to adopt any rule on this subject. 336 U.S. at 715. By directing us to adopt and apply *some* rule on this subject the Court determined only that the subject is before us; in other words, that the evidence to be ruled upon is evidence of an uncommunicated threat. Because the Court determined this latter question we do not discuss it.

The view that evidence of uncommunicated threats, including the evidence of Hunter's opened knife, should be admitted seems to us logical and humane. It is within the principle of admitting any type of evidence that may fairly be thought to have substantial probative value and is neither excluded by a settled rule nor particularly likely to be false, misleading, or unduly prejudicial. It is of course true that the apparent conduct of the deceased at the time of the homicide, rather than any concealed plan he may have had, bears directly on the question whether the accused acted in self-defense, but evidence that the deceased had a concealed plan of attack bears on the question what his apparent conduct was. We therefore adopt the following rule as the one we think should prevail in the District of Columbia. When a defendant claims self-defense and there is substantial evidence, though it be only his own testimony, that the deceased attacked him, evidence of uncommunicated threats of the deceased against the defendant is admissible. We agree with cases in which uncommunicated threats have been admitted although there were eye-witnesses.

The question remains whether a new trial should be granted. In remanding the case the Supreme Court said: "Were the Court of Appeals to declare that the controverted evidence was admissible according to the law prevailing in the District, it would have to consider further whether it would not be too dogmatic, on the basis of mere speculation, for any court to conclude that the jury would not have attached significance to the evidence favorable to the defendant had the evidence been before it." 336 U.S. at 708–709. We think it would be too dogmatic.[1] The appellant is therefore entitled to a new trial.

It would be unfair not to add that we have confidence in the good faith of the prosecution. Its opinion that evidence of the concealed knife was inadmissible was a reasonable opinion, which the District Court sustained and no court has overruled until today. However, the case emphasizes the necessity of disclosure by the prosecution of evidence that may reasonably be considered admissible and useful to the defense. When there is substantial room for doubt, the prosecution is not to decide for the court what is admissible or for the defense what is useful. "The United States Attorney is the representative not of an ordinary party to a controversy, but of a sovereignty whose obligation to govern impartially is as compelling as its obligation to govern at all; and whose interest, therefore, in a criminal prosecution is not that it shall win a case, but that justice shall be done." *Berger* v. *United States*, 295 U.S. 78, 88.

The order of the District Court is reversed and the case remanded with instructions to grant a new trial.

GEORGE H. CASH

v.

UNITED STATES OF AMERICA

Decided February 28, 1958

Before EDGERTON, *Chief Judge,* and PRETTYMAN and BURGER, *Circuit Judges*

George H. Cash and a codefendant were convicted of robbery. Cash applied to the District Court for leave to appeal *in forma*

[1] Though the evidence regarding the playing cards in Hunter's hand would, if believed, diminish the significance of the evidence regarding the knife in his pocket, it would not necessarily destroy that significance. Moreover a jury might believe the knife evidence but not the playing-card evidence.

pauperis—that is, to have the expenses of the appeal met by the Government. The District Court denied his petition, noting on it "not taken in good faith." A division of the Court of Appeals thought that the questions raised as grounds for appeal were without substance and could not lead to a reversal of the conviction. They found that the petition was, therefore, "without merit," "frivolous," "malicious," and "not taken in good faith." One judge took exception to Judge Edgerton's position as to the necessity of protecting the rights of the poor, stating that it related to a socially desirable goal rather than a standard of law.

On appeal the Supreme Court, on June 16, 1958, granted the petition, vacated the judgment of the Court of Appeals, and sent the case back for reconsideration in the light of two cases just decided, *Ellis* v. *United States* and *Hill* v. *United States*. In those cases the Court had ruled that a petition for leave to appeal *in forma pauperis* may not be dismissed "unless the issues raised are so frivolous that the appeal would be dismissed in the case of a non-indigent litigant." The Court said further that such an appeal may not be denied unless the appellant has had adequate representation by counsel who has acted "in the role of an advocate." *Ellis* v. *United States*, 356 U.S. 674.

On rehearing, the Court of Appeals granted the petition to proceed *in forma pauperis*, and after argument of the case affirmed the judgment of the District Court.

EDGERTON, *Chief Judge, dissenting:* Though I cannot concur in the judgment or in the court's opinion, I agree with much that is said, including the court's commendation of counsel whom we appointed to represent the petitioner. I find it hard to reconcile that commendation with the court's ruling. In my opinion the carefully documented contention which has been presented, after mature reflection, by competent counsel who has nothing to gain except a sense of duty well done, is not frivolous.

In discussing the "good faith" requirement of what is now 28 U.S.C. § 1915(a) Senator Bacon, a member of the Judiciary Committee, said: "When a judge has heard a case and it is about to be carried to an appellate court, he . . . is in a position to judge whether it is a case proceeding captiously, or viciously, or with prejudice, or from any other improper motive, or whether the litigant is proceeding in good faith." 45 Cong. Rec. 1533. No one suggests that petitioner or his counsel is proceeding captiously, or viciously, or with prejudice, or from any improper motive.

In another case the Solicitor General advised the Supreme Court: "We agree with petitioner that, as Mr. Justice Frankfurter pointed out on the application for bail in *Ward* v. *United States*, 76 S.Ct. 1063 (decided August 8, 1956), there is a qualitative distinction between 'frivolous' and 'lack of a substantial question.' We further agree that this Court has indicated in *Johnson* v. *United States*, 352 U.S. 565, and *Farley* v. *United States*, 354 U.S. 521, that 'frivolity' is the proper standard to be applied in determining lack of good faith under the *in forma pauperis* statute. . . . Neither case equated 'lack of a substantial question' with 'frivolous.' " In still another case, in which this court had applied the "substantial question" test, the Solicitor General advised the Supreme Court: "[W]e agree that the proper test to be applied in determining whether a defendant should be allowed to appeal *in forma pauperis* is whether the appeal is frivolous, not whether the question is substantial. We believe that there is a difference of substance, not merely of terminology, in these two standards, and that this Court has determined that the proper standard to be applied is that of lack of frivolity. . . . [W]e do not believe that here the question raised, that of probable cause for the arrest, can necessarily be characterized as frivolous, even though ultimately the appeal may prove unsuccessful. We therefore suggest that it would be appropriate to remand the cause for reconsideration by the Court of Appeals as to whether the appeal is frivolous."

An appeal may raise a substantial question and yet be unlikely to succeed. Obviously one that falls short of raising a substantial question is very unlikely to succeed. It does not follow that it is frivolous. Even when the costs of a criminal appeal are prepaid, if the appeal is obviously groundless it may be dismissed under Rule 39(a), F.R.Crim.P. I think it clear that if the costs of the appeal now proposed were prepaid, this court would not dismiss the appeal but would permit it to be briefed and argued in the usual way. If that be true, this court's action prevents the petitioner because he is poor from proceeding with an appeal he could proceed with if he were rich. Though full briefing and oral argument would probably not result in reversing petitioner's conviction, counsel's memorandum convinces me that there would be a possibility of reversal. I think it follows that we should allow an appeal *in forma pauperis*.

Some have urged that courts, government counsel, and counsel for poor defendants should not be burdened with appeals that are unlikely to succeed. To this there are several answers. The United States can afford to let poor defendants take criminal appeals that the rich could take. It cannot afford to do otherwise. And the burden of prosecuting, defending, and deciding appeals, though it is greater, is not inordinately greater than the burden of prosecuting and deciding disputes, such as this one, over the question whether an appeal should be made possible.

V

Aliens and Outcasts

The law as to immigration, naturalization, and nationality was developed over the years by a number of Acts of Congress and by court decisions until it became a maze in which even the specialist might lose his way. The problem was further complicated by special laws passed to help persons seeking political asylum, including displaced persons. In 1952 Congress passed the Immigration and Naturalization Act, which was intended to be a codification as well as a revision of existing law. This complex law, in turn, has had to be interpreted by the courts in the light of the earlier Acts and other relevant statutes.

LOUIS BERNARD LAPIDES

v.

THOMAS C. CLARK

Decided May 23, 1949

Before EDGERTON, CLARK, and PROCTOR,
Circuit Judges

Sections 804–806 of the Nationality Act of 1940 provide that a naturalized citizen loses his U.S. citizenship if he lives abroad continuously for a period of five years. Louis Bernard Lapides became a naturalized citizen of the United States in 1928. In 1934 he went to Palestine, where he stayed until 1947. When he returned to the United States on July 3, 1947, the immigration authorities at the Port of New York refused to admit him on the ground that by his long stay abroad he had expatriated himself. They said that he had become an alien who was attempting to enter the country without a quota immigration visa. Lapides brought suit, first in the District Court in New York and then in the District of Columbia, claiming that Section 804 was unconstitutional because it discriminated arbitrarily against naturalized citizens. In both jurisdictions the District Court dismissed his complaint, and the Court of Appeals affirmed that judgment.

The majority opinion found that expatriation was "a natural and inherent right of all peoples" for which Congress might provide and that Section 804 was intended "to lessen friction with foreign governments growing out of disputes as to the nationality of our naturalized citizens and their offspring residing for prolonged periods in foreign lands." Since Section 804 had "a purpose in the international policy of our government," it was not arbitrary or unreasonable. The Supreme Court refused to review the case.

EDGERTON, *J., dissenting:* In my opinion the appellant's expatriation and banishment are unconstitutional on two grounds. Congress may not discriminate against naturalized citizens. Arbitrary discrimination is not due process of law.

The Constitution empowers Congress "to establish an uniform rule of naturalization." Article I, § 8, Par. 4. A "rule of naturalization" regulates eligibility and procedure for becoming a citizen. It increases the number of citizens but does not divide them into classes. By authorizing Congress to prescribe who may be naturalized and how, the Constitution does not authorize it to deprive citizens either at or after naturalization of liberties that other citizens enjoy. "The power of naturalization, vested in Congress by the Constitution, is a power to confer citizenship, not a power to take it away." *United States* v. *Wong Kim Ark*, 169 U.S. 649,

703. Chief Justice Marshall said in 1824: "A naturalized citizen . . . becomes a member of the society, possessing all the rights of a native citizen, and standing, in the view of the constitution, on the footing of a native. The constitution does not authorize congress to enlarge or abridge those rights. The simple power of the national legislature is, to prescribe a uniform rule of naturalization, and the exercise of this power exhausts it, so far as respects the individual. The constitution then takes him up, and, among other rights, extends to him the capacity of suing in the courts of the United States, precisely under the same circumstances under which a native might sue." *Osborn* v. *United States Bank,* 9 Wheat. (22 U.S.) 737, 827. The Supreme Court said in 1913: "Under our Constitution, a naturalized citizen stands on an equal footing with the native citizen in all respects, save that of eligibility to the Presidency." *Luria* v. *United States,* 231 U.S. 9, 22. In the *Knauer* case in 1946 the Court pointed out that "there are other exceptions of a limited character" and, in a footnote, mentioned the Nationality Act. But in that case the Court was dealing with cancellation of an invalid naturalization because of fraud in its procurement. The Court had no opportunity to consider and decide whether a valid naturalization may be terminated because of residence abroad.

Deprivation of liberty by severe and arbitrary discrimination is not due process of law. Aside from the Nationality Act, citizens may live abroad. By imposing a heavy penalty on the exercise of this liberty the Nationality Act takes part of it away from all naturalized citizens, regardless of their devotion to America and their connections here. All native citizens, regardless of possible devotion to a foreign country and connections there, are exempt. Congress may expatriate citizens on reasonable grounds. No doubt these may include five years residence abroad. But it does not follow that Congress may expatriate some citizens and not others on this ground. The *Mackenzie* case upheld as reasonable a statute that expatriated women but not men who married aliens. Some distinctions between citizens solely because of their sex are still considered reasonable. *Goesaert* v. *Cleary*, 335 U.S. 464. But "distinctions between citizens solely because of their ancestry are by their very nature odious to a free people." *Hirabayashi* v. *United States*, 320 U.S. 81, 100. Distinctions because of birthplace are equally arbitrary. The fact that the appellant was born in Austria is no reason for penalizing his sojourn in Palestine. Together with the immigration law the Nationality Act makes it in effect a crime punishable by banishment, which may well be called cruel and unusual, for some citizens but not for others to live five years abroad. Even complete inability, from whatever cause, to return to the United States during the five-year period gives no immunity, and a considerable number of foreign-born Americans have therefore been banished by circumstances over which they had no control. . . .

SERGE RUBINSTEIN

v.

HERBERT BROWNELL, JR.

Decided June 11, 1953

Before EDGERTON, PROCTOR, and BAZELON,
Circuit Judges

Serge Rubinstein was convicted of filing false affidavits to escape the draft. When he had served his sentence, the Attorney General started proceedings to deport him on the ground that he had been convicted of a crime involving moral turpitude. He was arrested, but was released on bail during the period of administrative proceedings. On December 20, 1952, the Attorney General issued a final deportation order, and the Director of Immigration immediately ordered Rubinstein to be arrested. He brought suit, asking that the Attorney General be restrained from holding him in arrest while he appealed the deportation order.

The Government contended that under the Immigration and Naturalization Act of 1952 there could be no review of a deportation order in the courts except by habeas corpus. The earlier part of Judge Edgerton's opinion deals with this question. He found that there is a right of judicial review, a position taken by the Supreme Court in a later case, *O'Shaughnessy* v. *Pedreiro,* 349 U.S. 48. Having reached this conclusion, he went on to consider whether the Attorney General's order was a proper exercise of discretion.

The Supreme Court reviewed the *Rubinstein* case and sustained the Court of Appeals in a 4 to 4 decision.

EDGERTON, *Circuit Judge, dissenting:* . . .

In our opinion the appellant, if he were under arrest, would be entitled to release in habeas corpus. . . .

Section 242(a) authorizes the Attorney General to keep an alien in custody, release him on bond, or release him on conditional parole. The Attorney General arrested the appellant and released him on bond. It also authorizes the Attorney General "in his discretion" to revoke the bond or parole and take the alien into custody again. But discretion in this connection is a reasonable discretion, not an arbitrary and capricious one. *Carlson* v. *Landon,* 342 U.S. 524, was a habeas corpus case decided under a provision of the Internal Security Act of 1950, 64 Stat. 1010, 8 U.S.C. (Supp. V) § 156(a), which likewise authorized the Attorney General in his "discretion" to keep an alien in custody pending final determination of his deportability. The Court said: "Respondent filed returns defending his orders of detention on the ground that there was reasonable cause to believe that petitioners' release would be prejudicial to the public interest and would endanger the welfare and safety of the United States. . . . The Government does not urge that the Attorney General's discretion is not subject to any judicial review, but merely that his discretion can be overturned only on a showing of clear abuse. . . . When in the judgment of the Attorney General an alien Communist may so conduct himself pending deportation hearings as to aid in carrying out the objectives of the world communist movement, that alien may be detained. . . . This is a permissible delegation of legislative power because the executive judgment is limited by adequate standards." 342 U.S. at 529, 540, 544. . . .

The *Carlson* case governs this one. The assertions in his counsel's affidavit that appellant is not hostile to the Government or likely to engage in subversive, criminal, or reprehensible activities are undenied. As we noted in our order of January 26, 1953, appellee's counsel informed us that no injury to the public interest is to be anticipated from postponing appellant's arrest. There is no suggestion that he will flee or hide. Counsel suggest a desire to question him but do not show that he cannot be questioned without being arrested. The record shows no reason for the order of arrest, apart from the uncontradicted statements in the complaint that the original defendant, the former Attorney General, "received many letters, telegrams and other communications urging plaintiff's deportation" and his "attention was directed to newspaper columns urging plaintiff's deportation." Neither appellant's criminal record nor his unpopularity justifies imprisoning him. As far as the record shows, his arrest under § 242 (a) would be a clear abuse of discretion. We have shown that § 242 (c) does not authorize his arrest while judicial review of the deportation order is pending.

As we held on the former appeal, the question of detention must be decided in accordance with the principles applicable in habeas corpus proceedings. In accordance with those principles, the question of detention is entirely independent of the question who is likely finally to prevail in regard to the validity of the deportation order. If the order be upheld, that will not retroactively legalize a previous arrest. There is no occasion to balance equities. Even if there were, the record contains nothing that could outweigh the irreparable loss of personal liberty which would follow from an arrest.

In denying a preliminary injunction the District Court declared that the crime for which appellant had served a term involved moral turpitude. But this is only one of the issues, raised by the complaint, on which the validity of the deportation order will depend. To avoid piecemeal appeals, we shall not consider this issue until the others have been heard. The case is accordingly remanded to the District Court for further proceedings, with directions to issue a preliminary injunction restraining appellee from revoking appellant's bail and from taking him into custody on a warrant of arrest for deportation, pending final determination of this suit, unless the appellee shows to the court that there are adequate reasons for making the arrest.

HERBERT BROWNELL, JR.

v.

JOSEF MARION GUTNAYER

Decided April 22, 1954

Before EDGERTON, PRETTYMAN, and WASHINGTON,
Circuit Judges

EDGERTON, *Circuit Judge:* Section 4 of the Displaced Persons Act of 1948, 62 Stat. 1011, as amended, 64 Stat. 224, 66 Stat. 277, 50 U.S.C. App., Supp. V, § 1953, provides that "a displaced person residing in the United States" may apply to the Attorney General for an adjustment of his immigration status, and that "if the Attorney General shall, upon consideration of all the facts and circumstances of the case, determine that such alien has been of good moral character for the preceding five years and that such alien is qualified under the provisions of this section, the Attorney General shall report to the Congress all of the pertinent facts in the case." The term "displaced person residing in the United States" is defined, in substance, as a person who establishes "that he lawfully entered the United States as a non-immigrant," that he is displaced because of events subsequent to the outbreak of World War II, and that he cannot return home because of racial, religious, or political persecution.

It appears without dispute that appellee was admitted to the United States on January 25, 1946 as an accredited official of a foreign government, and that the Attorney General has denied adjustment of his immigration status on the ground that he entered the United States unlawfully in that at the time of his entry he intended to remain here permanently. In this suit, appellee asks a declaratory judgment that he is eligible for relief under the Displaced Persons Act and that he cannot be denied adjustment of status on the ground that he entered the United States unlawfully. The Attorney General appeals from a judgment "that the matter shall be referred back to the Attorney General for a consideration of all the facts and circumstances relevant to the status of the plaintiff under the Displaced Persons Act, but that plaintiff shall not be denied adjustment of status as a displaced person upon the sole ground that he entered the United States unlawfully."

Appellee's intention to remain permanently in the United States did not make it unlawful for him to enter the United States "as a non-immigrant" on being duly admitted as an accredited official of a foreign government under § 3 of the Immigration Act of 1924, 43 Stat. 154, as then amended, 54 Stat. 711. Cf. *United States* v. *Prince Line, Ltd.*, 189 F. 2d 386 (2d Cir., 1951). And the Attorney General's discretion under the Displaced Persons Act is subject to judicial review for plain error of law. Cf. *McGrath* v. *Kristensen*, 340 U.S. 162; *United States ex rel. Accardi* v. *Shaughnessy*, 347 U.S. 260, decided March 15, 1954. However, we think the final clause of the appealed judgment should provide only that the plaintiff is not to be denied adjustment of status as a displaced person upon the theory that an intention to remain permanently in the United States made his entry unlawful.

VI

Separate Is Not Equal

"No state shall make or enforce any law which shall abridge the privileges or immunities of citizens of the United States; nor shall any State deprive any person of life, liberty, or property without due process of law; nor deny to any person within its jurisdiction the equal protection of the laws." Many of those who voted for the Fourteenth Amendment doubtless believed that the foregoing clause was broad enough to bring about the removal of all legal distinctions between white and Negro citizens. Its very breadth has made it susceptible to widely differing interpretations. Beginning in 1873 with the *Slaughterhouse Cases*, 16 Wall. 36, the Supreme Court has been called upon to survey and resurvey the boundaries of the Amendment in the light of current social conditions, public policy, and the public conscience.

The first court decisions placed sharp limits upon the potential scope of the Amendment. The *Slaughterhouse Cases* involved a question of business monopoly and had nothing to do with the rights of Negroes. The Court's decision in the case nullified almost a third of the Amendment's basic provisions. It excluded from the phrase "privileges or immunities of citizens of the United States" the personal rights defined in the first eight amendments. Ten years later in the *Civil Rights Cases*, 109 U.S.

3, the Court ruled that the Amendment limited only the activities of states and of public officials and not those of private individuals, who were free to discriminate against Negroes if they chose to do so. These two cases have never been overruled.

When "Jim Crow" was born in the 1890's, the Court evolved a doctrine that enabled it to give him its blessing. In 1896 in *Plessy* v. *Ferguson*, 163 U.S. 537, it found that a state law requiring segregation on railroads did not deny equal protection of the laws, provided that the facilities offered to the two races were substantially equal. To the argument that segregation was unconstitutional the Court replied:

> We consider the underlying fallacy of the plaintiff's argument to consist in the assumption that the enforced separation of the two races stamps the colored race with a badge of inferiority. If this be so, it is not by reason of anything found in the act, but solely because the colored race chooses to put that construction on it.

From the time of *Plessy* v. *Ferguson* until 1954, cases involving segregation were considered in terms of "separate but equal," and for many years the Court's interpretation of "equal" was decidedly non-Euclidian, permitting deplorably substandard conditions for Negroes.

In the twentieth century the tide has flowed in the opposite direction. In a long series of cases, many of which, like the *Slaughterhouse Cases*, involved no racial issue and even no question of individual rights, the Supreme Court has interpreted the phrases "life, liberty or property" and "due process" so as to establish federal protection against "state action" of rights perhaps originally thought to be included in the privileges and immunities clause. The Court has looked behind the form to the substance of schemes intended to evade the requirement of equal protection of the laws, notably in cases dealing with voting and with exclusion of Negroes from service on grand and petit juries. The concept of "state action" has been expanded until it covers not only state and municipal laws and the acts of public officials, but any exercise of power derived from the state, including the orders of a court. Standards of equality of treatment have become steadily more exacting. Finally on May 7, 1954, in the case of *Brown* v. *Board of Education of Topeka*, 347 U.S. 483, and a companion case, *Bolling* v. *Sharpe*, 347 U.S. 497, that came to it from the District of Columbia, the Court specifically overruled *Plessy* v. *Ferguson*, saying, "We conclude that in the field of public education the doctrine of separate but equal has no place. Separate educational facilities are inherently unequal."

The Right to a Home

CLARA I. MAYS

v.

WILLIAM T. BURGESS

Decided January 29, 1945

Before GRONER, *Chief Judge*, MILLER and
EDGERTON, *Associate Justices*

In 1917 in the case of *Buchanan* v. *Warley*, 245 U.S. 60, the Supreme Court ruled that municipal ordinances providing for segregated living quarters for Negroes violated the Due Process Clause of the Constitution. Thereafter such segregation was achieved in many cities by means of private agreements called restrictive covenants, by which property owners agreed with each other not to sell or lease their land to Negroes. These agreements were usually incorporated in deeds of transfer, were recorded, and were enforceable in the courts.

On February 17, 1944, Clara I. Mays, a Negro woman who was the head of a large family, had tried to solve her housing problem by buying a house and lot in a section of Washington that had been reserved exclusively for whites. The former owners of the land had joined with their neighbors in a restrictive covenant, by which each agreed not to sell or rent his land to a Negro for 21 years, a period that was due to expire on September 1, 1946. Mrs. Mays knew of the covenant, which was duly recorded in the District of Columbia, but neither she nor the real-estate corporation that sold to her was a party to it. Four of the white neighbors on the block sued to enjoin her from using the property. The District Court granted the injunction and ordered Mrs. Mays to move out within 60 days. The Court of Appeals also found against her, and the Supreme Court refused to review the case. On September 3, 1945, Mrs. Mays was still living in the house she had purchased, and the neighbors again went to court to ask that she be judged in contempt. Again she was ordered to move, again she appealed, and again she lost. She was now told to move on November 1, 1945, just ten months before the covenant would expire.

In both cases the majority found that the court was bound by the established precedents and the settled law of the District of Columbia and that "rights created by covenants such as these have been so consistently enforced by us as to become a rule of property and within the accepted public policy of the District of Columbia." The only exception to the rule arises, the Court declared, when conditions have so changed that to enforce the covenant would be to defeat its purposes. This condition the judges did not believe existed. In both cases Judge Edgerton dissented.

EDGERTON, *J., dissenting:* I think the decision of the court is wrong for several reasons.

(1) I think this case is within the settled principle that when an agreement which restricts the use of real property can no longer serve its purpose it is not enforceable in equity. The parties to the agreement obviously wished to maintain the value

of their properties and doubtless also wished to live in an exclusively white neighborhood. Enforcement today of this agreement made many years ago will accomplish neither purpose.

The agreement was made in 1925 by owners of all the houses and lots in the 2200 block of First Street N.W. Like the rest of First Street this block runs north and south. Most if not all of the property immediately west of this block, and for a considerable distance beyond, is occupied by Negroes. Six consecutive blocks on First Street, including the 2200 block and the blocks immediately north and south of it, were occupied by white persons and were subject to restrictive agreements at the time of the trial in the District Court. So was, and apparently still is, a considerable area immediately east of these six blocks. But the 2100 block on First Street, which is immediately south of the 2200 block, ceased on November 1, 1944 to be covered by an agreement. When this suit was tried two houses in the 2100 block had already been sold to colored persons and suits regarding them were pending. The restrictive agreement with respect to the 2200 block itself will expire on September 1, 1946 and obviously will not be renewed. All of the property in the 2200 block is now more valuable for sale to Negroes than to white persons. There is ample testimony to that effect and there is no dispute about it. Real estate dealers testified that the houses in this block are worth about $7,500 for sale to white purchasers and about $10,000 for sale to colored purchasers. Appellants' house had been vacant for some time, and a white person had offered $7,500 for it, when appellant Mays bought it for $9,950. Performance of the restrictive agreement, instead of maintaining the value of property in the 2200 block, will actually depress it. The court should not enforce the agreement and defeat its most obvious purpose.

This is the more clearly true because enforcement of the agreement will not accomplish its other purpose. Since (1) the area immediately west of the 2200 block is largely occupied by colored people; (2) the block immediately south of the 2200 block is no longer restricted, and colored people have begun to buy homes there; (3) the 2200 block itself will cease to be restricted next year; (4) property in this block is more valuable to colored purchasers than to white purchasers; and (5) as a witness testified without dispute, the "trend" in the neighborhood is toward colored ownership and occupancy; it is evident that the neighborhood has lost the exclusively white character which the agreement sought to preserve, and that enforcement of the agreement during the short remainder of its life will not restore that character. As we said in *Hundley* v. *Gorewitz*, 132 F. 2d 23, "The trend is unmistakable, its effect is apparent, and . . . to grant an injunction enforcing the covenant would merely depreciate all the property in the block without accomplishing the purpose which originally impelled its making, while to deny an injunction will leave all of the properties with a value commensurate to the conditions as they now exist. In these circumstances the equities require that we refuse injunctive relief and leave the parties to such remedies as they may have at law."

(2) The effect of an injunction upon appellant Mays and her family must be considered. The family consists of appellant herself, a government employee; three sisters who are employed in Washington; and four nieces who attend school there. A house which they formerly rented was sold and they had to move. They had to break up their family, store their furniture, and rent rooms in various places until they bought the house in suit. According to appellant's undisputed testimony she "accepted this proposition because of an absolute lack of other available properties." To force her and her family to leave their home during the present acute housing emergency will subject them to very great hardship. It will probably compel them again to separate and rent such rooming space, if any, as they can find, and it may compel some of them to leave the District of Columbia and its vicinity. The chances are much against their being

able, without months of search, to find a single house or apartment here that will accommodate them as a family. None of the cases on which the court relies, in which agreements against sales to Negroes were enforced, involved any circumstance even remotely resembling this. In accordance with the familiar principle of "balancing equities," the fact that an injunction will cause extreme hardship to the defendant without *commensurate* benefit to the plaintiff is in itself a sufficient reason for denying an injunction.

(3) The restriction in suit was created by a contract among the owners of some 32 houses and lots. None of the appellants was a party to that contract. None of them has ever agreed to be bound by it. Whether they should be required to conform to this contract which they never made involves more than the balancing of particular equities. It involves a question of general policy. The question is not whether the operators of a public or private housing development, or other persons, may voluntarily select their tenants or their purchasers on the basis, among other things, of color. The question is whether a person who wishes to sell his house to a Negro and has contracted to do so, and has never contracted not to do so, should be prevented by a court from performing his contract because one of his predecessors in title once contracted with other property-owners that their property should not be sold to Negroes.

Since housing is a necessity of life, as an original question a contract of 32 property-owners that they and their successors will not sell houses to Negroes would seem to stand on much the same plane as a contract of 32 grocers that they and their successors will not sell food to Negroes. The ultimate purpose of the combination was the advantage of its members, but its immediate purpose was to withhold a necessity from many persons by limiting the capacity of owners to transfer their property. As an original question, the contract in suit would seem to be an unreasonable restraint on alienation and plainly contrary to public policy. The Committee on Negro Housing of the President's Conference on Home Building and Home Ownership said in its Report in 1932: "Segregation . . . has kept the Negro-occupied sections of cities throughout the country fatally unwholesome places, a menace to the health, morals and general decency of cities, and 'plague spots for race exploitation, friction and riots.' " It would seem clear, as an original question, that a court of equity would have nothing to do with such a contract unless to prevent its enforcement or performance.

(4) The decided cases do not clearly answer the question of policy on which, apart from the particular equities, this case turns. As long ago as 1917 the Supreme Court held in the *Buchanan* case that racial zoning of streets, by statute or ordinance, was unconstitutional. The Court held in 1926, in the *Corrigan* case, that an injunction to prevent a *party* to a contract like the one before us from conveying in breach of his contract did not violate the Constitution or the laws of the United States. *Corrigan* v. *Buckley*, 271 U.S. 323, 332. But the Court had no occasion to decide, and it expressly refrained from deciding, whether or not a contract of this sort was "void because contrary to public policy" or was "of such a discriminatory character that a court of equity will not lend its aid by enforcing the specific performance of the covenant." The Supreme Court has never decided whether this sort of contract is enforceable against anyone.

It would seem to be unsound policy for a court, in the exercise of its equitable discretion, to enforce a privately adopted segregation plan which would be unconstitutional if it were adopted by a legislature. Moreover the Supreme Court has recently said that "discriminations based on race alone are obviously irrelevant and invidious." *Steele* v. *Louisville & Nashville Railroad Co.*, 323 U.S. 192. That case dealt with contracts between employers and a union which represented employees. The Court held that "Congress plainly did not undertake to authorize the bargaining representative to make such discriminations." For the current fiscal year Congress has authorized expenditure of $500,000 by the President's Committee on Fair Employment Practice. Congress is the authoritative exponent of the public policy of the District of Columbia. I can see no sufficient distinction, from the point of view of policy, between discrimination in employment and discrimination in housing.

It is true that in 1924, in *Corrigan* v. *Buckley*, this court restrained a *party* to a contract like the one before us from making a conveyance in violation of his contract. And this court has enforced *covenants in deeds,* of like tenor, against subsequent owners of the land who, as far as appears, were not parties to the deeds. It does not follow that a mere *contract* like the one before us, against selling land to Negroes, is enforceable against a subsequent owner of the land who has notice of the contract but is not a party to it. Whether it is so enforceable is a question which this court has never had occasion to decide until now.

There is a substantial difference between the policy of enforcing against subsequent owners a restraint on alienation created by a deed and the policy of enforcing against them a restraint on alienation created only by a contract, though either policy, in my opinion, is thoroughly bad. If the restraint can be created only by a deed, that fact provides a substantial limitation on its spread; but if neighboring landowners, by merely making and recording a contract, may impose a restraint on alienation which is enforceable against subsequent landowners, unlimited quantities of land may rapidly be subjected to the restraint. By holding that such a restraint may be imposed in such a way this court is not simply following precedent. It is adding an unfortunate extension to an unfortunate doctrine.

(5) Quite aside from the fact that our *Corrigan* decision was probably unsound when it was rendered, and the fact that it would not cover this case even if general conditions in the District of Columbia had remained the same, I think it is quite inapplicable today because general conditions have not remained

the same. It was a decision on a question of policy. Questions of policy have no meaning in a vacuum but relate to particular situations. The housing situation in the District of Columbia has changed since 1924. Although the first World War created a temporary housing emergency, by 1924 the Supreme Court was prepared to take judicial notice of the fact that the emergency had ceased. It is a matter of common knowledge that the emergency is now acute and that the shortage of decent housing, or any housing, for Negroes is particularly acute. We cannot close our eyes to what is commonly known. The conditions in which many of the 187,000 Negroes in the District of Columbia have long been obliged to live are now worse than ever. Since restrictive contracts and covenants are among the factors which limit the supply of housing for Negroes and thereby increase its price, it cannot be sound policy to enforce them today, whatever may have been true in 1924.

In order to work people must live within reach of their work, and in order to work effectively they must live in some degree of comfort. Requiring Negroes to live according to their common color instead of their individual capacities hampers the war effort by interfering with their employment. Congress has declared in the Rent Control Act of the District that it is "the policy of the Congress during the existing emergency to prevent . . . practices relating to housing accommodations in the District of Columbia which may tend to increase the cost of living or otherwise impede the national-defense program. "Race restriction agreements, undertaking to do what the state cannot, must yield to the public interest in the sound development of the whole community."

(6) The majority opinion does not and consequently, on analysis, the concurring opinion does not contend that the Supreme Court has determined either the question of particular equities or the question of general policy on which this case turns. If, as the majority say, decisions of our court have deter-

mined those questions adversely to appellants, we should overrule the decisions. We cannot turn the Supreme Court's power of
review into a duty or our duty of reinterpreting the law into a
privilege.

James M. Hurd

v.

Frederic E. Hodge

Decided May 26, 1947

Before Edgerton, Clark, and Wilbur K. Miller,
Associate Justices

A year and a half after the final decision in the Mays case, the
Court of Appeals was again faced with almost the identical question.
In the same general area of the District of Columbia, Negroes had
bought and occupied houses that were subject to restrictive covenants
forbidding the lease or sale at any time to a Negro. The neighbors
had brought suit in the District Court to enforce the covenant, the
deeds to the Negroes had been declared void, and they had been
ordered to vacate the premises. The Court of Appeals sustained the
District Court on the authority of *Mays* v. *Burgess*. It again rejected the contention that the character of the neighborhood had
changed sufficiently to prevent enforcement of the covenant and
repeated that if it should now reverse decisions that had followed
the same course for 25 years it would "destroy contracts and titles
to valuable real estate made and taken on the faith of our decisions."
Again Judge Edgerton dissented, disagreeing as to both the facts
and the public policy.

In the interval, the concept of "state action," or "state responsibility," as Justice Frankfurter has preferred to call it, had been
extended in cases involving Negro voting and the powers of unions.
Judge Edgerton now made the point that enforcement of a restrictive
covenant based on race is as much a matter of state action as the
passing of a law by the legislature or the action of a police officer.

The Supreme Court this time agreed to review the decision of the Court of Appeals and considered it together with a similar case from the State of Missouri, *Shelley* v. *Kraemer,* 334 U.S. 1. On May 3, 1948, the Court reversed the Court of Appeals and agreed with Judge Edgerton's opinion as to the character of the covenants and the issues of state action and of public policy. Five years later, in *Barrows* v. *Jackson,* 346 U.S. 249, the Supreme Court took the next step and ruled that the courts will not recognize a covenant based on race by granting damages against a property owner who has broken his covenant and sold to a Negro.

EDGERTON, *Associate Justice (dissenting).*

The court holds that perpetual deed covenants forbidding sale of homes to Negroes are valid and enforceable by injunctions cancelling sales, evicting Negroes from homes that they have bought, and preventing sales to other Negroes. I think this erroneous for five reasons, each independent of the other four. The covenants are void as unreasonable restraints on alienation. They are void because contrary to public policy. Their enforcement by injunction is inequitable. Their enforcement by injunction violates the due process clause of the Fifth Amendment. Their enforcement by injunction violates the Civil Rights Act which requires that "All citizens of the United States shall have the same right, in every State and Territory, as is enjoyed by white citizens thereof to inherit, purchase, lease, sell, hold, and convey real and personal property." R.S. § 1978, 8 U.S.C.A. § 42.

Despite the great importance of the questions whether racial restrictive covenants are valid and whether they are enforceable by injunction, the Supreme Court has never ruled on either. The opposite is often assumed. In this court's recent case of *Mays* v. *Burgess* both the principal opinion and the concurring opinion appear to reflect a belief that the issues then and now before this court have been decided by the Supreme Court. The court now relies on that case among others.

The erroneous impression that the Supreme Court has ruled

on these questions results from misinterpretation of *Corrigan* v. *Buckley*, 1926, 271 U.S. 323. In that case a bill was filed in the trial court of the District of Columbia to enforce a racial restrictive covenant by injunction. The defendants moved to dismiss the bill on the sole ground that the "covenant is void" because in conflict with the Constitution and the laws of the United States and with public policy. The trial court overruled the motions and granted the injunction, and this court affirmed. This court ruled only that the covenant was not unconstitutional or contrary to public policy or void. The pleadings presented no other issue.

Corrigan v. *Buckley* reached the Supreme Court on *appeal* and not on certiorari. Section 250 of the Judicial Code as it read on the critical date authorized appeals in six sorts of cases, including (Third) "cases involving the construction or application of the Constitution of the United States . . ." and (Sixth) "cases in which the construction of any law of the United States is drawn in question by the defendant." The defendants based their appeal solely on the contention that the covenant was "void" because it violated the Fifth, Thirteenth and Fourteenth Amendments of the Constitution and also the Civil Rights Act, §§ 1977, 1978 and 1979 of the Revised Statutes, 8 U.S.C.A. §§ 41–43. The Supreme Court held that since the Fifth and Fourteenth Amendments dealt only with government action and not with action of private persons, and the Thirteenth only with involuntary servitude, the contention that these amendments made the *covenant void* raised no substantial question. One of the sections of the Civil Rights Act on which the appellants relied, R.S. § 1978, provides that all citizens shall have the same right as white citizens to purchase and hold property. The Court decided that the several sections, "like the Constitutional Amendment under whose sanction they were enacted, do not in any manner prohibit or invalidate contracts entered into by private individuals in respect to the control and disposition of their own property. There is no color for the contention that they rendered the indenture void. . . . We therefore conclude that neither the constitutional nor statutory questions relied on as grounds for the appeal to this Court have any substantial quality or color of merit, or afford any jurisdictional basis for the appeal." 271 U.S. 323, 324. For want of jurisdiction, therefore, and without at all implying that the appealed judgment was right, the Court dismissed the appeal. Since it had no jurisdiction it could decide no question that was not involved in reaching that conclusion. Accordingly it decided nothing with regard to racial restrictive covenants except that *the Constitution and the Civil Rights Act* plainly do not make them *void.*

No contention that either the Constitution or the Civil Rights Act prohibited *enforcement by injunction* of such covenants was raised by any pleading in any court, or was considered by the District Court, or was considered by this court. Despite that fact, by brief and argument the appellants undertook to raise in the Supreme Court the contention that *"the decrees* of the courts below constitute a violation of the Fifth and Fourteenth Amendments to the Constitution, in that they deprive the appellants of their liberty and property without due process of law." 271 U.S. 323, 324. The Court pointed out that since this contention was not raised by the pleadings it could not give the Court jurisdiction of the appeal, and then added, without a word of argument, six words of dictum adverse to the contention itself: "it likewise is lacking in substance."

The difference between the only point decided by the Supreme Court—that the Constitution and the Civil Rights Act plainly do not make a racial restrictive covenant void—and our own court's proposition that such a covenant is both valid and enforceable by injunction, is very great. Since the Supreme Court had no jurisdiction it could not decide even whether the covenant is void or valid, but necessarily left open the questions (1) whether it is "void because contrary to public policy" and (2) whether it is void as an unreasonable restraint on alienation. Regardless of whether damages can or cannot be recovered for its breach, its specific enforcement by injunction, which much more directly and effectively prevents Negroes from buying and using the property, may be forbidden either (3) by the Constitution, (4) by the Civil Rights Act, or (5) by principles of equity. The Supreme Court did not and could not decide any of these questions in *Corrigan* v. *Buckley*. Its dictum touched only the third of these questions.

Aside from that dictum and the narrow point on which the Supreme Court actually ruled, this court's present decision that racial restrictive covenants are valid and enforceable by injunction rests only on our own past decisions to like effect. In my opinion those decisions, which were reached without full consideration of the questions involved, are erroneous and should be overruled. I think all five of the questions enumerated in the preceding paragraph must be answered in appellants' favor. If any one of them is so answered the appealed judgments must be reversed.

The fifth question requires little discussion. It is enough to point out that the familiar principle of "balancing equities" precludes any injunction in this case because, in view of the present housing situation, the extreme hardship which injunctions will inflict upon the appellants greatly outweighs any benefits which the appellees may possibly derive from them; and that "especially courts of equity, may appropriately withhold their aid where the plaintiff is using the right asserted contrary to the public interest." I discuss the other four questions in the following order: I, the Constitution; II, the Civil Rights Act; III, restraint on alienation; IV, public policy.

I. The Constitution. In *Buchanan* v. *Warley*, 1917, 245 U.S. 60, the Supreme Court held that enforcement of a Louisville ordinance which forbade Negroes to move into predominantly white city blocks and whites to move into predominantly Negro city blocks would violate the Constitution and also, apparently, the Civil Rights Act. The Court said: "The concrete question here is: May the occupancy, and, necessarily, the purchase and sale of property of which occupancy is an incident, be inhibited by the States, or by one of its municipalities, solely because of the color of the proposed occupant of the premises?" 245 U.S. at page 75. "Colored persons are citizens of the United States and have the right to purchase property and enjoy and use the same without laws discriminating against them solely on account of color. . . . These enactments did not deal with the social rights of men, but with those fundamental rights in property which it was intended to secure upon the same terms to citizens of every race and color. . . . The Fourteenth Amendment and these statutes enacted in furtherance of its purpose operate to qualify and entitle a colored man to acquire property without state legislation discriminating against him solely because of color." 245 U.S. at pages 78, 79. "We think this attempt to prevent the alienation of the property in question to a person of color was not a legitimate exercise of the police power of the State, and is in direct violation of the fundamental law enacted in the Fourteenth Amendment of the Constitution preventing state interference with property rights except by due process of law." 245 U.S. at page 82. The Court held that the ordinance invaded even the rights of a white vendor, who could therefore avoid it and enforce performance of a colored purchaser's contract.

But "so far as the requirement of due process is concerned, and in the absence of other constitutional restriction, a state is free to adopt whatever economic policy may reasonably be deemed to promote public welfare, and to enforce that policy by legislation adapted to its purpose." *Nebbia* v. *People of the State of New York*, 291 U.S. 502, 537. Specifically, ordinances that limit what may be done with property in a given area are constitutional and enforceable unless they "are clearly arbitrary and unreasonable, having no substantial relation to the public health, safety, morals, or general welfare." *Euclid* v. *Ambler Realty Co.*, 272 U.S. 365, 395. So, as the Court held in the *Euclid* case, a city may exclude businesses and even apartment houses from a residence area merely because the city thinks it best to segregate them elsewhere. In the light of the *Euclid* case, therefore, *Buchanan* v. *Warley* determines among other things that it is clearly arbitrary and unreasonable, having no substantial relation to the public health, safety, morals, or general welfare, to prevent property in a white neighborhood from being transferred to and used by Negroes.

The upshot is that Negroes have a constitutional right to buy and use, and whites to sell to Negroes, whatever real property they can without direct government interference based on race.

Such interference is forbidden even when it accords with the wishes of the inhabitants of a neighborhood as well as the act of a legislature. A New Orleans ordinance forbade Negroes to establish residence in a white community and whites to establish residence in a Negro community (as defined), "except on the written consent of a majority of the persons of the opposite race inhabiting such community." On the authority of the *Buchanan* case the Supreme Court held this ordinance void. *Harmon* v. *Tyler*, 273 U.S. 668. If an ordinance forbade Negroes to buy a house in a white community against the written dissent of a former owner of the house and a present owner of a neighboring house, obviously the ordinance and any injunction based upon it would be unconstitutional. The present question is whether an injunction which does the same thing without the support of an ordinance is constitutional.

The specific rule, adjudged by the Supreme Court in the *Buchanan* and *Harmon* cases, that it is arbitrary to exclude a race from a neighborhood is an instance of the general rule that "discriminations based on race alone are obviously irrelevant and invidious." *Steele* v. *Louisville & Nashville Railroad Co.*, 323 U.S. 192, 203. It has been contended that enforcement of covenants which exclude a race from a neighborhood does not involve discrimination because it permits reciprocity. This amounts to saying that if Negroes are excluded from decent housing they may retaliate by excluding whites from slums. Such reciprocity is not merely imaginary and unequal but irrelevant. Because appellants are Negroes the court deprives them of homes which they could keep if they were white. Discrimination against them because of color is not merely relative but absolute. The imagined possibility that others may suffer similar discrimination because they are white is as irrelevant as the certainty that others will suffer it because they are Negroes. Both the Louisville ordinance and the New Orleans ordinance which excluded Negroes from white neighborhoods also excluded whites from Negro neighborhoods. Since they undertook to discriminate because of race against members of both races they had a formal reciprocity that restrictive covenants lack. This did not reconcile their enforcement with the requirements of due process.

Restrictive covenants are not self-executing. This case arises because persons whom they purport to bind have violated them. The white appellants have sold restricted property to the colored appellants. The appellees, neighbors not directly involved in the sales, seek to set them aside. For that purpose they necessarily invoke the aid of a court of equity. If all persons whom the covenants purport to bind had refused to sell to Negroes, no government action would be involved but only the action of private individuals, and no question of due process of law would arise. The situation then would be comparable to the refusal of the innkeeper in the Civil Rights Cases to serve Negroes. Even if some landowners had persuaded or hired others not to sell to Negroes, or Negroes not to buy, there would still be only private action, whether legal or illegal, and no due process question. But in this case private means have failed to produce compliance with the covenant and a court has been asked to enforce it. If the colored appellants refuse to vacate the premises in obedience to the court's decree it will be enforced against them through the court's power to punish for contempt; they may be imprisoned or fined, and dispossessed by force if necessary. The action that begins with the decree and ends with its enforcement is obviously direct government action. As this court said in *Corrigan* v. *Buckley*, 299 F. 901, no Negro has "the constitutional power to compel sale and conveyance to him of any particular private property." But no such question was before the court then or is before it now. Appellants claim no constitutional power to compel sale and conveyance of any property. The question is whether a court of the United States has the constitutional power to cancel deeds which willing sellers have made to willing buyers, and evict the buyers from the property, because the buyers are Negroes.

Since courts are arms of government they are subject, like legislatures and executive officers, to the restrictions that the Constitution imposes on government. Every case that holds legislation unconstitutional holds in terms or in effect that its judicial enforcement would be unconstitutional. The Constitution does not exempt any kind of judicial action from the requirements of due process of law. Not only legislation and procedure but judicially adopted rules of substantive law, including equity, are invalid when they conflict with these requirements. Rules which the due process clause forbids legislatures to enact it forbids courts to adopt, for substantive due process is not a matter of method. A judicial decree which would be invalid if it had legislative sanction is not validated by lack of legislative sanction. Since racial restrictions on transfer and use of property are "clearly arbitrary and unreasonable" and do not promote the general welfare, the Constitution forbids courts to enforce such restrictions even when a legislature, for supposed public purposes, has attempted to impose them. Such restrictions are not less arbitrary and unreasonable, and not more conducive to the general welfare, when private persons acting without legislative sanction have attempted to impose them for private purposes. It follows that the Constitution forbids courts to enforce such restrictions in the second case, which is this case, as clearly as in the first, which is *Buchanan* v. *Warley*. It is strangely inconsistent to hold as this court does that although no legislature can authorize a court, even for a moment, to prevent Negroes from acquiring and using particular property, a mere owner of property at a given moment can authorize a court to do so for all time. Either the due process clauses of the Constitution do not forbid governments to prevent Negroes from acquiring and using particular property, in which case they do not forbid courts to enforce racial restrictions which statutes have imposed; or these clauses do forbid governments to prevent Negroes from acquiring and using particular property, in which case they forbid courts to enforce racial restrictions which covenants have imposed. *Buchanan* v. *Warley* rules out the first alternative. . . .

All this is said with due deference to the rule of the *Corrigan* case that the Constitution does not make racial convenants *void*.

II. The Civil Rights Act. White citizens have, beyond question, the right to purchase the property in suit from willing sellers and to hold it. This court forbids colored citizens to do so. It thereby rules that they have no right to do so. The court does not say, and it would be a contradiction in terms to say, "Despite the fact that we forbid colored citizens to purchase and hold this property they have a right to do so." I see no possible escape from the fact that the court's ruling violates not only the due process clause of the Fifth Amendment but also the Civil Rights Act, which expressly provides that "All citizens of the United States shall have the same right, in every State and

Territory, as is enjoyed by white citizens thereof to inherit, purchase, lease, sell, hold, and convey real and personal property." A statute which declares or confers a right means, if it means anything, that courts shall recognize and protect the right. Since (1) appellants are citizens of the United States, (2) the Act assures all citizens the same right as white citizens to purchase and hold property, and (3) white citizens have the right to purchase and hold the property in suit, the Act requires the courts to recognize and protect the very right which this court denies and destroys.

Nothing is alleged or found against appellants except their color. Since the injunctions are based on covenants alone and the covenants are based on color alone, ultimately the injunctions are based on color alone. Even if they were based on color in combination with other factors they would still violate the Act. The Act prohibits injunctions which depend in any degree upon the fact that the persons enjoined are colored, for any restriction which is imposed upon the right of colored citizens to purchase and hold property and would not be imposed upon the right of white citizens to purchase and hold the same property denies to colored citizens "the same right . . . as is enjoyed by white citizens."

It makes no difference that the court denies the right of Negroes to purchase and hold certain property only and not all the property in the District of Columbia. Much of the land in the District is covered by covenants like those in suit. Though these injunctions refer only to appellants' land, denying the right of appellants and other Negroes to buy this land has the practical effect of denying the right of any Negro to buy any land covered by any such covenant. Moreover, the conflict between the Act and the injunctions does not depend upon the fact that the injunctions have a general effect. If a municipal legislature were to pass an ordinance forbidding Negroes to purchase and hold precisely the land in suit, and no other, obviously the court could not prevent them from purchasing and holding it, since such prevention would violate the Act of Congress. I think it quite as plain that the court violates the Act of Congress when, without even the excuse of municipal legislation, it prevents Negroes from purchasing and holding this property. The expressed will of a former property-owner cannot authorize the court to deny a right which the expressed will of a legislature could not authorize it to deny.

Any opinion as to the reasonableness or desirability of preventing Negroes from purchasing and holding this property is irrelevant to the present point. The Constitution and the Civil Rights Act have foreclosed the matter. The right to buy and use anything that whites may buy and use is conferred upon Negroes implicitly by the due process clauses of the Fifth and Fourteenth Amendments and explicitly by the Civil Rights Act. Of the civil rights so conferred, none is clearer and few are more vital than the right to buy a home and live in it.

The *Corrigan* case holds that the Civil Rights Act does not make racial covenants *void*, but the Supreme Court has never held that the Act does not forbid direct governmental denial and destruction of the right of Negroes to acquire property. The *Buchanan* case holds the contrary. . . .

IV. Public Policy. Racial restrictive covenants have been defended on two grounds. They are said to increase the value, i.e. the price, of the restricted property, and to prevent racial conflict. If the first proposition is true, which is very doubtful in the District of Columbia, it is no defense of these covenants from the point of view of public policy, but quite the contrary, since the prices of homes are inflated above any level that can be thought socially desirable. The second proposition assumes that racial conflict is likely to result when whites and Negroes live near each other. Familiar facts refute this assumption. In unrestricted areas within the economic reach of Negroes, and particularly along the boundaries between restricted and unrestricted areas, whites and Negroes do live near each other and racial conflict does not result. Serious students of the subject believe that enforced housing segregation increases rather than diminishes the possibility of racial conflict. If the satisfaction which many of the whites in restricted areas may derive from excluding Negroes is to be given weight, it must be weighed against the dissatisfaction which Negroes may feel at being excluded.

Any contention that public welfare is on the whole promoted by preventing Negroes from buying homes in white neighborhoods is refuted as a matter of law by *Buchanan* v. *Warley*. 245 U.S. 60. If it were not "clearly arbitrary and unreasonable, having no substantial relation to the public health, safety, morals, or general welfare" to prevent Negroes from buying homes in white neighborhoods, legislation directed to that end would be due process of law. *Buchanan* v. *Warley* determines that it is not due process of law. Since racial restrictive covenants are directed to the same end, it follows that they also do not promote the general welfare. *Buchanan* v. *Warley* does not exclude the theoretical possibility that these covenants might be merely neutral in relation to the general welfare. But the fact is that they do great and varied harm, are therefore clearly contrary to public policy, and should be held void for that reason. Moreover the Civil Rights Act discussed in part II of this opinion would be, if it were nothing more, a declaration by Congress that the public policy of the United States forbids preventing Negroes from buying homes because they are Negroes.

The housing shortage in the District of Columbia has long been acute. The shortage of decent housing, or any housing, for Negroes is particularly acute. They are largely confined to wretched quarters in overcrowded ghettoes. These facts are commonly known and undisputed. The correlation of bad and overcrowded housing with delinquency, disease and death has often been proved. The Negro death rate from tuberculosis in the District of Columbia is 4½ times the white, the Negro maternity death rate 5 times the white, and the Negro death rate from all causes 40 per cent higher than the white. Though these differences are not due entirely to the inferiority of Negro housing no one questions the fact that they are due partly to that cause.

The inferiority of Negro housing is not due entirely to racial covenants, but no one questions the fact that it is due in part to racial covenants. Covenants prevent free competition for a short supply of housing and curtail the supply available to Negroes. They add an artificial and special scarcity to a general scarcity, particularly where the number and purchasing power of Negroes as well as whites have increased as they have recently in the District of Columbia. The effect is qualitative as well as quantitative. Exclusion from decent housing confines Negroes to slums to an even greater extent than their poverty makes necessary. Covenants exclude Negroes from a large fraction— no one knows just how large—of the decent housing in the District of Columbia. Some of it is within the economic reach of some of them. Because it is beyond their legal reach, relatively well-to-do Negroes are compelled to compete for inferior housing in unrestricted areas, and so on down the economic scale. That enforced housing segregation, in such circumstances, increases crowding, squalor, and prices in the areas where Negroes are compelled to live is obvious. It results in " 'doubling up,' scandalous housing conditions for Negroes, destroyed home life, mounting juvenile delinquency, and other indications of social pathology which are bound to have their contagious influence upon adjoining white areas." Gunnar Myrdal, *An American Dilemma: The Negro Problem and Modern Democracy* (1944), p. 626.

Neither the present nor any previous opinion of this court questions or considers these facts. The judgments appear to rest upon the theory that they are unimportant.

As long ago as 1932, when the situation was less acute, the

Committee on Negro Housing of the President's Conference on Home Building and Home Ownership said in its Report: "Segregation . . . has kept the Negro-occupied sections of cities throughout the country fatally unwholesome places, a menace to the health, morals and general decency of cities, and 'plague spots for race exploitation, friction and riots.'" Racial restrictive covenants "exist today in thousands of American communities." Housing segregation may therefore be expected to continue in thousands of communities as long as courts continue to enforce racial restrictive covenants by injunctions. But "If the Court should follow up its action of declaring all local laws to segregate Negroes unconstitutional by declaring illegal also the private restrictive covenants, segregation in the North would be nearly doomed, and segregation in the South would be set back slightly." Myrdal, *op. cit.*, p. 378, note 36.

The Charter of the United Nations provides that "the United Nations shall promote . . . universal respect for, and observance of, human rights and fundamental freedoms for all without distinction as to race . . ." and that "all Members pledge themselves to take joint and separate action" for that purpose. In ruling that racial covenants are contrary to current public policy, a Canadian court relies in part on Canada's adherence to this Charter. *Re Drummond Wren,* [1945] 4 D.L.R. 674 (Ontario High Court). America's adherence to this Charter, the adherence of other countries to it, and our American desire for international good will and co-operation cannot be neglected in any consideration of the policy of preventing men from buying homes because they are Negroes. In many countries the color of a man's skin is little more important than the color of his hair and in many others the favored color is not white. In western Europe, to say nothing of other parts of the world, the position of Negroes in America is widely advertised and widely resented. . . .

Suits like these, and the ghetto system they enforce, are among our conspicuous failures to live together in peace. In another such suit, this court recently argued that "if ever the two races are to meet upon mutually satisfactory ground, it cannot be through legal coercion. . . ." *Mays* v. *Burgess*, 147 F. 2d 869, 873. This premise, instead of supporting the court's conclusion that racial restrictive covenants should be enforced by injunctions, is one more argument against it. The question in these cases is not whether law should punish racial discrimination, or even whether law should try to prevent racial discrimination, or whether law should interfere with it in any way. The question is whether law should affirmatively support and enforce racial discrimination. Appellants do not ask that appellees be forced to sell them houses. Appellees alone have come into court with a claim. They ask the court to take away appellants' homes by force because they are Negroes. There is no other issue in the case.

Equal Education

MARGUERITE DAISY CARR

v.

ROBERT M. CORNING

Decided February 14, 1950

Before EDGERTON, CLARK, and PRETTYMAN,
Circuit Judges

From its establishment by Congress in 1862 until the decision of the Supreme Court in the cases of *Brown* v. *Board of Education of Topeka* and *Bolling* v. *Sharpe* in 1954, the public school system in the District of Columbia was operated upon a segregated basis. Successive Acts of Congress of 1862, 1864, 1866, and 1874 provided specifically for separate schools for white and Negro children, and later laws endorsed such a system by implication. The practice was generally accepted by the community as natural and proper, and it was taken for granted that the Board of Education was complying with the requirement that the two sets of schools should be equal. At the time that the case of *Carr* v. *Corning* was brought in the District Court, the population shifts and increases in the city of Washington, similar to those taking place in other metropolitan areas, had had an important impact on the school system. White families had moved in large numbers to the suburbs. Negroes had crowded into the city to take advantage of new job opportunities and in many cases had settled in areas previously reserved for whites and far from the schools provided for Negroes. White schools were no longer filled to capacity, whereas the Negro schools were seriously overcrowded. An obvious inequality of educational facilities in their physical and tangible aspects had developed. The Board of Education recognized this fact and attempted to overcome it. The Negroes began to demand that their children, who were receiving a substandard education, be admitted to the white schools in their own neighborhoods.

In September, 1947, the parents of Marguerite Carr asked that she be transferred from an overcrowded Negro junior high school, operating on a double shift, to a nearby white one that did not have its quota of pupils. When this request was denied, her father brought suit in her behalf and in behalf of other Negro children of school age in the District of Columbia, asking that the Board of Education be required to permit colored children to attend nearby schools that provided the full-time education required by law, regardless of whether these schools had been designated for white or Negro children. The following January the Parent-Teacher Association of the same junior high school sued to prevent their children from being transferred to elementary school buildings that lacked the facilities needed for the junior high years and to permit them to attend nearby white junior high schools. Both suits were dismissed in the District Court, and the appeals were consolidated for hearing in the Court of Appeals.

In the interval Congress had ordered a survey to be made of the public school system in the District of Columbia. The resulting report, known as the Strayer Report, revealed that there were greater inequalities between white and Negro schools than were shown in the affidavits filed in the case by the Board of Education. The report was not made public until the spring of 1949 and was not before the court.

Judge Prettyman wrote the majority opinion in the case, sustaining the action of the District Court. He dealt solely with the question of whether, in fact, equal educational opportunities were afforded to white and Negro school children. In doing so he relied upon the affidavits in the record and refused to take judicial notice of the Strayer Report. He found that the existing practices of which the Negroes complained had been applied at times to overcrowded schools allotted to white children, so that they could not be said to involve any discrimination as to race.

Judge Edgerton in a dissenting opinion also dealt at length with the factual question of equality of tangible school facilities. He relied upon the Strayer Report, of which he felt the court could take judicial notice, analyzed its findings with minute care, and reached the conclusion, diametrically opposite to that of his colleagues, that even if one relied only on the affidavits of the Board of Education the tangible educational facilities were glaringly unequal. He then struck out on a pioneering venture of the law and was the first judge in a United States court to find that today segregation of Negroes in schools amounts to an unconstitutional denial of their rights without due process.

The plaintiffs in this case did not appeal from the decision of the Court of Appeals. In 1954, however, the Supreme Court had before it four cases, from four different states, involving the constitutionality of segregated school systems. A fifth case, *Bolling* v. *Sharpe,* had been brought in the District of Columbia in which the Supreme Court permitted an appeal directly from an adverse judgment of the District Court, bypassing the Court of Appeals, in order that all the cases involving the issue of segregated schools might be brought before it at one time. In some of the cases there were findings that the various school boards either had achieved substantial equality or were making every effort to achieve it in the near future. The Court refused to deal only with the question of equality of tangible facilities and asked whether "segregation of children in public schools solely on the basis of race, even though the physical facilities and other 'tangible' factors may be equal [does] deprive the children of the minority group of equal educational opportunities." The Court answered simply, "We believe that it does."

The Court then invited all states requiring or permitting racial discrimination in public education to present their views as to the manner in which this decision should be implemented. After hearing their arguments, the Court made the now-famous order that segregation should be abolished "with all deliberate speed." It placed upon the district courts that had first heard the cases the duty of enforcing this order.

In the District of Columbia desegregation has been peacefully achieved. In the process ample evidence was uncovered of how unequal in fact was the separate education formerly offered to white and Negro children.

The first part of Judge Edgerton's opinion in the *Carr* case is a detailed factual analysis, based largely on the Strayer Report, of the inequalities of the educational facilities available to white and Negro children in the District of Columbia.

EDGERTON, *Circuit Judge, dissenting:* . . .

IV. *Unconstitutionality of racial discrimination in public schools.* It is plain that pupils represented in these appeals are denied better schooling and given worse because of their color. This the Constitution forbids. "Distinctions between citizens solely because of their ancestry are by their very nature odious to a free people whose institutions are founded upon the doctrine of equality. For that reason, legislative classification or discrimination based on race alone has often been held to be a denial of equal protection." *Hirabayashi* v. *United States,* 320 U.S. 81, 100. "Discriminations based on race alone are obviously irrelevant and invidious," *Steele* v. *Louisville & Nashville Rail-*

road Co., 323 U.S. 192, 203, and therefore arbitrary and unreasonable. Their imposition upon any citizen by any agency of government is reconcilable neither with due process of law nor with the equal protection of the laws.

The Supreme Court has applied this general principle to public education in a number of familiar cases. The Court of Appeals for the Fourth Circuit has recently applied it as between segregated high schools. The leading cases have been based on the Fourteenth Amendment of the Constitution, which is not directly applicable in the District of Columbia. The Fifth Amendment, which is directly applicable here, contains no equal protection clause. But the Supreme Court has held that governmentally enforced racial discrimination in housing violates not only the equal protection clause but also the due process clause of the Fourteenth Amendment, and the Court has repeatedly indicated that arbitrary and injurious discrimination may violate the due process clause of the Fifth Amendment. As long ago as 1896 the Court said "the Constitution . . . forbids, so far as civil and political rights are concerned, discrimination by the General Government, or by the States, against any citizen because of his race." *Gibson* v. *Mississippi*, 162 U.S. 565, 591.

It is said there are not enough vacancies in the better schools for all pupils. This is no answer to these complaints of racial discrimination. As long as good schools cannot accommodate all, the pupils who attend them may be chosen on any reasonable basis, including proximity, intelligence, and conduct. They may not be chosen for the color of their hair or their skin.

Appellees say in effect: (1) We try to avoid discrimination against colored pupils, but (2) the rapid growth of the colored population, its location, its movement, and the war, have made this impossible; yet (3) in general, we do avoid discrimination against colored pupils. The first proposition is immaterial except as it tends to support the second, for the question is not whether appellees have good intentions but whether appellants have equal schooling. The second proposition supports appellants' case, not appellees', for the more clearly segregation precludes equality the more clearly it must go. The third proposition contradicts not only the second but the facts, and would not conclude the rights of any pupil even if it were true. It may be that the same segregated system which discriminates against most colored pupils discriminates, or has sometimes discriminated, against some white pupils. But in the restrictive covenant case, as in others, the Supreme Court pointed out that the rights created by the Fourteenth Amendment "are, by its terms, guaranteed to the individual. The rights established are personal rights. It is, therefore, no answer to these petitioners to say that the courts may also be induced to deny white persons rights . . . on grounds of race or color. Equal protection of the laws is not achieved through indiscriminate imposition of inequalities." *Shelley* v. *Kraemer*, 334 U.S. 1, 22. This is also true of the right to due process of law created by the Fifth Amendment. While many children are handicapped in their schooling because of their race it is no defense to say that some children of the same race are not, and some children of a different race are, so handicapped.

Two railroad cars may be, in themselves, exactly alike. But two schools are seldom if ever fully equal to each other in location, environment, space, age, equipment, size of classes, and faculty. Therefore it follows from the mere number of public schools, at every level, in the District of Columbia that discrimination against many individual pupils of one race or the other because of their race cannot be avoided while segregation is maintained. In other words objective equality, which is clearly required, cannot here be attained without abolishing segregation. The appellees should therefore be required to cease to exclude any pupil from any school because of color.

V. *Unconstitutionality of racial segregation in public schools.*

If it be assumed that objective equality *could* be attained, the question whether enforced segregation in public schools would then be valid becomes one upon which the Supreme Court has never squarely ruled, although the Court has repeatedly spoken of segregation as valid. Since *Plessy* v. *Ferguson,* enforced segregation in travel has been upheld as "reasonable," though it is now under attack by the United States. But the Supreme Court held over thirty years ago that an ordinance forbidding Negroes to move into predominantly white city blocks and whites to move into predominantly Negro city blocks was a denial of due process of law. The Court thereby recognized that enforced racial segregation in housing is arbitrary and cannot reasonably be thought to serve a public purpose. I submit that enforced racial segregation in schooling is even more arbitrary. Instead of serving a public purpose it fosters prejudice and obstructs the education of whites and Negroes by endorsing prejudice and preventing mutual acquaintance. Adults are not restricted in their contacts to people who live in the same block, but many children are practically restricted in their contacts to children who attend the same school. The education required for living in a cosmopolitan community, and especially for living in a humane and democratic country and promoting its ideals, cannot be obtained on either side of a fence that separates a more privileged majority and a less privileged minority. Segregation in travel is intermittent and affects chiefly adults. Segregation in colleges and universities affects young people whose patterns of feeling and behavior have been formed. But segregation in public schools affects children during their formative years and does so continually.

It also affects them unequally. Here at least, as a current brief for the United States says of segregation in general, " 'separate but equal' is as much a contradiction in terms as 'black but white': facilities which are segregated by law solely on the basis of race or color, cannot in any real sense be regarded as equal." It is notorious that segregated colored schooling is never equal to segregated white schooling in objectively measurable ways. Independently of objective differences between white and colored schooling, school segregation means discrimination against Negroes for two distinct reasons. (1) By preventing a dominant majority and a depressed minority from learning each other's ways, school segregation inflicts a greater economic and social handicap on the minority than on the majority. It aggravates the disadvantages of Negroes and helps to preserve their subordinate status. (2) School segregation is humiliating to Negroes. Courts have sometimes denied that segregation implies inferiority. This amounts to saying, in the face of the obvious fact of racial prejudice, that the whites who impose segregation do not consider Negroes inferior. One might as well say that the whites who apply insulting epithets to Negroes do not consider them inferior. Not only words but acts mean what they are intended and understood to mean. Segregation of the Czar of Russia meant that others were not thought fit to associate with him. Segregation of a depressed minority means that it is not thought fit to associate with others. Both whites and Negroes know that enforced racial segregation in schools exists because the people who impose it consider colored children unfit to associate with white children. As the President's Committee on Civil Rights said of the "separate but equal" policy in general, it "brands the Negro with the mark of inferiority and asserts that he is not fit to associate with white people. . . . No argument or rationalization can alter this basic fact: a law which forbids a group of American citizens to associate with other citizens in the ordinary course of daily living creates inequality by imposing a caste status on the minority group." One of the recommendations of the President's Committee was that Congress prohibit segregation in the public schools of the District of Columbia. In my opinion the Constitution does not permit courts to wait for Congress to act.

Appellees say that Congress requires them to maintain segregation. The President's Committee concluded that congressional legislation "assumes the fact of segregation but nowhere makes it mandatory." I think the question irrelevant, since legislation cannot affect appellants' constitutional rights.

When the Fifth Amendment was adopted Negroes in the District of Columbia were slaves, not entitled to unsegregated schooling or to any schooling. Congress may have been right in thinking Negroes were not entitled to unsegregated schooling when the Fourteenth Amendment was adopted. But the question what schooling was good enough to meet their constitutional rights 160 or 80 years ago is different from the question what schooling meets their rights now. "It is of the very nature of a free society to advance in its standards of what is deemed reasonable and right. Representing as it does a living principle, due process is not confined within a permanent catalogue of what may at a given time be deemed the limits of the essentials of fundamental rights." *Wolf* v. *Colorado*, 338 U.S. 25, 27.

It is sometimes suggested that due process of law cannot require what law cannot enforce. No such suggestion is relevant here. When United States courts order integration of District of Columbia schools they will be integrated. It has been too long forgotten that the District of Columbia is not a provincial community but the cosmopolitan capital of a nation that professes democracy.

Index

Date Due